BUSINESS ISSUES, COMPETITION AND ENTREPRENEURSHIP

SMALL BUSINESS ISSUES

CONTRACTING, COMPLIANCE AND TAX BENEFITS

BUSINESS ISSUES, COMPETITION AND ENTREPRENEURSHIP

Additional books and e-books in this series can be found on Nova's website under the Series tab.

BUSINESS ISSUES, COMPETITION AND ENTREPRENEURSHIP

SMALL BUSINESS ISSUES

CONTRACTING, COMPLIANCE AND TAX BENEFITS

ANDREA MOELLER
EDITOR

snova
New York

Library of Congress Cataloging-in-Publication Data

ISBN: 978-1-53615-870-0

Published by Nova Science Publishers, Inc. † New York

CONTENTS

PREFACE

Congress has broad authority to impose requirements upon the federal procurement process, that is, the process whereby agencies obtain goods and services from the private sector. One way in which Congress has exercised this authority is by adopting measures to promote contracting and subcontracting between "small businesses" and federal agencies. Chapter 1 describes the various federal programs, requirements, procurement officers, and procurement offices involved in promoting federal contracting and subcontracting with small businesses, small disadvantaged businesses (SDBs), SDBs participating the SBA's "8(a) Program," Historically Underutilized Business Zone (HUBZone) small businesses, women-owned small businesses (WOSBs), and service-disabled veteran-owned small businesses (SDVOSBs). Chapter 2 discusses the extent to which selected federal agencies demonstrated compliance with thirteen section 15(k) requirements for OSDBUs and SBPAC review process results. Chapter 3 examines what contracting officers consider when assigning NAICS codes to federal contracts and the status of efforts to clarify code assignment and industry views on NAICS code assignment and the number and outcomes of appeals. Chapter 4 reports on SBA's development of criteria and guidance on using a risk-based approach for certifying and recertifying HUBZone firms, and SBA's implementation of the revised policies and procedures for firms located in Puerto

Rico. Chapter 5 examines the extent to which SBA and the participating agencies have implemented these benchmarks, including assessing businesses against them and establishing the consequence of not meeting them. The federal tax burden on small firms and its effects on their formation and growth have long been matters of legislative concern for Congress. This abiding interest has helped pave the way for the enactment of a series of tax laws in recent years that included targeted tax relief for a number of small businesses as discussed in chapter 6.

Chapter 1 - Congress has broad authority to impose requirements upon the federal procurement process, that is, the process whereby agencies obtain goods and services from the private sector. One way in which Congress has exercised this authority is by adopting measures to promote contracting and subcontracting between "small businesses" and federal agencies. These measures, among other things, declare a congressional policy of ensuring that a "fair proportion" of federal contract and subcontract dollars is awarded to small businesses; establish government-wide and agency-specific goals for the percentage of federal contract and subcontract dollars awarded to small businesses; establish an annual Small Business Goaling Report to measure progress in meeting these goals; generally require federal agencies, under specified circumstances, to reserve contracts that have an anticipated value greater than the micro-purchase threshold (currently $10,000), but not greater than the simplified acquisition threshold (currently $250,000) exclusively for small businesses; authorize federal agencies, under specified circumstances, to set aside contracts that have an anticipated value greater than the simplified acquisition threshold exclusively for small businesses; authorize federal agencies to make sole source awards to small businesses when the award could not otherwise be made (e.g., only a single source is available, under urgent and compelling circumstances); authorize federal agencies to set aside contracts for, or grant other contracting preference to, specific types of small businesses (e.g., 8(a) small businesses, HUBZone small businesses, women-owned small businesses (WOSBs) and service-disabled veteran-owned small businesses (SDVOSBs)); and task the Small Business Administration (SBA) and other federal procurement officers with reviewing and restructuring proposed procurements to maximize opportunities for small business participation. Small business contracting programs generally have strong bipartisan support. However, that does not mean that these programs face no opposition, or that issues have not been raised concerning the impact and operations of specific programs. For example, small business advocates note that implementing regulations in the Federal Acquisition Regulation (FAR) narrow the reach (and impact) of some small business contracting preferences by excluding specific types of contracts, such as those listed in the Federal Supply Schedules, from FAR requirements pertaining to small business contracting. Advocates want the federal government to enact policies that reduce or eliminate such exclusions. Critics have questioned some of these programs' effectiveness, in terms of both promoting small business opportunities to win federal contracts and promoting a more diversified, robust economy. Many observers judge the relative success or failure of federal efforts to enhance small business contracting opportunities by whether federal government and individual federal agencies meet the predetermined procurement goals in the annual Small Business Goaling Report. In recent years, the federal government has generally succeeded in meeting the government-wide goals of awarding 23% of the total value of all small business eligible prime contract awards to small businesses, 5% to small disadvantaged businesses (SDBs), and 3% to SDVOSBs. It has had difficulty meeting the goals of 5% to WOSBs and 3% to HUBZone small businesses. The Small Business Goaling Report is the most convenient measure available to compare federal small business contracting performance over time, but it has limitations. For example, the SBA excludes some contracts from the report in its determination of what is "small business eligible" and some federal procurement activities are not included because they are not recorded in the Federal Procurement Data System—Next Generation. It also does not evaluate the effect these contracts have on small businesses, industry competitiveness, or the overall economy.

Chapter 2 - Section 15(k) of the Small Business Act requires federal agencies with procurement powers to establish an OSDBU to advocate for small businesses. The National Defense Authorization Act for Fiscal Year

2013 established additional requirements for OSDBUs and required SBPAC to review OSDBU compliance with section 15(k) requirements. This testimony is based on a report GAO issued in August 2017 (GAO-17- 675). For that report, GAO examined (1) the extent to which selected federal agencies demonstrated compliance with thirteen section 15(k) requirements for OSDBUs and (2) SBPAC review process results. GAO selected 10 agencies, based on contracting obligations, to review a reporting requirement for OSDBU directors. For the other 12 requirements, GAO surveyed OSDBU directors at 24 agencies, selected based on contracting obligations (100 percent response rate). To review and augment survey responses, GAO also analyzed guidance and documents and interviewed OSDBU directors.

Chapter 3 - Federal regulations require that contracting officers assign the NAICS code that best describes the principal purpose of the acquisition. SBA's OHA is responsible for reviewing appeals of NAICS code assignments. Questions have been raised about whether agencies assign the appropriate NAICS codes to ID/IQ contracts with multiple task orders. GAO was asked to review several issues related to NAICS codes. In this chapter, GAO examines (1) what contracting officers consider when assigning NAICS codes to federal contracts and the status of efforts to clarify code assignment and (2) industry views on NAICS code assignment and the number and outcomes of appeals. GAO reviewed policies and procedures of the four agencies with the highest ID/IQ obligations from fiscal years 2011–2015: Army, Navy, Department of Homeland Security (DHS), and Department of Health and Human Services (HHS); reviewed one contract and 10 related task orders at each of the selected agencies and interviewed the related contracting officers; analyzed 2016 federal contracting data to identify commonly used NAICS codes and size standards; interviewed three industry groups and five firms that filed appeals for industry views on NAICS code assignment; and analyzed SBA decisions on NAICS code appeals in 2014–2016. The Department of Defense, DHS, and SBA had no comments on the report. The General Services Administration and HHS had technical comments, which we incorporated as appropriate.

Chapter 4 - The HUBZone program is intended to stimulate economic development in economically distressed areas. Certified HUBZone firms are eligible for federal contracting benefits, including limited competition awards such as set-aside contracts, and are required to be recertified every 3 years. The Puerto Rico Oversight, Management, and Economic Stability Act of 2016 required SBA to develop criteria and guidance for a risk-based approach to verify firm eligibility for the program and included a provision for GAO to review SBA's development and implementation of the required criteria and guidance. This chapter examines, among other objectives, (1) SBA's development of criteria and guidance on using a risk-based approach for certifying and recertifying HUBZone firms, and (2) SBA's implementation of the revised policies and procedures for firms located in Puerto Rico. GAO analyzed SBA documents and reviewed files of a non-generalizable sample of 12 firms located in Puerto Rico that received certification between March 2017 and March 2018. GAO also interviewed SBA officials, representatives from HUBZone certified firms in Puerto Rico, and local economic development agencies in Puerto Rico.

Chapter 5 - Through the SBIR and STTR programs, federal agencies have awarded about 162,000 contracts and grants totaling $46 billion to small businesses to help them develop and commercialize new technologies. Eleven federal agencies participate in the SBIR program, and 5 agencies also participate in the STTR program. Each program has three phases, which take projects from initial feasibility studies through commercialization activities. SBA oversees both programs. In response to the 2011 reauthorization of the programs, SBA and the participating agencies developed benchmarks to measure small businesses' progress in developing and commercializing technologies. GAO was asked to review SBA's and the agencies' efforts related to these benchmarks. This chapter examines the extent to which SBA and the participating agencies have implemented these benchmarks, including assessing businesses against them and establishing the consequence of not meeting them. GAO analyzed award data and interviewed officials from SBA and the 11 participating agencies.

Chapter 6 - The federal tax burden on small firms and its effects on their formation and growth have long been matters of legislative concern for Congress. This abiding interest has helped pave the way for the enactment of a series of tax laws in recent years that included targeted tax relief for a number of small businesses. This chapter describes the main federal tax preferences that benefit small firms and examines the main arguments for and against government support for small firms in general and for tax benefits targeted at such firms in particular. It addresses the tax preferences that can be claimed only by small firms in a wide range of industries and excludes those targeted at small firms in specific industries, such as the special deduction for small life insurance companies under Section 806 of the federal tax code. The small business tax preferences discussed here reflect the changes in the tax code under P.L. 115-97. The following small business tax benefits are examined here:

- Expensing allowance for machinery and equipment under Section 179 of the Internal Revenue Code;
- Cash-basis accounting under Section 446;
- Tax credit for a portion of the costs incurred by small firms in establishing pension funds for employees under Section 45E;
- Tax credit for costs incurred by small firms in complying with the Americans with Disabilities Act under Section 44;
- Full exclusion from the capital gains tax on the sale or exchange of qualified small business stock under Section 1202;
- Exemption from the limitation on the deduction for business interest expenses under Section 163;
- Tax credit for small firms that offer qualified health insurance coverage to employees under Section 45R;
- Simplified dollar-value last-in-last-out accounting under Section 474;
- Deduction for and amortization of business start-up expenses under Section 195;

- Ordinary income treatment of losses on the sale of certain small business stock under Section 1244;
- Treating losses on the sale of Small Business Investment Company stock as ordinary losses under Section 1242;
- Exemption from the uniform capitalization rule under Section 263A; and
- Use of research tax credit to reduce payroll tax for certain small firms under Section 41.

While available information does not allow for an estimate of the federal revenue cost of the small business tax preferences examined here, a recent estimate by the Joint Committee on Taxation suggests that the cost might exceed $17 billion in FY2018. Tax preferences for small businesses raise several policy issues. For some, a key question is whether they can be justified on economic grounds. In the absence of such a justification, small business tax benefits, while promoting the survival and growth of firms that can take advantage of them, may cause more economic harm than good by distorting the allocation of domestic economic resources.

In: Small Business Issues
Editor: Andrea Moeller
ISBN: 978-1-53615-870-0

Chapter 1

AN OVERVIEW OF SMALL BUSINESS CONTRACTING*

Robert Jay Dilger

SUMMARY

Congress has broad authority to impose requirements upon the federal procurement process, that is, the process whereby agencies obtain goods and services from the private sector. One way in which Congress has exercised this authority is by adopting measures to promote contracting and subcontracting between "small businesses" and federal agencies.

These measures, among other things, declare a congressional policy of ensuring that a "fair proportion" of federal contract and subcontract dollars is awarded to small businesses; establish government-wide and agency-specific goals for the percentage of federal contract and subcontract dollars awarded to small businesses; establish an annual Small Business Goaling Report to measure progress in meeting these goals; generally require federal agencies, under specified circumstances, to reserve contracts that have an anticipated value greater than the micro-

---

* This is an edited, reformatted and augmented version of Congressional Research Service, Publication No. R45576, dated March 8, 2019.

purchase threshold (currently $10,000), but not greater than the simplified acquisition threshold (currently $250,000) exclusively for small businesses; authorize federal agencies, under specified circumstances, to set aside contracts that have an anticipated value greater than the simplified acquisition threshold exclusively for small businesses; authorize federal agencies to make sole source awards to small businesses when the award could not otherwise be made (e.g., only a single source is available, under urgent and compelling circumstances); authorize federal agencies to set aside contracts for, or grant other contracting preference to, specific types of small

businesses (e.g., 8(a) small businesses, HUBZone small businesses, women-owned small businesses (WOSBs) and service-disabled veteran-owned small businesses (SDVOSBs)); and task the Small Business Administration (SBA) and other federal procurement officers with reviewing and restructuring proposed procurements to maximize opportunities for small business participation.

Small business contracting programs generally have strong bipartisan support. However, that does not mean that these programs face no opposition, or that issues have not been raised concerning the impact and operations of specific programs. For example, small business advocates note that implementing regulations in the Federal Acquisition Regulation (FAR) narrow the reach (and impact) of some small business contracting preferences by excluding specific types of contracts, such as those listed in the Federal Supply Schedules, from FAR requirements pertaining to small business contracting. Advocates want the federal government to enact policies that reduce or eliminate such exclusions. Critics have questioned some of these programs' effectiveness, in terms of both promoting small business opportunities to win federal contracts and promoting a more diversified, robust economy.

Many observers judge the relative success or failure of federal efforts to enhance small business contracting opportunities by whether federal government and individual federal agencies meet the predetermined procurement goals in the annual Small Business Goaling Report. In recent years, the federal government has generally succeeded in meeting the government-wide goals of awarding 23% of the total value of all small business eligible prime contract awards to small businesses, 5% to small disadvantaged businesses (SDBs), and 3% to SDVOSBs. It has had difficulty meeting the goals of 5% to WOSBs and 3% to HUBZone small businesses.

The Small Business Goaling Report is the most convenient measure available to compare federal small business contracting performance over time, but it has limitations. For example, the SBA excludes some contracts from the report in its determination of what is "small business eligible" and some federal procurement activities are not included because they are not recorded in the Federal Procurement Data System—

Next Generation. It also does not evaluate the effect these contracts have on small businesses, industry competitiveness, or the overall economy.

INTRODUCTION

During World War II and then again after the outbreak of fighting in Korea, Congress found that the existence of thousands of small business concerns was being threatened by war-induced shortages of materials coupled with an inability to obtain defense contracts or financial assistance.[1] Concerned that many small businesses might fail without government assistance, in 1953, Congress passed and President Dwight Eisenhower signed into law the Small Business Act (P.L. 83-163), which authorized the Small Business Administration (SBA).[2] The act specifies that it is the declared policy of Congress to promote the interests of small businesses to "preserve free competitive enterprise." Congress specified that one of the ways to preserve free competitive enterprise was to insure that small businesses received a "fair proportion" of federal contracts and subcontracts:

It is the declared policy of the Congress that the Government should aid, counsel, assist, and protect, insofar as is possible, the interests of small-business concerns in order to preserve free competitive enterprise, to insure that a fair proportion of the total purchases and contracts or subcontracts for property and services for the Government (including but

---

[1] U.S. Congress, Senate Select Committee on Small Business, Small Business Administration, committee print, 83rd Cong., 1st sess., August 10, 1953 (Washington: GPO, 1953), p. iii. Also, see U.S. Congress, House Committee on Banking and Currency, Small Business Act of 1953, report to accompany H.R. 5141, 83rd Cong., 1st sess., May 28, 1953, H.Rept. 83-494 (Washington: GPO, 1953).

[2] On July 31, 1951, the Small Defense Plants Administration (SDPA) was created by an amendment to P.L. 81-774, the Defense Production Act of 1950, and was given "primary responsibility in the field of channeling defense contracts to small producers." As hostilities with Korea subsided, so did the perceived need for the SDPA. Congress granted the Small Business Administration (SBA) similar authority to promote small business contracting with federal agencies, but with all federal agencies, as opposed to focusing on the Department of Defense. See U.S. Congress, Senate Select Committee on Small Business, Small Business Administration, committee print, 83rd Cong., 1st sess., August 10, 1953 (Washington: GPO, 1953), p. iv.

not limited to contracts or subcontracts for maintenance, repair, and construction) be placed with small-business enterprises, to insure that a fair proportion of the total sales of Government property be made to such enterprises, and to maintain and strengthen the overall economy of the Nation.[3]

Congress indicated that its intent in supporting small businesses was not to "favor small business at the expense of its larger competitors. Our only purpose in supporting the creation and effective operation of the SBA is to equalize the scales when necessary to guarantee the continued vigor of our competitive free enterprise system."[4]

More recently, a House committee report indicated that the primary rationale for small business contracting programs

> is the positive economic benefits they provide, as well as assisting small businesses overcome the complexities of the system. The economic benefits of these programs can be seen in two primary areas—market competition and local economic development. First, [these] programs ... are designed to increase and diversify small contractors with the intent of expanding the federal supplier base. This leads to increased competition, which results in higher quality, greater product variety, and lower prices. Second, these contracting initiatives lower barriers to entry in a wide range of markets for small businesses. This provides greater market access for small firms' goods and services. From an economic perspective, such access is critical to generating positive macroeconomic benefits, including higher job creation, wage growth, and greater income distribution.[5]

Over the years, Congress has approved legislation to support small business in various ways. For example, the SBA administers several types of programs to support small businesses, including loan guaranty and

---

[3] 15 U.S.C. §631(a); and P.L. 83-163, the Small Business Act of 1953 (as amended), see http://legcounsel.house.gov/ Comps/Small%20Business%20Act.pdf.

[4] U.S. Congress, Senate Select Committee on Small Business, Small Business Administration, committee print, 83rd Cong., 1st sess., August 10, 1953 (Washington: GPO, 1953), p. v.

[5] U.S. Congress, House Committee on Small Business, Small Business Contracting Program Improvements Act, report to accompany H.R. 3867, 110th Cong., 1st sess., October 22, 2007, H.Rept. 110-400 (Washington: GPO, 2007), p. 4.

venture capital programs to enhance small business access to capital; contracting programs to increase small business opportunities in federal contracting; direct loan programs for businesses, homeowners, and renters to assist their recovery from natural disasters; and small business management and technical assistance training programs to assist business formation and expansion. In recent years, congressional interest in these programs has increased, primarily because assisting small businesses is viewed as a means to stimulate economic activity and create jobs.

This chapter describes the various federal programs, requirements, procurement officers, and procurement offices involved in promoting federal contracting and subcontracting with small businesses, small disadvantaged businesses (SDBs), SDBs participating the SBA's "8(a) Program," Historically Underutilized Business Zone (HUBZone) small businesses, women-owned small businesses (WOSBs), and service-disabled veteran-owned small businesses (SDVOSBs). The SBA administers many, but not all, of these programs.

It examines the following federal requirements and authorities in promoting contracting and subcontracting with small businesses:

1) The requirement that federal agencies generally reserve contracts that have an anticipated value greater than the micro-purchase threshold (currently $10,000) but not greater than the simplified acquisition threshold (currently $250,000) exclusively for small businesses unless the contracting officer is unable to obtain offers from two or more small businesses that are competitive with market prices and the quality and delivery of the goods or services being purchased.[6]
2) The establishment of small business procurement goals, both government-wide and agency specific, to promote the awarding of contracts to small businesses.
3) The requirement that federal agencies generally set aside contracts that have an anticipated value exceeding the simplified acquisition

[6] Federal Acquisition Regulation (FAR) §19.502-2.

threshold exclusively for small businesses when there is a reasonable expectation that offers will be obtained from at least two responsible small businesses offering the products of different small businesses (Rule of Two) and the award will be made at a fair market price.[7]

4) The authority provided federal agencies to make sole source awards to small businesses when the award could not otherwise be made (e.g., only a single source is available, under urgent and compelling circumstances).
5) The authority provided federal agencies to set aside contracts for, or grant other contracting preference to, specific types of small businesses (e.g., 8(a) small businesses, HUBZone small businesses, WOSBs, and SDVOSBs).

It discusses the SBA's oversight and responsibilities concerning the small business goaling program, small business mentor-protégé programs, the 7(j) management and training program, and the surety bond guaranty program.

It also discusses the role of the Office of Small and Disadvantaged Business Utilization (OSDBU), located in each federal agency, in promoting contracting with small businesses, and examines the role and responsibilities of various federal procurement officers, including procurement center representatives, commercial market representatives, and business opportunity specialists, in promoting small business contracting opportunities.

This chapter concludes with a brief discussion of the strong bipartisan support for small business contracting programs. However, that does not mean that these programs face no opposition, or that issues have not been raised concerning the impact and operations of specific programs. For

---

[7] "For acquisitions of supplies or services that have an anticipated dollar value exceeding the simplified acquisition threshold ... the contracting officer shall first consider an acquisition for the small business socioeconomic contracting programs (i.e., 8(a), HUBZone, SDVOSB, or WOSB programs) before considering a small business set-aside (see 19.502-2(b)). However, if a requirement has been accepted by the Small Business Administration (SBA) under the 8(a) Program, it must remain in the 8(a) Program unless the SBA agrees to its release in accordance with 13 C.F.R. parts 124, 125, and 126." FAR §19.203(c).

example, small business advocates note that implementing regulations in the Federal Acquisition Regulation (FAR) narrow the reach (and impact) of some small business contracting preferences by excluding specific types of contracts, such as those listed in the Federal Supply Schedules, from FAR requirements pertaining to small business contracting.[8] Advocates want the federal government to enact policies that reduce or eliminate exclusions that narrow the reach of small business contracting preferences. Critics have questioned some of these programs' effectiveness, in terms of promoting both small business opportunities to win federal contracts and a more diversified, robust economy.[9]

---

[8] FAR §8.405-5 indicates that the small business preference programs are not mandatory in this subpart (blanket purchase agreements and Federal Supply Schedules). Federal agencies may, at their discretion, set aside orders under the Federal Supply Schedules and blanket purchase agreements for small businesses.

The Federal Supply Schedule program "provides Federal agencies with a simplified process of acquiring commercial supplies and services in varying quantities while obtaining volume discounts. Indefinite-delivery contracts are awarded using competitive procedures to firms. The firms provide supplies and services at stated prices for given periods of time, for delivery within a stated geographic area such as the 48 contiguous states, the District of Columbia, Alaska, Hawaii, and overseas. ...Although GSA [General Services Administration] awards most Federal Supply Schedule contracts, it may authorize other agencies to award schedule contracts and publish schedules. For example, the Department of Veterans Affairs awards schedule contracts for certain medical and nonperishable subsistence items." FAR §38.101.

A blanket purchase agreement (BPA) is "a simplified method of filling anticipated repetitive needs for supplies or services by establishing "charge accounts" with qualified sources of supply. ...BPAs should be established for use by an organization responsible for providing supplies for its own operations or for other offices, installations, projects, or functions. Such organizations, for example, may be organized supply points, separate independent or detached field parties, or one-person posts or activities. ...The use of BPAs does not exempt an agency from the responsibility for keeping obligations and expenditures within available funds." FAR §13.303-1.

For an argument advocating regulatory changes that might require the mandatory application of set-asides to orders in the same manner that law and regulation currently require for contracts, see Interagency Task Force on Federal Contracting Opportunities for Small Businesses, Report, September 2010, pp. 8-10, at https://www.sba.gov/document/support—interagency-task-force-federal-contracting-opportunities-small-businesses.

The U.S. Supreme Court ruled in 2016, in Kingdomware Technologies, Inc. v. United States, that the Department of Veterans Affairs (VA) cannot continue its former practice of making purchases through the Federal Supply Schedules without first considering whether the contract could be set aside for veteran-owned small businesses (VSOBs) due to language in P.L. 109-461, the Veterans Benefits, Health Care, and Information Technology Act of 2006, that required VA specifically to promote contract awards to VOSBs.

[9] For example, see Henry Beale and Nicola Deas, "The HUBZone Report," prepared for the SBA, Office of Advocacy, May 2008, pp. i, ii, 124-131, at https://www.sba.gov/sites/default/files/rs325tot.pdf; and Clifford A. Grammich, Thomas R. Edison, Jr., Nancy

BASIC CONTRACTING REQUIREMENTS

Federal Contractors

With a few exceptions, businesses interested in bidding on a federal contract must obtain a Dun & Bradstreet Data Universal Numbering System (DUNS) number (i.e., a unique nine-digit identification number) for each of the business's physical locations, and register with the federal government's System for Award Management (SAM).[10] SAM is used by government agencies for several purposes, including to find contractors.[11]

Businesses also must match their products and services to a North American Industry Classification System (NAICS) code. Businesses generally have a primary NAICS code, and may have multiple NAICS codes if they sell multiple products and services.[12]

Businesses that identify themselves as a small business in SAM must (1) meet the Small Business Act's definition of a small business and (2) not exceed size standards established, and updated periodically, by the SBA.[13]

The Small Business Act defines a small business as one that

- is organized for profit;
- has a place of business in the United States;

Young Moore, and Edward G. Keating, Small Business and Defense Acquisitions: A Review of Policies and Current Practices (Santa Monica, CA: RAND, 2011), p. xii, 15, 16, at https://www.rand.org/ content/dam/rand/pubs/monographs/2011/RAND_MG443.pdf.

[10] SBA, "Federal Contracting Guide: Basic Requirements," at https://www.sba.gov/federal-contracting/contractingguide/basic-requirements. For additional information and analysis, see CRS Report R44490, Unique Identification Codes for Federal Contractors: DUNS Numbers and CAGE Codes, by L. Elaine Halchin; and CRS Report RS22536, Overview of the Federal Procurement Process and Resources, by L. Elaine Halchin.

[11] SBA, "Register with SAM," at https://www.sba.gov/federal-contracting/contracting-guide/basicrequirements#section-header-8.

[12] U.S. Bureau of the Census, "North American Industry Classification System," at https://www.census.gov/eos/www/naics/.

[13] P.L. 111-240, the Small Business Jobs Act of 2010, requires the SBA to conduct a detailed review of not less than one-third of the SBA's industry size standards every 18 months beginning on the new law's date of enactment (September 27, 2010) and ensure that each size standard is reviewed at least once every five years.

- operates primarily within the United States or makes a significant contribution to the U.S. economy through payment of taxes or use of American products, materials, or labor;
- is independently owned and operated; and
- is not dominant in its field on a national basis.[14]

The business may be a sole proprietorship, partnership, corporation, or any other legal form.[15]

The Small Business Act authorizes the SBA to establish size standards to ensure that only small businesses are provided SBA assistance. The SBA currently uses two types of size standards to determine SBA program eligibility: *industry-specific size standards* and *alternative size standards*, for some lending and venture capital investment programs based on the applicant's maximum tangible net worth and average net income after federal taxes.[16] The SBA's industry-specific size standards are used to determine eligibility for federal small business contracting purposes.

---

[14] 15 U.S.C. §632(a); and 13 C.F.R. §121.105. Affiliations between businesses, or relationships allowing one party control or the power of control over another, generally count in size determinations. Businesses can thus be determined to be other than small because of their involvement in joint ventures, subcontracting arrangements, or franchise or license agreements, among other things, provided that their employment or income, plus those of their affiliate(s), exceed the pertinent size threshold. See 13 C.F.R. §121.103.

[15] For additional information and analysis of the SBA's size standards, see CRS Report R40860, Small Business Size Standards: A Historical Analysis of Contemporary Issues, by Robert Jay Dilger.

[16] The SBA's 7(a) loan guarantee program allows businesses to qualify as small if they meet the SBA's size standard for the industry in which the applicant is primarily engaged, or a maximum tangible net worth of not more than $15 million and average after-tax net income after federal taxes (excluding any carry-over losses) of not more than $5 million for two full fiscal years before the date of application. 15 U.S.C. §632(a)(2-3) and 15 U.S.C. §632(a)(5)(B).

Businesses participating in the SBA's 504/Certified Development Company (504/CDC) loan guaranty program are deemed small if they did not have a tangible net worth in excess of $15 million and did not have an average net income in excess of $5 million after taxes (excluding any carry-over losses) for the preceding two years before the date of application. 15 U.S.C. §632(a)(5)(B).

The SBA's Small Business Investment Company (SBIC) program allows businesses to qualify as small if they meet the SBA's size standard for the industry in which the applicant is primarily engaged, or a maximum tangible net worth of not more than $19.5 million and average after-tax net income for the preceding two years of not more than $6.5 million. 15 U.S.C. §662(12)(A-B); and SBA, "Small Business Size Standards: Inflation Adjustment to Monetary Based Size Standards," 79 Federal Register 33647-33669, June 12, 2014.

The SBA determines if a business is small by comparing that business's economic characteristics (typically number of employees or average annual receipts) to size standards listed in the SBA's Table of Small Business Size Standards. The table has size standards for 1,036 industrial classifications in the North American Industrial Classification System. Businesses that exceed the applicable size standard for their primary industry do not meet the requirement of being small.

The SBA's size standards are designed to (1) encourage competition within each industry and (2) ensure that SBA assistance is provided only to firms that are not dominant in their field on a national basis. The size standards are derived through an assessment of four economic factors: (1) the average firm size, (2) the average assets size as a proxy of start-up costs and entry barriers, (3) the four-firm concentration ratio (the cumulative share of total industry receipts of that industry's four biggest firms) as a measure of industry competition, and (4) the size distribution of firms.[17] The SBA also considers the ability of small businesses to compete for federal contracting opportunities and, when necessary, several secondary factors "as they are relevant to the industries and the interests of small businesses, including technological change, competition among industries, industry growth trends, and impacts of size standard revisions on small businesses."[18]

Historically, the SBA has used the number of employees to determine if manufacturing and mining companies are small (ranging from fewer than 50 employees for some industries to fewer than 1,500 employees for others) and average annual receipts for most other industries (ranging from

---

[17] SBA, Office of Government Contracting and Business Development, "SBA Size Standards Methodology," April 27, 2018, pp. 29, 30, at https://www.sba.gov/document/support—size-standards-methodology-white-paper.

[18] Ibid., p. 1. Any changes to size standards must follow the rulemaking procedures of the Administrative Procedure Act. A proposed rule changing a size standard is first published in the Federal Register, allowing for public comment. It must include documentation establishing that a significant problem exists that requires a revision of the size standard, plus an economic analysis of the change. Comments from the public, plus any other new information, are reviewed and evaluated before a final rule is promulgated establishing a new size standard.

no more than $1 million for some industries to no more than $40 million for others).[19]

Federal Agencies

To make it easier to determine if an offeror meets the SBA's definition of a small business, prior to soliciting bids, federal agencies are required to classify a product or service being acquired in only one (NAICS code) industry, "whose definition best describes the principal nature of the product or service being acquired even though for other purposes it could be classified in more than one."[20] When acquiring a product or service that could be classified in two or more industries with different size standards, contracting officers must "apply the size standard for the industry accounting for the greatest percentage of the contract price."[21] If a solicitation calls for more than one item and allows offers to be submitted on any or all of the items, "an offeror must meet the size standard for each item it offers to furnish."[22] If a solicitation calling for more than one item requires offers on all or none of the items, "an offeror may qualify as a small business by meeting the size standard for the item accounting for the greatest percentage of the total contract price."[23]

With several notable exceptions (e.g., HUBZone small businesses, SBA 8(a) program participants, and veteran-owned small businesses [VOSBs] and SDVOSBs seeking contracts with the Department of Veterans Affairs), businesses generally self-certify their status as small when they register their business in the SAM database.

The contracting officer is required to accept an offeror's representation in a specific bid or proposal that it is a small business unless "(1) another offeror or interested party challenges the concern's small business

---

[19] Ibid., p. 28.
[20] FAR §19.102(c).
[21] FAR §19.102(d).
[22] FAR §19.102(e).
[23] FAR §19.102(e).

representation or (2) the contracting officer has a reason to question the representation."[24]

If an offeror's small business status is challenged, the contracting officer is generally not allowed to award the contract until the SBA has made a size determination or 15 business days after the SBA receives the protest, whichever occurs first.[25] The SBA's Office of Government Contracting Area Office (Area Office) serving the area in which the headquarters of the offeror is located initially reviews the protest.[26] The Area Office is required, by regulation, to determine the offeror's size status within 15 business days after receipt of the protest, or "within any extension of time granted by the contracting officer."[27] If the SBA does not make a determination within the required time, the contracting officer "may award the contract after determining in writing that there is an immediate need to award the contract and that waiting until SBA makes its determination will be disadvantageous to the government."[28]

An appeal of the Area Office's decision may be filed with the SBA's Office of Hearings and Appeals (OHA). If the OHA accepts the appeal for consideration and finds the protested concern to be ineligible for award, the contracting officer must "terminate the contract unless termination is not in the best interests of the government, in keeping with the circumstances

---

[24] FAR §19.301-1(b).

[25] The contracting officer may award the contract if he or she "determines in writing that an award must be made to protect the public interest." FAR §19.302(g)(1).

[26] FAR §19.302(c)(1). "An offeror, the SBA, or another interested party may protest the small business representation of an offeror in a specific offer. However, for competitive 8(a) contracts, the filing of a protest is limited to an offeror, the contracting officer, or the SBA." FAR §19.302(a)(2). "The protest, or confirmation if the protest was initiated orally, shall be in writing and shall contain the basis for the protest with specific, detailed evidence to support the allegation that the offeror is not small. The SBA will dismiss any protest that does not contain specific grounds for the protest." FAR §19.302(c)(2). "The protest shall include a referral letter written by the contracting officer with information pertaining to the solicitation." FAR §19.302(c)(3). "In order to affect a specific solicitation, a protest must be timely." FAR §19.302(d). "To be timely, a protest ... must be received ... by the close of business of the fifth business day after bid opening (in sealed bid acquisitions) or receipt of the special notification from the contracting officer that identifies the apparently successful offeror (in negotiated acquisitions)." FAR §19.302(d)(1). "...a protest filed by the contracting officer or the SBA is generally always considered timely whether filed before or after award." FAR §19.302(d)(2).

[27] FAR §19.302(f)(1).

[28] FAR §19.302(g)(2).

described in the [aforementioned] written determination. However, the contracting officer shall not exercise any options or award further task or delivery orders."[29] Furthermore, a concern cannot become eligible for a specific award after the SBA has determined that it is not a small business, even if the concern takes action to meet the definition of a small business.[30]

The SBA or the federal agency may suspend or debar a firm from future government contracts for misrepresenting its size status. In addition, individuals that knowingly misrepresent a business's size to secure a federal contract can be subject to civil and criminal penalties.[31]

THE PRE-AWARD PROCESS

Federal Agency Requirements

15 U.S.C. §644(e)(1) states, "To the maximum extent practicable, procurement strategies used by a Federal department or agency having contracting authority shall facilitate the maximum participation of small business concerns as prime contractors, subcontractors, and suppliers." To accomplish this goal, FAR regulations (FAR §19.202-1) require contracting officers, when applicable, to take the following actions prior to awarding a federal contract:

1) "Divide proposed acquisitions of supplies and services (except construction) into reasonably small lots (not less than economic production runs) to permit offers on quantities less than the total requirement."
2) "Plan acquisitions such that, if practicable, more than one small business concern may perform the work, if the work exceeds the amount for which a surety may be guaranteed by the SBA against

[29] FAR §19.302(h).
[30] FAR §19.301-1(c).
[31] 13 C.F.R. §121.108; 18 U.S.C. §287; and 18 U.S.C. §1001. For additional information and analysis, see CRS Report R45322, Selected Legal Tools for Maintaining Government Contractor Accountability, by David H. Carpenter and Kathleen Ann Ruane.

loss under 15 U.S.C. §694b [generally $6.5 million, or $10 million if the contracting officer certifies that the higher amount is necessary]."

3) "Ensure that delivery schedules are established on a realistic basis that will encourage small business participation to the extent consistent with the actual requirements of the Government."
4) "Encourage prime contractors to subcontract with small business concerns [primarily through the agency's role in negotiating an acceptable small business subcontracting plan with prime contractors on contracts anticipated to exceed $700,000 or $1.5 million for construction contracts]."[32]
5) "Provide a copy of the proposed acquisition package to the SBA procurement center representative [PCR, duties are described later]" for his or her review, comment and recommendation, or, if a PCR is not assigned, to the SBA Area Office serving the area in which the procuring activity is located "at least 30 days prior to the issuance of the solicitation if (i) The proposed acquisition is for supplies or services currently being provided by a small business and the proposed acquisition is of a quantity or estimated dollar value, the magnitude of which makes it unlikely that small businesses can compete for the prime contract; (ii) The proposed acquisition is for construction and seeks to package or consolidate discrete construction projects and the magnitude of this consolidation makes it unlikely that small businesses can compete for the prime contract; or (iii) The proposed acquisition is for a consolidated or bundled requirement.... The contracting officer

[32] Subcontracting plans are not required from small businesses, for personal services contracts, for contracts or contract modifications that will be performed entirely outside of the United States and its outlying areas, or for modifications that were within the scope of the contract. "[A]ny contractor or subcontractor failing to comply in good faith with the requirements of the subcontracting plan is in material breach of its contract." FAR §19.702(c). In addition, "Any contractor receiving a contract with a value greater than the simplified acquisition threshold must agree in the contract that small business, veteran-owned small business, service-disabled veteran-owned small business, HUBZone small business, small disadvantaged business, and women-owned small business concerns will have the maximum practicable opportunity to participate in contract performance consistent with its efficient performance." FAR §19.702.

shall provide all information relative to the justification for the consolidation or bundling, including the acquisition plan or strategy and if the acquisition involves substantial bundling, the information identified in [FAR] 7.107-4.[33] The contracting officer shall also provide the same information to the agency Office of Small and Disadvantaged Business Utilization [duties are described later]."

6) "Provide a statement explaining why the (i) Proposed acquisition cannot be divided into reasonably small lots (not less than economic production runs) to permit offers on quantities less than the total requirement; (ii) Delivery schedules cannot be established on a realistic basis that will encourage small business participation to the extent consistent with the actual requirements of the government; (iii) Proposed acquisition cannot be structured so as to make it likely that small businesses can compete for the prime contract; (iv) Consolidated construction project cannot be acquired as separate discrete projects; or (v) Consolidation or bundling is necessary and justified."
7) "Process the 30-day notification concurrently with other processing steps required prior to the issuance of the solicitation."
8) "If the contracting officer rejects the SBA procurement center representative's recommendation ... document the basis for the rejection and notify the SBA procurement center representative [who (as described later) may appeal the rejection to the chief of the contracting office and, ultimately, to the agency head]."[34]

---

[33] FAR §7.017-4(2)(b) states "...when the proposed acquisition strategy involves substantial bundling, the agency shall document in its strategy—(1) The specific benefits anticipated to be derived from substantial bundling; (2) An assessment of the specific impediments to participation by small business concerns as contractors that result from substantial bundling; (3) Actions designed to maximize small business participation as contractors, including provisions that encourage small business teaming; (4) Actions designed to maximize small business participation as subcontractors (including suppliers) at any tier under the contract, or order, that may be awarded to meet the requirements; (5) The determination that the anticipated benefits of the proposed bundled contract or order justify its use; and (6) Alternative strategies that would reduce or minimize the scope of the bundling, and the rationale for not choosing those alternatives."

[34] FAR §19.202-1. See FAR §19.505 for a description of the appeals process.

The Role of SBA Procurement Center Representatives

The SBA may assign one or more procurement center representatives (PCRs) to any contracting activity or contract administration office to implement the SBA's policies and programs. The SBA currently has 49 PCRs located in the SBA's six Area Offices.[35] PCRs are required to comply with the contracting agency's directives governing the conduct of contracting personnel and the release of contract information.[36]

PCR duties include the following:

- Review proposed acquisitions to recommend "the setting aside of selected acquisitions not unilaterally set aside by the contracting officer;" new qualified small business sources; and the feasibility of breaking out components of the contract for competitive acquisitions.[37]
- Review proposed acquisition packages. If the PCR (or, if a PCR is not assigned, the SBA Area Office serving the area in which the procuring activity is located) "believes that the acquisition, as proposed, makes it unlikely that small businesses can compete for the prime contract," the PCR can recommend any alternate contracting method that he or she "reasonably believes will increase small business prime contracting opportunities." The recommendation must be made to the contracting officer within 15 days after the package's receipt.[38]
- Recommend small businesses "for inclusion on a list of concerns to be solicited in a specific acquisition."[39]
- Appeal to the contracting office's chief "any contracting officer's determination not to solicit a concern recommended by the SBA for a particular acquisition, when not doing so results in no small

[35] SBA, "Procurement Center Representative Directory," at https://www.sba.gov/federal-contracting/counseling-help/ procurement-center-representative-directory.
[36] FAR §19.402(a)(1).
[37] FAR §19.402(c)(1).
[38] FAR §19.402(c)(2).
[39] FAR §19.402(c)(3).

business being solicited." This appeal may be further appealed to the agency head.[40]

- Conduct periodic reviews of the agency's contracting activity, including the agency's assessment of any required small business subcontracting plan, "to ascertain whether the agency is complying with the small business policies in this regulation."[41]
- Sponsor and participate in conferences and training "designed to increase small business participation in the contracting activities of the office."[42]

The Role of the Office of Small and Disadvantaged Business Utilization

Every federal agency (except the SBA) that has procurement powers is required to have an OSDBU, whose director, by statute, reports directly to the head of the agency and has supervisory authority over agency staff performing certain procurement functions.[43] The OSDBU's primary responsibility is to ensure that small businesses, SDBs, WOSBs, SDVOSBs, and HUBZone small businesses are treated fairly and that they have an opportunity to compete and be selected for a fair amount of the agency's contract dollars. Among its statutory responsibilities are the following:

- "Identify proposed solicitations that involve significant bundling of contract requirements, and work with the agency acquisition officials and the Administration to revise the procurement strategies for such proposed solicitations where appropriate to

[40] FAR §19.402(c)(4). See FAR §19.505 for a description of the appeals process.

[41] FAR §19.402(c)(5).

[42] FAR §19.402(c)(6).

[43] For a discussion of the extent to which Offices of Small and Disadvantaged Business Utilization have implemented these statutory requirements, see U.S. Government Accountability Office (GAO), Small Business Contracting: Actions Needed to Demonstrate and Better Review Compliance with Select Requirements for Small Business Advocates, GAO-17-675, August 25, 2017, pp. 1-4, at https://www.gao.gov/assets/690/686766.pdf.

increase the probability of participation by small businesses as prime contractors, or to facilitate small business participation as subcontractors and suppliers, if a solicitation for a bundled contract is to be issued."[44]

- Assist small businesses "to obtain payments, required late payment interest penalties, or information regarding payments due to the concern from an executive agency or a contractor."[45]
- Assign "a small business technical adviser to each office to which the SBA has assigned" a PCR. The small business technical advisor "shall be a full-time employee of the procuring activity, well qualified, technically trained and familiar with the supplies or services purchased at the activity; and whose principal duty shall be to assist" the PCR.[46]
- Provide the agency's "Chief Acquisition Officer and senior procurement executive ... with advice and comments on acquisition strategies, market research, and justifications [related to limitations on the consolidation of contracts as a means to provide small businesses appropriate opportunities to participate as prime contractors and subcontractors]."[47]
- Provide training to small businesses and contract specialists, provided that the training does not interfere with the director carrying out his or her other responsibilities.[48]
- Ensure that a small business that notifies the PCR prior to a contract's award that "a solicitation, request for proposal, or request for quotation unduly restricts [its] ability ... to compete for the award ... is aware of other resources and processes available to address unduly restrictive provisions ... even if such resources and processes are provided by such agency, the Administration, the

---

[44] 15 U.S.C. §644(k)(5).
[45] 15 U.S.C. §644(k)(6).
[46] 15 U.S.C. §644(k)(8).
[47] 15 U.S.C. §644(k)(12).
[48] 15 U.S.C. §644(k)(13).

Comptroller General, or a Department of Defense (DOD) procurement technical assistance program [described below]."[49]

- Review all subcontracting plans "to ensure that the plan provides maximum practicable opportunity for small business concerns to participate in the performance of the contract to which the plan applies."[50]

In accordance with P.L. 109-163, the National Defense Authorization Act of 2006, the DOD renamed its OSDBU the Office of Small Business Programs (OSBP). The act also redesignated the Army, Navy, and Air Force's OSDBUs to OSBPs of the Department of the Army, Navy, and Air Force, respectively.

The Roles of Other Procurement Officers and Offices

At the agency level, procurement department heads (sometimes titled *senior procurement executive*) are responsible for implementing small business programs at their agencies, including achieving program goals. In general, procurement department staff who work on small business issues (often titled *small business specialists*) coordinate with OSDBU directors on their agencies' small business programs.[51]

Chief acquisition officers provide a focal point for acquisition in agency operations. Their key functions include "monitoring and evaluating agency acquisition activities, increasing the use of full and open competition, increasing performance-based contracting, making acquisition decisions, managing agency acquisition policy, acquisition career management, acquisition resources planning, and conducting acquisition assessments."[52]

---

[49] 15 U.S.C. §644(k)(17).

[50] 15 U.S.C. §644(k)(20).

[51] GAO, Small Business Contracting: Actions Needed to Demonstrate and Better Review Compliance with Select Requirements for Small Business Advocates, GAO-17-675, August 25, 2017, p. 7, at https://www.gao.gov/assets/690/ 686766.pdf.

[52] Ibid., pp. 7-8.

The SBA must assign a *breakout procurement center representative* (breakout PCR) to each major procurement center. A major procurement center is, in the opinion of the SBA Administrator, a procurement center that purchases substantial dollar amounts of other than commercial items, and has the potential to incur significant savings as a result of the placement of a breakout PCR.[53]

The breakout PCR advocates for (1) the appropriate use of full and open competition, and (2) the breakout of items, "when appropriate and while maintaining the integrity of the system in which such items are used."[54] The breakout PCR is in addition to the PCR.

When a breakout PCR is assigned, the SBA must assign at least two co-located small business technical advisors. SBA breakout PCRs and technical advisors must comply with the contracting agency's directives governing the conduct of contracting personnel and the release of contract information. The SBA must obtain security clearances for its breakout PCRs and technical advisors as required by the contracting agency.[55]

The SBA has four *commercial market representatives* who, among other duties, help prime contractors find small businesses that are capable of performing subcontracts; provide counseling on the contractor's responsibility to maximize subcontracting opportunities for small businesses; and conduct periodic reviews of contractors awarded contracts requiring an acceptable subcontracting plan that provides small businesses "the maximum practicable opportunity to participate in contract performance consistent with its efficient performance" (generally any solicitation to perform a contract that is expected to exceed $700,000 ($1.5 million for construction) and that has subcontracting possibilities).[56]

The SBA's *business opportunity specialists* provide, among other duties, guidance, counseling, and referrals for assistance with technical, management, financial, or other matters intended to improve the competitive viability of SBA 8(a) program participants. They provide 8(a)

---

[53] 15 U.S.C. §644(l)(6); and FAR §19.403(a).
[54] FAR §19.403(a).
[55] FAR §19.403(a).
[56] 15 U.S.C. §633(h)(1). For additional information on subcontracting plan requirements, see FAR §19.702(a)(1); and 15 U.S.C. §637(d)(3).

program participants comprehensive assessments of the firm's strengths and weaknesses; monitor and document their compliance with 8(a) program requirements; advise them on compliance with contracting regulations after the award of a 8(a) program contract or subcontract; review and monitor their compliance with mentor-protégé agreements; represent the interests of the SBA Administrator and small businesses in the award, modification, and administration of 8(a) program contracts and subcontracts; and report fraud or abuse involving the 8(a) program.[57]

The *Small Business Procurement Advisory Council* (SBPAC), whose members are composed of the SBA Administrator (or his or her designee), the director of the Minority Business Development Agency, and the head of each OSDBU in each federal agency having procurement powers, has the following statutory duties:

1) Develop positions on proposed procurement regulations affecting the small business community.
2) Submit comments reflecting such positions to appropriate regulatory authorities.
3) Conduct reviews of each OSDBU to determine the office's compliance with its statutory requirements.
4) Identify best practices for maximizing small business utilization in federal contracting that may be implemented by federal agencies having procurement powers.
5) Submit annually, to the House Committee on Small Business and Senate Committee on Small Business and Entrepreneurship, a report describing (1) the comments submitted to appropriate regulatory authorities, including any outcomes related to the comments; (2) the results of its review of each OSDBU; and (3) best practices identified for maximizing small business contracting.[58]

---

[57] 15 U.S.C. §633(g)(1).
[58] 15 U.S.C. §644a(b).

The Defense Logistic Agency's *Procurement Technical Assistance Program* (PTAC) helps "businesses pursue and perform under contracts with the Department of Defense, other federal agencies, state and local governments and with government prime contractors. Most of the assistance the PTACs provide is free. PTAC support to businesses includes registration in systems such as the System for Award Management (SAM), identification of contract opportunities, and help in understanding requirements and in preparing and submitting bids."[59]

SET-ASIDES AND SOLE SOURCE AWARDS

The Competition in Contracting Act of 1984 generally requires "full and open competition" for government procurement contracts.[60] However, various provisions of the Small Business Act authorize or, in some cases, require federal agencies to provide for other than "full and open competition through the use of competitive procedures" when contracting with small businesses. For example, as mentioned previously, federal agencies are generally required to reserve contracts that have an anticipated value greater than the micro-purchase threshold (currently $10,000), but not greater than the simplified acquisition threshold (currently $250,000) exclusively for small businesses unless the contracting officer is unable to obtain offers from two or more small businesses that are competitive with market prices and the quality and delivery of the goods or services being purchased.[61] In addition, federal agencies

---

[59] DOD, Defense Logistics Agency, "Procurement Technical Assistance Program," at http://www.dla.mil/. SmallBusiness/PTAP/. For a list of Procurement Technical Assistance Centers, see SBA, "Procurement Technical Assistance Center," at https://www.sba.gov/tools/local-assistance/ptac.

[60] 41 U.S.C. §253(b)(1); 41 U.S.C. §259(b); and P.L. 98-369, the Deficit Reduction Act of 1984 (Title VII, the Competition in Contracting Act).

[61] 15 U.S.C. §644(j)(1). As mentioned previously, certain regulations implementing this provision of the Small Business Act effectively narrows its scope. For example, certain small business contracts awarded or performed overseas are not necessarily required to be set aside for small businesses, and the small business provisions contained in Part 19 of the FAR generally do not apply to blanket purchase agreements and orders placed against Federal Supply Schedule contracts.

- are generally required to set aside contracts that have an anticipated value exceeding the simplified acquisition threshold exclusively for small businesses when there is a reasonable expectation by the contracting officer that offers will be obtained by at least two responsible small businesses offering the products of different small businesses (Rule of Two) and the award will be made at a fair market price;[62]
- may similarly set aside contracts exceeding the simplified acquisition threshold for competition reserved for specific types of small businesses (e.g., 8(a) small businesses, HUBZone small businesses, WOSBs and SDVOSBs);[63]
- may enter into negotiations directly with particular types of small businesses (e.g., a sole source award) when the award could not otherwise be made (e.g., only a single source is available or under urgent and compelling circumstances);[64] and
- are required to grant HUBZone small businesses a price evaluation preference of not more than 10% in open and unrestricted competitions.[65]

SBA CONTRACTING PROGRAMS[66]

Several SBA programs assist small businesses in obtaining and performing federal contracts and subcontracts. These include various prime

---

[62] 15 U.S.C. §644(a). A set-aside is commonly used to refer to a competition in which only small businesses may compete. However, some set-asides involve small purchases that may be made by means of simplified acquisition procedures that entail less than "full and open competition," and by sealed bidding or contracting by negotiation that is more commonly associated with set-asides of larger contracts.

[63] 15 U.S.C. §637(a) for 8(a) participants; 15 U.S.C §657a for HUBZone small businesses; 15 U.S.C §637(m) for WOSBs; and 15 U.S.C §657f for SDVOSBs.

[64] 15 U.S.C. §637(a) for 8(a) participants; 15 U.S.C §657a for HUBZone small businesses; 15 U.S.C §637(m) for WOSBs; and 15 U.S.C §657f for SDVOSBs.

[65] 15 U.S.C. §657a(b)(3).

[66] These programs apply government-wide but are implemented under the authority of the Small Business Act, pursuant to regulations promulgated by the SBA that determine, in part, eligibility for the programs.

contracting programs; subcontracting programs; and other assistance (e.g., contracting technical training assistance and oversight of the federal small business goaling program and the Surety Bond Guarantee program).

Prime Contracting Programs

Several contracting programs allow small businesses to compete only with similar firms for government contracts or receive sole source awards in circumstances in which such awards could not be made to other firms. These programs provide small businesses an opportunity to win government contracts without having to compete against larger and more experienced companies.

8(a) Program[67]

The 8(a) Minority Small Business and Capital Ownership Development Program (named for the section of the Small Business Act from which it derives its authority) provides business development assistance to businesses owned and controlled by persons who are socially and economically disadvantaged.[68] African Americans, Hispanics, Native Americans (including American Indians, Eskimos, Aleuts, and Native Hawaiians), Asian-Pacific Americans, and Subcontinent Asian Americans are presumed to be socially and economically disadvantaged.[69] Other individuals can also qualify as socially and economically disadvantaged on a case-by-case basis. To be considered economically disadvantaged, an

---

[67] For additional information and analysis, see CRS Report R44844, SBA's "8(a) Program": Overview, History, and Current Issues, by Robert Jay Dilger.

[68] Section 8(a) of the Small Business Act, P.L. 85-536, as amended, can be found at 15 U.S.C. §637(a). Regulations are in 13 C.F.R. §124.

[69] Asian Pacific Americans are those whose country of origin is Burma, Thailand, Malaysia, Indonesia, Singapore, Brunei, Japan, China (including Hong Kong), Taiwan, Laos, Cambodia, Vietnam, Korea, the Philippines, U.S. Trust Territory of the Pacific Islands (Republic of Palau), Republic of the Marshall Islands, Federated States of Micronesia, Commonwealth of the Northern Mariana Islands, Guam, Samoa, Macao, Fiji, Tonga, Kiribati, Tuvalu, or Nauru. Subcontinent Asian Americans are those whose country of origin is India, Pakistan, Bangladesh, Sri Lanka, Bhutan, the Maldives Islands, or Nepal. 13 C.F.R. §124.103(b).

individual's net worth, excluding ownership interest in the 8(a) firm and equity in his or her primary personal residence, must be less than $250,000 at the time of application to the 8(a) Program, and less than $750,000 thereafter.

Federal agencies are authorized to award contracts for goods or services, or to perform construction work, to the SBA for subcontracting to 8(a) firms. The SBA is authorized to delegate the function of executing contracts to the procuring agencies and often does so. Once the SBA has accepted a contract for the 8(a) Program, the contract is awarded through either a set-aside or on a sole source basis, with the contract amount generally determining the acquisition method used. When the contract's anticipated total value, including any options, is less than $4 million ($7 million for manufacturing contracts), the contract is normally awarded without competition (as a sole source award). In contrast, when the contract's anticipated value exceeds these thresholds, the contract generally must be awarded via a set-aside with competition limited to 8(a) firms so long as there is a reasonable expectation that at least two eligible and responsible 8(a) firms will submit offers and the award can be made at fair market price.[70] The SBA also provides technical assistance and training to 8(a) firms. Firms may participate in the 8(a) Program for no more than nine years.

In FY2017, the federal government awarded $27.2 billion to 8(a) firms.

- $16.4 billion was awarded with an 8(a) preference ($8 billion through an 8(a) set-aside and $8.4 billion through an 8(a) sole source award);
- $4.8 billion was awarded to an 8(a) firm in open competition with other firms; and
- $6 billion was awarded with another small business preference (e.g., set-asides and sole source awards for small businesses

[70] 15 U.S.C. §637(a)(1)(D)(ii); and SBA, "Conforming Statutory Amendments and Technical Corrections to Small Business Government Contracting Regulations," 83 Federal Register 12849, March 26, 2018.

generally and for HUBZone firms, women-owned small businesses, and service-disabled veteran-owned small businesses).[71]

Historically Underutilized Business Zone Program[72]

This program assists small businesses located in Historically Underutilized Business Zones (HUBZones) through set-asides, sole source awards (so long as the award can be made at a fair and reasonable price, and the anticipated total value of the contract, including any options, is below $4 million, or $7 million for manufacturing contracts) and price evaluation preferences (of up to 10%) in full and open competitions.[73] The HUBZone program targets assistance to small businesses located in areas with low income, high poverty, or high unemployment.[74] To be certified as a HUBZone small business, at least 35% of the small business's employees must generally reside in a HUBZone.

In FY2017, the federal government awarded $7.53 billion to HUBZone-certified small businesses.

- $1.90 billion was awarded with a HUBZone preference ($1.49 billion through a HUBZone set-aside, $65.3 million through a HUBZone sole source award, and $346.9 million through a HUBZone price-evaluation preference);
- $1.53 billion was awarded to HUBZone-certified small businesses in open competition with other firms; and
- $4.10 billion was awarded with another small business preference (e.g., set-asides and sole source awards for small businesses

---

[71] U.S. General Services Administration (GSA), Federal Procurement Data System—Next Generation, June 5, 2018, at https://www.fpds.gov/fpdsng/.

[72] For additional information and analysis, see CRS Report R41268, Small Business Administration HUBZone Program, by Robert Jay Dilger.

[73] 15 U.S.C. §657a(b)(2-3); and SBA, "Conforming Statutory Amendments and Technical Corrections to Small Business Government Contracting Regulations," 83 Federal Register 12849, March 26, 2018.

[74] For specific criteria, see 15 U.S.C. §632(p)(4); and 13 C.F.R. §126.103.

generally and for 8(a), women-owned, and service-disabled veteran-owned small businesses).[75]

Service-Disabled Veteran-Owned Small Business Program

This program allows agencies to set aside contracts for SDVOSBs. Also, federal agencies may award sole source contracts to SDVOSBs so long as the award can be made at a fair and reasonable price, and the anticipated total value of the contract, including any options, is below $4 million ($6.5 million for manufacturing contracts).[76] For purposes of this program, veterans and service-related disabilities are defined as they are under the statutes governing veterans affairs.[77]

In FY2017, the federal government awarded $18.2 billion to SDVOSBs.

- $6.8 billion was awarded through a SDVOSB set-aside award;
- $4.3 billion was awarded to a SDVOSB in open competition with other firms; and
- $7.1 billion was awarded with another small business preference (e.g., set-asides and sole source awards for small businesses generally and for HUBZone firms, 8(a) firms, and WOSBs).[78]

Women-Owned Small Business Program

Under this program, contracts may be set aside for economically disadvantaged WOSBs in industries in which women are underrepresented and substantially underrepresented. Federal agencies may award sole

---

[75] GSA, Federal Procurement Data System—Next Generation, June 5, 2018, at https://www.fpds.gov/fpdsng/.

[76] 15 U.S.C. §657f(a-b); and SBA, "Conforming Statutory Amendments and Technical Corrections to Small Business Government Contracting Regulations," 83 Federal Register 12849, March 26, 2018.

[77] 38 U.S.C §8127(f). Veteran-owned small businesses and service-disabled veteran-owned small businesses are eligible for separate preferences in procurements conducted by the Department of Veterans Affairs under the authority of P.L. 109-461, the Veterans Benefits, Health Care, and Information Technology Act of 2006, as amended by P.L. 110-389, the Veterans' Benefits Improvements Act of 2008.

[78] GSA, Federal Procurement Data System—Next Generation, June 5, 2018, at https://www.fpds.gov/fpdsng/.

source contracts to WOSBs so long as the award can be made at a fair and reasonable price, and the anticipated total value of the contract, including any options, is below $4 million ($6.5 million for manufacturing contracts).[79]

In FY2017, the federal government awarded $21.3 billion to WOSBs.

- $648.9 million was awarded with a WOSB preference ($580.5 million through a WOSB set-aside and $68.4 million through a WOSB sole source award);
- $7.0 billion was awarded to a WOSB in open competition with other firms; and
- $13.7 billion was awarded with another small business preference (e.g., set-asides and sole source awards for small businesses generally and for HUBZone firms, 8(a) firms, and SDVOSBs).[80]

Subcontracting Programs

Federal contracting officers are required to provide the SBA's PCR (or, if a PCR is not assigned, the SBA Area Office serving the procuring activity area) a "reasonable period of time" to review any solicitation requiring submission of a small business subcontracting plan and to submit advisory findings before the solicitation is issued.[81] The PCR's advisory comments regarding the small business subcontracting plan's acceptability must be submitted, in writing, to the appropriate contracting officer within five working days after the plan's receipt.[82]

As mentioned previously, the SBA's commercial market representatives help prime contractors find small businesses to perform

---

[79] 15 U.S.C. §637(m); and SBA, "Conforming Statutory Amendments and Technical Corrections to Small Business Government Contracting Regulations," 83 Federal Register 12849, March 26, 2018.

[80] GSA, Federal Procurement Data System—Next Generation, June 5, 2018, at https://www.fpds.gov/fpdsng/.

[81] FAR §19.705-3.

[82] SBA, "Prime Contracts Program," SOP 60 02 8, effective October 27, 2013, p. 15, at https://www.sba.gov/document/ sop-60-02-prime-contracts-program.

subcontracts; counsel contractors on their responsibility to maximize subcontracting opportunities for small businesses; and conduct periodic reviews, often in concert with a SBA PCR, of contractors awarded contracts that require an acceptable small business subcontracting plan.[83]

OTHER FEDERAL AGENCY CONTRACTING PROGRAMS

Federal agencies may also set aside contracts or make sole source awards to small businesses not participating in any other program under certain conditions.

Department of Transportation Disadvantaged Business Enterprise Program

The Department of Transportation's (DOT's) Disadvantaged Business Enterprise (DBE) Program originally began in 1980 as a minority/women's business enterprise program "established by regulation under the authority of Title VI of the Civil Rights Act of 1964 and other nondiscrimination statutes that apply to DOT financial assistance programs."[84] Congress has reauthorized the DBE program several times since its inception; most recently in P.L. 114-94, the Fixing America's Surface Transportation Act (FAST-Act).

The FAST-Act provides, that, except to the extent the Secretary of Transportation determines otherwise, not less than 10% of the amounts made available for any program under Titles I (federal-aid highways), II (innovative project finance), III (public transportation) and VI (innovation) of the act and 23 *U.S. Code* 403 (highway safety research and

---

[83] 15 U.S.C. §633(h)(1). For additional information on subcontracting plan requirements, see FAR §19.702(a)(1); and 15 U.S.C. §637(d)(3).

[84] Department of Transportation (DOT), "Disadvantaged Business Enterprise (DBE) Program," at https://www.transportation.gov/civil-rights/disadvantaged-business-enterprise.

development), shall be expended with DBEs. DOT also has a separate DBE program for airport concessions.[85]

A DBE is a for-profit small business owned and controlled by socially and economically disadvantaged individuals.[86] Eligibility for the DBE program differs somewhat from the 8(a) program. For example, under the DBE program, women are presumed to be socially and economically disadvantaged individuals. Also, to be regarded as economically disadvantaged, an individual must have a personal net worth (excluding ownership interest in the firm and equity in his or her primary personal residence) that does not exceed $1.32 million. The DBE must also meet SBA size criteria and have average annual gross receipts not exceeding $23.98 million. Size limits for the airport concessions DBE program are higher.[87]

The DBE program's eight objectives are to

1) ensure nondiscrimination in the award and administration of DOT-assisted contracts in the department's highway, transit, and airport financial assistance programs;
2) create a level playing field on which DBEs can compete fairly for DOT-assisted contracts;
3) ensure that the department's DBE program is narrowly tailored in accordance with applicable law;

---

[85] 49 C.F.R. Part 23. "As recipients of DOT financial assistance, state and local transportation agencies ... certify the eligibility of DBE firms to participate in their DOT-assisted contracts; establish narrowly-tailored goals for the participation of disadvantaged entrepreneurs; and evaluate their DOT-assisted contracts throughout the year and establish contract-specific DBE subcontracting goals as necessary to achieve the overall goal of the agency.... DOT is responsible for developing the rules and regulations for the national DBE program; providing guidance and conducting oversight to make sure that these rules and regulations are followed by the recipients of DOT funds; and considering appeals from state/local certification decisions." DOT, "Definition of a Disadvantaged Business Enterprise," at https://www.transportation.gov/civil-rights/disadvantaged-business-enterprise/definition-disadvantaged-businessenterprise.

[86] DOT, "Definition of a Disadvantaged Business Enterprise," at https://www.transportation.gov/civil-rights/disadvantaged-business-enterprise/definition-disadvantaged-business-enterprise.

[87] Ibid.

4) ensure that only firms that fully meet the program's eligibility standards are permitted to participate as DBEs;
5) help remove DBE-participation barriers in DOT-assisted contracts;
6) promote the use of DBEs in all types of federally-assisted contracts and procurement activities conducted by recipients;
7) assist the development of firms that can compete successfully in the marketplace outside the DBE program; and
8) provide appropriate flexibility to recipients of federal financial assistance in establishing and providing opportunities for DBEs.[88]

Subcontracting Programs for Small Disadvantaged Businesses

Other federal programs promote subcontracting with small disadvantaged businesses (SDBs). SDBs include 8(a) participants and other small businesses that are at least 51% unconditionally owned and controlled by socially or economically disadvantaged individuals or groups. Individuals owning and controlling non-8(a) SDBs may have net worth of up to $750,000 (excluding ownership interests in the SDB firm and equity in their primary personal residence). Otherwise, however, SDBs must generally satisfy the same eligibility requirements as 8(a) firms, although they do not apply to the SBA to be designated SDBs in the same way that 8(a) firms do.

Federal agencies must negotiate "subcontracting plans" with the apparently successful bidder or offeror on eligible prime contracts prior to awarding the contract. Subcontracting plans set goals for the percentage of subcontract dollars to be awarded to SDBs, among others, and describe efforts that will be made to ensure that SDBs "have an equitable opportunity to compete for subcontracts."[89] Federal agencies may also consider the extent of subcontracting with SDBs in determining to whom to award a contract or give contractors "monetary incentives" to subcontract with SDBs.

---

[88] 49 C.F.R. §26.1.

[89] 15 U.S.C. §637(d)(6)(c).

As of February 11, 2019, the SBA's Dynamic Small Business Search database included 2,538 SBA-certified SDBs and 100,595 self-certified SDBs.[90]

Other Small Business Programs of Interest

The SBA 7(j) Management and Technical Assistance Program

The SBA's 7(j) Management and Technical Assistance program provides "a wide variety of management and technical assistance to eligible individuals or concerns to meet their specific needs, including: (a) counseling and training in the areas of financing, management, accounting, bookkeeping, marketing, and operation of small business concerns; and (b) the identification and development of new business opportunities."[91] Eligible individuals and businesses include "8(a) certified firms, SDBs, businesses operating in areas of high unemployment, or low income or firms owned by low income individuals."[92]

In FY2017, the 7(j) Management and Technical Assistance program assisted 4,100 small businesses.[93]

SBA Surety Bond Guarantee Program[94]

The SBA's Surety Bond Guarantee program aims to increase small businesses' access to federal, state, and local government contracting, as

---

[90] SBA, "Dynamic Small Business Search," at http://dsbs.sba.gov/dsbs/search/dsp_dsbs.cfm.

[91] 13 C.F.R. §124.702.

[92] SBA, FY2018 Congressional Budget Justification and FY2016 Annual Performance Report, p. 44, at https://www.sba.gov/sites/default/files/aboutsbaarticle/FINAL_SBA_FY_2018_CBJ_May_22_2017c.pdf.

[93] SBA, FY2019 Congressional Budget Justification and FY2017 Annual Performance Report, p. 74, at https://www.sba.gov/sites/default/files/aboutsbaarticle/SBA_FY_2019_CBJ_APR_2_12_post.pdf.

[94] For additional information and analysis, see CRS Report R42037, SBA Surety Bond Guarantee Program, by Robert Jay Dilger.

well as private-sector contracts, by guaranteeing bid, performance, and payment bonds for small businesses that cannot obtain surety bonds through regular commercial channels.[95] The program guarantees individual contracts of up to $6.5 million and up to $10 million if a federal contracting officer certifies that such a guarantee is necessary. The SBA's guarantee ranges from not to exceed 80% to not to exceed 90% of the surety's loss if a default occurs.[96] In FY2017, the SBA guaranteed 10,397 bid and final surety bonds with a total contract value of more than $6.3 billion.[97]

A surety bond is a three-party instrument between a surety (someone who agrees to be responsible for the debt or obligation of another), a contractor, and a project owner. The agreement binds the contractor to comply with the terms and conditions of a contract. If the contractor is unable to successfully perform the contract, the surety assumes the contractor's responsibilities and ensures that the project is completed. The surety bond reduces the risk associated with contracting.[98]

Surety bonds are meant to encourage project owners to contract with small businesses that may not have the credit history or prior experience of larger businesses and may be at greater risk of failing to comply with the contract's terms and conditions.[99]

Surety bonds are important to small businesses interested in competing for federal contracts because the federal government requires prime contractors—prior to the award of a federal contract exceeding $150,000 for the construction, alteration, or repair of any building or public work of

---

[95] Ancillary bonds are also eligible if they are incidental and essential to a contract for which the SBA has guaranteed a final bond. A reclamation bond is eligible if it is issued to reclaim an abandoned mine site and for a project undertaken for a specific period of time.

[96] P.L. 114-92, the National Defense Authorization Act for Fiscal Year 2016, includes a provision that increased the Preferred Surety Bond Guarantee Program's guarantee rate from not to exceed 70% to not to exceed 90% of losses starting one year from enactment (effective November 25, 2016). For additional information and analysis, see CRS Report R42037, SBA Surety Bond Guarantee Program, by Robert Jay Dilger.

[97] SBA, FY2019 Congressional Budget Justification and FY2017 Annual Performance Report, p. 66, at https://www.sba.gov/sites/default/files/aboutsbaarticle/SBA_FY_2019_CBJ_APR_2_12_post.pdf.

[98] SBA, "Surety Bonds," at https://www.sba.gov/category/navigation-structure/loans-grants/bonds/surety-bonds.

[99] Ibid.

the United States—to furnish a performance bond issued by a surety satisfactory to the contracting officer in an amount that the officer considers adequate to protect the government.[100]

Small Business Mentor-Protégé Programs[101]

Small business mentor-protégé programs typically seek to pair new businesses with more experienced businesses in mutually beneficial relationships. Protégés may receive financial, technical, or management assistance from mentors in obtaining and performing federal contracts or subcontracts, or serving as suppliers under such contracts or subcontracts. Mentors may receive credit toward subcontracting goals, reimbursement of certain expenses, or other incentives.

The federal government currently has several mentor-protégé programs to assist small businesses in various ways.

- The *8(a) Mentor-Protégé Program* is a government-wide program designed to assist small businesses "owned and controlled by socially and economically disadvantaged individuals" participating in the SBA's Minority Small Business and Capital Ownership Development Program (commonly known as the 8(a) program) in obtaining and performing federal contracts. For that purpose, mentors may (1) form joint ventures with protégés that are eligible to perform federal contracts set aside for small businesses; (2)

---

[100] The threshold amount was originally set at $2,000 in 1935 under P.L. 74-321, An Act Requiring Contracts for the Construction, Alteration, and Repair of Any Public Building or Public Work of the United States to be Accompanied by a Performance Bond Protecting the United States and an Additional Bond for the Protection of Persons Furnishing Material or Labor for the Construction, Alteration, or Repair of Said Public Buildings or Public Work [the Miller Act of 1935], 49 Stat. 793 (August 24, 1935) (codified at 40 U.S.C. §3131(a)(b)). Also, see Department of Defense, General Services Administration, and National Aeronautics and Space Administration, "Federal Acquisition Regulation; Inflation Adjustment of Acquisition-Related Thresholds," 75 Federal Register 53130, August 30, 2010.

[101] For additional information and analysis of federal small business mentor-protégé programs, see CRS Report R41722, Small Business Mentor-Protégé Programs, by Robert Jay Dilger.

make certain equity investments in protégé firms; (3) lend or subcontract to protégé firms; and (4) provide technical or management assistance to their protégés.[102]

- The *SBA's All Small Business Mentor-Protégé Program* is a government-wide mentor-protégé program for all small business concerns, consistent with the SBA's mentor-protégé program for participants in the SBA's 8(a) Business Development program.[103]
- The *Department of Defense (DOD) Mentor-Protégé Program*, in contrast, is agency-specific. It assists various types of small businesses and other entities in obtaining and performing DOD subcontracts and serving as suppliers on DOD contracts. Mentors may (1) make advance or progress payments to their protégés that DOD reimburses; (2) award subcontracts to their protégés on a noncompetitive basis when they would not otherwise be able to do so; (3) lend money to or make investments in protégé firms; and (4) provide or arrange for other assistance.[104]

Other agencies also have agency-specific mentor-protégé programs to assist various types of small businesses or other entities in obtaining and performing subcontracts under agency prime contracts. The Department of Homeland Security (DHS), for example, has a mentor-protégé program wherein mentors may provide protégés with rent-free use of facilities or equipment, temporary personnel for training, property, loans, or other assistance. Because these programs are not based in statute, unlike the SBA and DOD programs, they generally rely upon preexisting authorities (e.g., authorizing use of evaluation factors) or publicity to incentivize mentor participation. Currently, more than 1,200 mentor-protégé agreements are in place, even though there are issues with the accuracy and thoroughness of some federal agency records.[105]

---

[102] 15 U.S.C. §636(j)(10); and 13 C.F.R. §124.520.

[103] 15 U.S.C. §657r; SBA, "Small Business Mentor Protégé Programs," 81 Federal Register 48558-48595, July 25, 2016; and 13 C.F.R. §125.9.

[104] 10 U.S.C. §2302note: Mentor-Protégé Pilot Program.

[105] As of February 27, 2018, there were 493 active 8(a) mentor-protégé agreements. See Small Business Procurement Advisory Council, "All Small Mentor Protégé Program," February 27, 2018.

SMALL BUSINESS PROCUREMENT GOALS

Since 1978, federal agency heads have been required to establish federal procurement goals, in consultation with the SBA, "that realistically reflect the potential of small business concerns and small business concerns owned and controlled by socially and economically disadvantaged individuals" to participate in federal procurement. Each agency is required, at the conclusion of each fiscal year, to report its progress in meeting the goals to the SBA.[106]

In 1988, Congress authorized the President annually to establish government-wide minimum participation goals for procurement contracts awarded to small businesses and small businesses owned and controlled by socially and economically disadvantaged individuals. Congress required the government-wide minimum participation goal for small businesses to be "not less than 20% of the total value of all prime contract awards for each fiscal year" and "not less than 5% of the total value of all prime contract and subcontract awards for each fiscal year" for small businesses owned and controlled by socially and economically disadvantaged individuals.[107]

Each federal agency was also directed to "have an annual goal that presents, for that agency, the maximum practicable opportunity for small business concerns and small business concerns owned and controlled by socially and economically disadvantaged individuals to participate in the performance of contracts let by such agency."[108] The SBA was also

---

As of December 5, 2018, there were 644 active all small business mentor-protégé agreements. See SBA, "Active mentor-protégé agreements," at https://www.sba.gov/document/support—active-mentor-protege-agreements.

As of January 1, 2018, there were 63 active Department of Defense (DOD) mentor-protégé agreements. See DOD, Office of Small Business Programs, "Active MPP [Mentor-Protégé Program] Agreements," at http://business.defense.gov/Programs/Mentor-Protege-Program/Protege-Eligibility-Requirements/.

[106] 15 U.S.C. §644(g)(2); and P.L. 95-507, a bill to amend the Small Business Act and the Small Business Investment Act of 1958.

[107] 15 U.S.C. §644(g)(1); and P.L. 100-656, the Business Opportunity Development Reform Act of 1988. The government-wide minimum participation goal for small businesses was increased from 20% to 23% by P.L. 105-135, the Small Business Reauthorization Act of 1997.

[108] Ibid.

required to report to the President annually on the attainment of the goals and to include the information in an annual report to Congress.[109] The SBA negotiates the goals with each federal agency and establishes a *small business eligible* baseline for evaluating the agency's performance.[110] The agency head is required to "make consistent efforts to annually expand participation by small business concerns from each industry category."[111] If the SBA and the agency cannot agree on the goals, the agency may submit the case to the Office of Management and Budget (OMB) Office of Federal Procurement Policy (OFPP) for resolution.[112]

The small business eligible baseline excludes certain contracts that the SBA has determined do not realistically reflect the potential for small business participation in federal procurement (such as those awarded to mandatory and directed sources), contracts funded predominately from agency-generated sources (i.e., non-appropriated funds), contracts not covered by the FAR, acquisitions on behalf of foreign governments, and contracts not reported in the Federal Procurement Data System – Next Generation, or FPDS-NG (such as government procurement card purchases and contracts valued less than $10,000).[113] These exclusions typically account for 18% to 20% of all federal prime contracts each year.

The SBA then evaluates the agencies' performance against their negotiated goals annually, using FPDS-NG data, managed by the U.S. General Services Administration (GSA), to generate the small business

---

[109] Ibid.

[110] According to a 2001 GAO report, the SBA began to specify what types of contracts the Federal Procurement Data System would exclude when determining agency compliance with federal contracting goals in FY1998. Prior to FY1998, "agencies reported their small business achievements directly to SBA and excluded from their calculations certain types of contracts, such as those for which small businesses had a limited or no chance to compete. SBA then published an annual report summarizing each agency's achievements. SBA officials said that in some cases they were not aware of all exclusions the agencies made when reporting their numbers." GAO, Small Business: More Transparency Needed in Prime Contract Goal Program, GAO-01-551, August 1, 2001, pp. 9-10, at http://www.gao.gov/assets/240/231854.pdf.

[111] 15 U.S.C. §644(g)(2).

[112] SBA, Office of Policy, Planning & Liaison, Office of Government Contracting & Business Development, "FY 2018 Goaling Guidelines," August 30, 2017, p. 4, at https://www.sba.gov/document/report—sba-goaling-guidelines.

[113] Ibid., p. 3; and GSA, Federal Procurement Data System—Next Generation, "What's In FPDS-NG," at https://www.fpds.gov/wiki/index.php/FPDS-NG_FAQ.

eligible baseline. This information is compiled into the official Small Business Goaling Report, which the SBA releases annually. Each agency that fails to achieve any proposed prime or subcontract goal is required to submit a justification to the SBA on why it failed to achieve a proposed or negotiated goal with a proposed plan of corrective action.[114]

Agencies can take credit in every category that is applicable to the recipient of the contract. For example, "when counting goaling achievements, a contract awarded to a service-disabled Veteran-Owned Woman-Owned Small Business would be counted toward the Small Business (SB) goal, the Service-Disabled Veteran-Owned Small Business (SDVOSB) goal and the Women-Owned Small Business (WOSB) goal. However, these category counts are not summed to triple the total count. *The Sum of Parts Does Not Equal the Whole* (italics in original)."[115]

Over the years, federal government-wide procurement goals have been established for small businesses generally (P.L. 100-656, the Business Opportunity Development Reform Act of 1988, and P.L. 105-135, the HUBZone Act of 1997—Title VI of the Small Business Reauthorization Act of 1997); small businesses owned and controlled by socially and economically disadvantaged individuals (P.L. 100-656); women (P.L. 103-355, the Federal Acquisition Streamlining Act of 1994); small businesses located within a HUBZone (P.L. 105-135); and small businesses owned and controlled by a service-disabled veteran (P.L. 106-50, the Veterans Entrepreneurship and Small Business Development Act of 1999).

The current federal small business procurement goals are

- at least 23.0% of the total value of all small business eligible prime contract awards to small businesses for each fiscal year;

---

[114] SBA, Office of Policy, Planning & Liaison, Office of Government Contracting & Business Development, "FY 2018 Goaling Guidelines," August 30, 2017, p. 6, at https://www.sba.gov/document/report—sba-goaling-guidelines.

[115] Ibid., p. 5. "The exception to this non-additive rule is for total Small Disadvantaged Business (SDB) which is the sum of 8(a) and non-8(a) SDBs. Each special type of small business is first of all a small business. That also means Federal procurements awarded to SDVOSB will also have been awarded to Veteran-Owned Small Business (VOSB)."

- 5.0% of the total value of all small business eligible prime contract awards and subcontract awards to small disadvantaged businesses (including participants in the SBA's 8(a) Program) for each fiscal year;[116]
- 5.0% of the total value of all small business eligible prime contract awards and subcontract awards to women-owned small businesses;
- 3.0% of the total value of all small business eligible prime contract awards and subcontract awards to HUBZone small businesses;[117] and
- 3.0% of the total value of all small business eligible prime contract awards and subcontract awards to service-disabled veteran-owned small businesses.[118]

There are no punitive consequences for not meeting these goals. However, the SBA's Small Business Goaling Report is distributed widely, receives media attention, and serves to heighten public awareness of the issue of small business contracting. For example, agency performance as reported in the SBA's Small Business Goaling Report is often cited by Members during their questioning of federal agency witnesses during congressional hearings.

As shown in Table 1, the *FY2017 Small Business Goaling Report*, using FPDS-NG data, indicates that federal agencies met the federal procurement goal for small businesses generally, small disadvantaged businesses, and service-disabled veteran-owned small businesses in FY2017.

Table 1 also provides, for comparative purposes, the percentage of total reported federal contracts (without exclusions) awarded to those small businesses in FY2017.

---

[116] For additional information and analysis of the SBA's 8(a) Program, see CRS Report R44844, SBA's "8(a) Program": Overview, History, and Current Issues, by Robert Jay Dilger.

[117] For additional information and analysis of the HUBZone program, see CRS Report R41268, Small Business Administration HUBZone Program, by Robert Jay Dilger.

[118] 15 U.S.C. §644(g)(1)-(2).

Table 1. Federal Procurement Goals and Percentage of FY2017 Federal Contract Dollars Awarded to Small Businesses, by Type

Business Type	Federal Goal	Percentage of Federal Contracts (small business eligible)	Percentage of Federal Contracts (all reported contracts)
Small Businesses	23.0%	23.88%	21.70%
Small Disadvantaged Businesses	5.0%	9.10%	8.41%
Women-Owned Small Businesses	5.0%	4.71%	4.20%
HUBZone Small Businesses	3.0%	1.65%	1.48%
Service-Disabled Veteran-Owned Small Businesses	3.0%	4.05%	3.59%

Sources: U.S. Small Business Administration, "Statutory Guidelines," at https://www.sba.gov/content/statutoryguidelines-0 (federal goals); U.S. General Services Administration, Federal Procurement Data System—Next Generation, "Small Business Goaling Report: Fiscal Year 2017," at https://www.fpds.gov/downloads/ top_requests/FPDSNG_SB_Goaling_FY_2017.pdf and U.S. General Services Administration, Federal Procurement Data System—Next Generation, at https://www.fpds.gov/fpdsng/ (contract dollars).

Notes: The Small Business Goaling Report for FY2017 reports that small business eligible contracts, as of May 18, 2018, totaled $442.5 billion and that $105.7 billion was awarded to small businesses, $40.2 billion to small disadvantaged businesses, $20.8 billion to women-owned small businesses, $7.3 billion to SBA-certified HUBZone small businesses, and $17.9 billion to service-disabled veteran-owned small businesses. The Small Business Goaling Report for FY2017 does not indicate the total amount of federal contracts reported in the FPDS-NG on May 18, 2018. The percentages provided in the column for all reported contracts in FY2017 were calculated using FPDS-NG data for all contracts as reported on May 30, 2018: $508.8 billion in total contracts; $110.4 billion to small businesses, $42.8 billion to small disadvantaged businesses, $21.4 billion to women-owned small businesses, $7.5 billion to SBA-certified HUBZone small businesses, and $18.3 billion to service-disabled veteran-owned small businesses.

CERTIFICATE OF COMPETENCY PROGRAM

Before awarding a federal contract, the contracting officer must affirmatively determine that the business is responsible to perform the contract. If the contracting officer determines that an apparent successful small business offeror lacks certain elements of responsibility (e.g., is unable to fulfill the requirements of a specific government procurement because it lacks capability, competency, capacity, credit, integrity, perseverance, tenacity, or limitations on subcontracting), the officer is required to refer the matter in writing to the SBA for review and a possible Certificate of Competency (COC), even if the next acceptable offer is also from a small business.[119] The COC certifies in writing that the small business meets all required elements of responsibility for the purpose of receiving and performing a specific government contract. The "COC program empowers the SBA to certify to contracting officers as to all elements of responsibility of any small business concern to receive and perform a specific government contract. The COC program does not extend to questions concerning regulatory requirements imposed and enforced by other federal agencies."[120]

POST-AWARD REQUIREMENTS

As mentioned previously, the SBA's commercial market representatives conduct periodic compliance reviews of contractors awarded contracts that require an acceptable small business subcontracting plan.[121] In addition, once the contract is completed, federal agencies are required to pay the contractor on a timely basis and pay interest penalties for late payments. Under specified circumstances, federal agencies may also pay contractors before the contract's payment's due date.

Small Business Subcontracting Plan Reviews

The periodic compliance review can take place on-site, at the contracting agency, or virtual.[122] Materials that may be reviewed include

---

[119] 15 U.S.C. §637(b)(7); and FAR §19.601(a-e).

[120] FAR §19.601(b).

[121] 15 U.S.C. §633(h).

[122] SBA, "Subcontracting Assistance Program Post Award," SOP 60 03 7, effective July 17, 2018, p. 11, at https://www.sba.gov/document/sop-60-03-subcontracting-assistance-program-post-award.

the contractor's contract files, correspondence that is directly or indirectly related to the contract, IT systems, subcontracting methods, and procedures.[123] Contractors are selected randomly for audit.[124] The SBA may enter into agreements with other federal agencies to conduct these assessments.[125]

The compliance report includes compliant and non-compliant items found during the assessment of the contractor's subcontracting activities and a rating indicating the contractor's level of compliance or non-compliance, ranging from unsatisfactory to outstanding.[126] If any deficiencies are found, the contractor is required to submit, within 30 days of the compliance review rating letter date, a corrective action plan (CAP).[127] The CAP is submitted to the SBA Area Office via email, or any method designated by the SBA. The commercial market representative conducts a follow-up compliance report within six months to a year of the date the SBA acknowledges receipt of the contractor's CAP to ensure that corrective actions have been taken to eliminate the deficiencies. The SBA keeps the federal agency that awarded the contract informed of the contractor's adherence to correcting the deficiencies.[128]

If the contractor refuses to provide or address all deficiencies in the CAP, a delinquent CAP letter is sent advising the contractor that it has 15 days from the letter's date to comply with federal regulations. If an acceptable CAP is not received in the allotted time frame the case is escalated to the SBA's subcontracting program manager who informs the SBA's Office of Government Contracting director and works with the SBA's Office of General Counsel and the federal agency that awarded the contract for resolution or to begin accessing liquidated damages.[129]

---

[123] Ibid.

[124] Ibid., p. 12.

[125] Ibid., p. 14.

[126] 13 C.F.R. §125.3(e)(3).

[127] SBA, "Subcontracting Assistance Program Post Award," SOP 60 03 7, effective July 17, 2018, p. 12, at https://www.sba.gov/document/sop-60-03-subcontracting-assistance-program-post-award.

[128] Ibid., p. 13.

[129] Ibid. Liquidated damages are predetermined sums a contractor must pay the procuring agency for specified contract breaches or performance failures. For additional information and

Prompt Payments

Once a contract is awarded, federal agencies are generally required to pay interest to prime contractors on any invoice payments the agency fails to make by the date(s) specified in the contract, or within 30 days of receipt of a *proper invoice* for the amount due if no date is specified in the contract.[130]

Similar requirements exist for prime contractors in paying subcontractors on construction contracts. These requirements are especially important for small businesses in the construction industry. Specifically, every construction contract awarded by a federal agency must contain clauses obligating the prime contractor to (1) pay the subcontractor for "satisfactory performance" under the subcontract within seven days of receiving payment from the agency and (2) pay interest on any amounts that are not paid within the proper time frame.[131] The contract must also obligate the prime contractor to include similar payment and interest penalty terms in its subcontracts, as well as require its subcontractors to impose these terms on *their* subcontractors. This latter provision ensures that the payment and interest penalty requirements *flow down* to all tiers of construction subcontractors.

In addition, required subcontracting plans must incorporate terms obligating the prime contractor to notify the agency awarding the contract in writing if a subcontractor is paid a reduced price for goods supplied or services completed under the contract, or if payment is made to the subcontractor more than 90 days past due. The prime contractor must include the reason for the reduction in payment or failure to pay a

---

analysis, see CRS Report R45322, Selected Legal Tools for Maintaining Government Contractor Accountability, by David H. Carpenter and Kathleen Ann Ruane.

[130] 31 U.S.C. §3903(a); and P.L. 97-177, the Prompt Payment Act. Among other things, a proper invoice contains (1) the name of the contractor, the invoice date, and the contract number; (2) a description of the goods rendered and the shipping and payment terms; (3) other substantiating documentation or information required under the contract; and (4) the name, title, telephone number, and complete mailing address of the person to whom payment should be sent. 31 U.S.C. §3901(a); and 48 C.F.R. §32.905(b)(1)(i)-(x). The interest rate to be used is that determined by the Secretary of the Treasury twice a year under the Contract Disputes Act. 31 U.S.C. §3902(a).

[131] 31 U.S.C. §3905(b); and P.L. 100-496, the Prompt Payment Act Amendments of 1988.

subcontractor within 90 days.[132] If the contracting officer for a *covered contract* (a contract that requires an acceptable subcontracting plan) determines that a prime contractor has a history of unjustified, untimely payments to contractors, the contracting officer shall record the contractor's identity, describe the circumstances under which the contractor may be determined to have a history of unjustified, untimely payments to subcontractors, and include the contractor's identity in, and make publicly available through, the Federal Awardee Performance and Integrity Information System, or any successor.[133] This information is used by federal agencies to "evaluate the business ethics and quality of prospective contractors competing for Federal contracts and to protect taxpayers from doing business with contractors that are not responsible sources."[134]

Accelerated Payments

Federal agencies are permitted to make an accelerated payment up to seven days before the required payment date in a federal contract, or earlier if the agency deems it necessary on a case-by-case basis if, after receiving a proper invoice, it is in the best interest of the government, and any of the following is true:

- the invoice in under $2,500;
- the payment is to a small business; or

---

[132] 15 U.S.C. §637(d)(13)(A-B); and U.S. Department of the Treasury, Bureau of the Fiscal Service, "Prompt Payment," at https://www.fiscal.treasury.gov/fsservices/gov/pmt/promptPayment/promptPayment_home.htm. Under a construction contract, an agency may withhold payment to a prime vendor if it learns that the prime vendor has failed to pay subcontractors in accordance with the terms of the contract.

[133] 15 U.S.C. §637(d)(13)(C-E).

[134] Department of Defense, General Services Administration, and National Aeronautics and Space Administration, "Federal Acquisition Regulation; FAR Case 2008-027, Federal Awardee Performance and Integrity Information System," 75 Federal Register 14059, March 23, 2010.

- the payment is related to an emergency, disaster, or military deployment.[135]

In addition, the Secretary of Defense is required, to the fullest extent permitted by law, to establish an accelerated payment date for its small business prime contractors, with a goal of 15 days after receipt of a proper invoice for the amount due if a specific payment date is not established by contract.[136]

The Secretary of Defense is also required to establish, to the fullest extent permitted by law, an accelerated payment date for its prime contractors that subcontract with small businesses, with a goal of 15 days after receipt of a proper invoice for the amount due if a specific payment date is not established by contract and the prime contractor agrees to make payments to the subcontractor "in accordance with the accelerated payment date, to the maximum extent practicable, without any further consideration from or fees charged to the subcontractor."[137]

CONCLUSION

The small business contracting programs described in this chapter generally have strong bipartisan support. However, that does not mean that these programs face no opposition or that issues have not been raised concerning the impact or operations of specific programs. For example, small business advocates

- seek policies that reduce or eliminate exclusions that narrow the reach of small business contracting preferences,

---

[135] 31 U.S.C. §3903(a)(8); Office of Management and Budget, "Prompt Payment," 64 Federal Register 52582-52583, September 29, 1999; and 5 C.F.R. §1315.5.

[136] 10 U.S.C. §2307(2)(A); and P.L. 115-232, the John S. McCain National Defense Authorization Act for Fiscal Year 2019.

[137] 10 U.S.C. §2307(2)(B); and P.L. 115-232, the John S. McCain National Defense Authorization Act for Fiscal Year 2019.

- want the SBA to use the total value of all prime contract awards in the Small Business Goaling Report,[138] and
- want the SBA to use a more discerning methodology for awarding performance grades to federal agencies in meeting its small business contracting goals.[139]

Critics have questioned some of these programs' effectiveness, in terms of both promoting small business opportunities to win federal contracts and a more diversified, robust economy.[140]

Many observers judge the relative success or failure of federal efforts to enhance small business contracting opportunities by whether the federal government and individual federal agencies meet the procurement goals in the annual Small Business Goaling Report. In recent years, the federal government has generally succeeded in meeting the government-wide

---

[138] See American Small Business League v. Maria Contreras-Sweet in her capacity as Administrator of the United States Small Business Administration, May 3, 2016, at http://www.asbl.com/documents/ Filed_Complaint_For_Injunctive_Relief.pdf.

The federal government awarded more than $508.8 billion in federal contracts in FY2017. About $442.5 billion of that amount was deemed small business eligible. GSA, Federal Procurement Data System—Next Generation, at https://www.fpds.gov/fpdsng/ (contract dollar amount); and GSA, Federal Procurement Data System—Next Generation, "Small Business Goaling Report: Fiscal Year 2017," at https://www.fpds.gov/ downloads/top_requests/ FPDSNG_SB_Goaling_FY_2017.pdf.

[139] See Steven Koprince, "Let's Replace SBA Small Business Goaling Grades with Participation Trophies," SmallGovCon, May 29, 2018, at http://smallgovcon.com/uncategorized/lets-replace-sba-small-business-goaling-gradeswith-participation-trophies/.

The SBA's small business contracting scorecard methodology has four weighted components: 50% based on prime contracting achievement, 20% based on subcontracting achievement, 10% based on a comparison of the number of small business prime contractors in each of the five small business categories in the agency's top 100 small business NAICS codes between FY2016 and FY2017, and 20% based on each Office of Small and Disadvantaged Business Utilization (OSDBU) peer review on agency compliance with section 15(k) of the Small Business Act (18 requirements in FY2017, 21 in FY2018). SBA, "Contracting Scorecard Grading Methodology," at https://www.sba.gov/document/ support—contracting-scorecard-grading-methodology. For additional information and analysis of the SBA's methodology, see GAO, Small Business Administration: Actions Needed to Improve Confidence in Small Business Procurement Scorecard, GAO-18-672, September 27, 2018, at https://www.gao.gov/assets/700/694777.pdf.

[140] For example, see Henry Beale and Nicola Deas, "The HUBZone Report," prepared for the SBA, Office of Advocacy, May 2008, pp. i, ii, 124-131, at https://www.sba.gov/sites/ default/files/rs325tot.pdf; and Clifford A. Grammich, Thomas R. Edison, Jr., Nancy Young Moore, and Edward G. Keating, Small Business and Defense Acquisitions: A Review of Policies and Current Practices (Santa Monica, CA: RAND, 2011), pp. xii, 15, 16, at https://www.rand.org/content/dam/rand/pubs/ monographs/2011/RAND_MG443.pdf.

goals of awarding 23% of the total value of all small business eligible prime contract awards to small businesses generally, 5% to SDBs, and 3% to SDVOSBs. However, it has had difficulty meeting the goals of 5% to WOSBs and 3% to HUBZone small businesses.[141]

The Small Business Goaling Report is the most convenient measure available to compare federal small business contracting performance over time, but it has limitations. For example, the report does not include all federal contracts, because some are not deemed to be small business eligible and others are not recorded in the FPDS-NG. In addition, the report does not evaluate the effect these contracts have on small businesses, industry competitiveness, or the overall economy. As one group of researchers has argued,

> the entire goal-setting process ... is geared to measuring the dollars and contracts awarded to small business, and pays little attention to the effect that access to government contracts has on small business starts, growth, and wealth generation. Results of the program are also hard to isolate, difficult to measure, and generally not judged against the next best or other alternative policies [emphasis in original].142

Comprehensive studies examining the effect of small business contracting preferences on small business startups, growth, wealth generation, and industry competitiveness may prove useful for congressional oversight. In the meantime, although the Small Business Goaling Report has its limitations, it can help policymakers identify programs most in need of examination. For example, the SBA has announced that it is focusing additional efforts on promoting the HUBZone program to federal contracting officials, primarily due to the continuing

---

141 SBA, "The Federal Government Achieves Small Business Contracting Goal for the Fifth Consecutive Year with Record-Breaking $105 Billion to Small Businesses," at https://www.sba.gov/about-sba/sba-newsroom/press-releases-media-advisories/federal-government-achieves-small-business-contracting-goal-fifth-consecutive-year-record-breaking.

142 Clifford A. Grammich, Thomas R. Edison, Jr., Nancy Young Moore, and Edward G. Keating, Small Business and Defense Acquisitions: A Review of Policies and Current Practices (Santa Monica, CA: RAND, 2011), p. 15, at https://www.rand.org/content/dam/rand/pubs/monographs/2011/RAND_MG443.pdf.

difficulties federal agencies have had in meeting the 3% goal for HUBZone small businesses.[143]

[143] SBA, FY2019 Congressional Budget Justification and FY2017 Annual Performance Report, pp. 75-77, at https://www.sba.gov/sites/default/files/aboutsbaarticle/SBA_FY_19_508-Final-FINAL.PDF.

In: Small Business Issues
Editor: Andrea Moeller
ISBN: 978-1-53615-870-0

Chapter 2

SMALL BUSINESS CONTRACTING: ACTIONS NEEDED TO DEMONSTRATE COMPLIANCE WITH REQUIREMENTS FOR SMALL BUSINESS ADVOCATES*

William B. Shear

WHY GAO DID THIS STUDY

Section 15(k) of the Small Business Act requires federal agencies with procurement powers to establish an OSDBU to advocate for small businesses. The National Defense Authorization Act for Fiscal Year 2013 established additional requirements for OSDBUs and required SBPAC to review OSDBU compliance with section 15(k) requirements.

* This is an edited, reformatted and augmented version of United States Government Accountability Office; Testimony Before the Subcommittee on Contracting and Workforce, Committee on Small Business, House of Representatives, Publication No. GAO-18-191T, dated October 25, 2017.

This testimony is based on a report GAO issued in August 2017 (GAO-17- 675). For that report, GAO examined (1) the extent to which selected federal agencies demonstrated compliance with thirteen section 15(k) requirements for OSDBUs and (2) SBPAC review process results. GAO selected 10 agencies, based on contracting obligations, to review a reporting requirement for OSDBU directors. For the other 12 requirements, GAO surveyed OSDBU directors at 24 agencies, selected based on contracting obligations (100 percent response rate). To review and augment survey responses, GAO also analyzed guidance and documents and interviewed OSDBU directors.

What GAO Recommends

In GAO-17-675, GAO made recommendations to 20 agencies, including that agencies not demonstrating compliance with section 15(k) requirements comply or report to Congress on why they had not, and that SBA provide more detailed guidance for the new SBPAC review process. Agency responses to the recommendations varied. As discussed in the report, GAO maintains that implementation of each of its recommendations is warranted.

What GAO Found

Demonstrated compliance with selected section 15(k) requirements for the Office of Small and Disadvantaged Business Utilization (OSDBU) varied across the 24 agencies GAO surveyed. Examples of GAO findings (which relate to both OSDBU directors and OSDBU functions) include the following:

- Five agencies did not demonstrate compliance with a requirement to limit collateral duties of OSDBU directors.
- Six agencies did not demonstrate compliance with a requirement for compensation and seniority of OSDBU directors.
- Twenty-three agencies demonstrated compliance for four requirements on OSDBU director experience, supervisory duties of the OSDBU director, identifying and addressing significant bundling of contracts (consolidation of procurement requirements into a solicitation for a single contract), and providing assistance on payments.
- Fifteen agencies demonstrated compliance with a requirement to respond to notification by a small business that a solicitation unduly restricts the ability of the small business to compete for the award.
- Four OSDBU directors did not report directly to the agency head or deputy head (the one requirement for which GAO reviewed only 10 agencies).

Noncompliance with section 15(k) requirements may limit the extent to which an OSDBU can advocate for small businesses. For example, OSDBU influence in agencies might be limited if directors reported to lower levels of management. Directors with other duties might be less able to carry out all section 15(k) duties.

Results of the Small Business Procurement Advisory Council's (SBPAC) annual review of compliance with section 15(k) requirements differed from GAO's assessments. The Small Business Administration (SBA) chairs SBPAC, and its members are nearly all OSDBU directors. All agencies in the most recent review scored 94–98 percent (of 100 percent). But where GAO's review considered the same section 15(k) requirements as the SBPAC review, GAO found some agencies had not demonstrated compliance with multiple requirements. Other than reviewing documentation agencies choose to provide, SBA's guidance for the review panel does not indicate any other means by which reviewers could obtain or clarify information. GAO's review included follow-up discussions with agency officials to obtain or clarify information.

SBA has been developing a new review process, but preliminary information GAO reviewed indicates the process will be similar to the current one. According to federal standards for internal control, management should use quality information to make informed decisions. Under the new process, the review results (which SBA uses in another process that determines an agency's overall grade for small business contracting) also will carry twice as much weight as under the current process—underscoring the importance of the review results. A new review process substantially similar to the old one (especially in relation to guidance) may not provide a reliable indicator of OSDBU compliance with section 15(k) requirements.

Chairman Knight, Ranking Member Murphy, and Members of the Subcommittee:

I am pleased to be here today to discuss our recent work on the Offices of Small and Disadvantaged Business Utilization (OSDBU). As you know, the federal government has a long-standing policy to maximize contracting opportunities for small businesses. To help increase small business visibility among federal agencies, in 1978 Congress amended the Small Business Act to require that all federal agencies with procurement powers establish an OSDBU, which would advocate for small businesses in procurement and contracting processes.[1] Section 15(k) of the act contains provisions related to OSDBUs.

The National Defense Authorization Act for Fiscal Year 2013 further amended the Small Business Act with provisions intended to strengthen the position of the OSDBU director (director-related requirements). Section

[1] The provisions for OSDBUs were further amended, including in the National Defense Authorization Act for Fiscal Year 2013 (Pub. L. No. 112-239, § 1691, 126 Stat. 1632, 2087 (2013)); the National Defense Authorization Act for Fiscal Year 2016 (Pub. L. No. 114-92, § 870, 129 Stat. 726, 938 (2015)); and the National Defense Authorization Act for Fiscal Year 2017 (Pub. L. No. 114-328, §§ 1812, 1813, 1821, 130 Stat. 2000, 2652, 2654 (2016)). Our report, upon which this testimony is based, did not include amendments in the National Defense Authorization Act of Fiscal Year 2017 because the statute was amended during the time GAO was conducting the report review.

15(k) of the Small Business Act also includes required functions and duties of OSDBUs (functional requirements).

My testimony is based on our August 2017 report (GAO-17-675) that examined (1) the extent to which selected federal agencies demonstrated compliance with five section 15(k) requirements relating to the OSDBU director; (2) the extent to which selected federal agencies demonstrated compliance with eight section 15(k) requirements on OSDBU functions or activities; and (3) the review by the Small Business Procurement Advisory Council (SBPAC) of OSDBU compliance with section 15(k) requirements.[2]

For the August 2017 report, we reviewed 24 agencies (civilian and military). For one director-related requirement (that the OSDBU director report to the agency head or deputy head), we reviewed 10 of the 24 agencies and analyzed reports, position descriptions, and performance appraisals and interviewed OSDBU directors and agency officials. For the rest of the requirements in our review, we surveyed the 24 OSDBU directors, reviewed agency documents, and interviewed OSDBU directors and agency officials. To make our determinations of demonstrated compliance, we used agency documentation, survey responses, follow-up with agency officials, or some combination of the three. See appendix I for more information.

The work on which this statement is based was performed in accordance with generally accepted government auditing standards. Those standards require that we plan and perform the audit to obtain sufficient, appropriate evidence to provide a reasonable basis for our findings and conclusions based on our audit objectives. We believe that the evidence obtained provides a reasonable basis for our findings and conclusions based on our audit objectives.

---

[2] See GAO, Small Business Contracting: Actions Needed to Demonstrate and Better Review Compliance with Select Requirements for Small Business Advocates, GAO-17-675 (Washington, D.C.: Aug. 25, 2017).

Background

Section 15(k)(3) of the Small Business Act, as amended, requires that OSDBU directors generally be responsible only to and report directly to agency heads or their deputies.[3] The purpose of this provision is to help ensure OSDBU directors have direct access to agencies' top decision makers to advocate effectively for small businesses. Subsequent amendments specify minimum seniority or pay levels for directors, enumerate qualifying work experience, specify who must sign the director's performance appraisals, and outline position responsibilities.

Section 15(k), as amended, also establishes functions for which OSDBU directors are responsible, which include identifying proposed solicitations that bundle contract requirements; working with agency acquisitions officials to revise solicitations to increase the probability of small business participation; and assisting small businesses in obtaining payments from agencies.[4] OSDBUs also are to provide senior agency officials with advice on acquisition strategies and market research. See appendix II for more information.

SBPAC annually reviews each OSDBU to determine compliance with section 15(k) requirements.[5] The reviews are used to help determine the annual scorecard grade that the Small Business Administration (SBA)

---

[3] All references to section 15(k) are to section 15 of the Small Business Act, codified at 15 U.S.C. § 644(k).

[4] The Small Business Reauthorization Act of 1997 defines the bundling of contract requirements as the consolidation of 2 or more procurement requirements for goods or services previously provided or performed under separate smaller contracts into a solicitation of offers for a single contract likely to be unsuitable for award to a small business due to (1) the diversity, size, or specialized nature of the elements of the performance specified; (2) the aggregate dollar value of the anticipated award; (3) the geographical dispersion of the contract performance sites; or (4) any combination of the factors described. Pub. L. No. 105-135, § 412, 111 Stat. 2592, 2617 (1997), codified at 15 U.S.C. § 632(o).

[5] SBPAC comprises the Administrator of the Small Business Administration (SBA), or the designee of the administrator, the director of the Minority Business Development Agency, and the heads of each OSDBU. SBA chairs the council, which assists agencies in their acquisition planning efforts. The council also is to identify best practices for maximizing small business utilization in federal contracting.

gives each agency.[6] SBPAC also must report the results of the review to the House and Senate Small Business committees.

AGENCIES DEMONSTRATED MIXED LEVELS OF COMPLIANCE WITH OSDBU DIRECTOR REQUIREMENTS

Of the five director-related requirements we reviewed, the level of demonstrated compliance varied, but was not universal for any one requirement (see Table 1):

- Four of the 10 agencies we reviewed for the requirement that the director report to the head or deputy head of the agency did not demonstrate compliance.
- Twenty-three of the 24 agencies we reviewed demonstrated compliance for two requirements on director experience and supervisory duties.
- Nineteen of 24 agencies demonstrated compliance with a requirement limiting collateral duties of the director.
- Eighteen of 24 agencies demonstrated compliance with a requirement for the director's compensation and seniority.

Noncompliance with section 15(k) requirements may limit the extent to which an OSDBU can successfully advocate for small businesses. For example, OSDBU influence in agencies might be limited if directors reported to lower levels of management. Directors with other duties might be less able to carry out all section 15(k) duties.

In our August 2017 report, we made recommendations to 12 agencies to address demonstrated noncompliance with director-related requirements of section 15(k) or report to Congress on why they had not complied,

---

[6] According to SBA, the annual scorecard measures how well federal agencies reach small business contracting goals and reports agency-specific progress. Scorecard grades are based on the extent to which (or how well) agencies met goals for prime contracts and subcontracts and their progress plans for meeting goals.

including seeking any statutory flexibilities or exceptions believed appropriate. Agency responses to our recommendations varied. For example, the U.S. Agency for International Development agreed with our recommendation relating to section 15(k)(15), which requires that the OSDBU director not have collateral duties beyond those needed to carry out the responsibilities of section 15(k). We found that the agency had not demonstrated compliance with section 15(k)(15) because its OSDBU director had responsibility for the Minority Serving Institution program which is outside of the statutorily defined OSDBU duties. The agency stated that moving responsibility for the program from the OSDBU would not gain efficiencies and the agency will explore requesting an exception to allow the OSDBU director to continue to advocate for that program. The Department of Defense disagreed with the part of the recommendation to the Defense Logistics Agency about section 15(k)(7), supervisory duties. The Department noted the agency had numerous field offices, and thus supervisory authority was divided (headquarters did not supervise each field office). But this resulted in an OSDBU director not supervising all staff carrying out OSDBU responsibilities, which is required by section 15(k)(7), and we maintained our recommendation.

AGENCY COMPLIANCE VARIED BY FUNCTIONAL REQUIREMENT

Levels of demonstrated compliance were high for five of eight functional requirements, but were much lower for the remaining three requirements (see Table 2).

- All 24 agencies demonstrated compliance with requirements for providing advice to officials, providing training to small businesses or acquisition personnel, and receiving unsolicited proposals and forwarding them when appropriate.

Table 1. Agencies' Demonstrated Compliance with Section 15(k) Requirements Related to OSDBU Director as of May 19, 2017

Agency	Demonstrated compliance with section 15(k)				
	15(k): Director experience	15(k)(2): Compensation/ seniority	15(k)(3): Reporting requirement (head of agency or deputy head)[a]	15(k)(7): Supervisory duties	15(k)(15): Collateral duties
Defense Logistics Agency	✓	☒	N/A	☒	✓
Department of Agriculture	✓	☒	N/A	✓	☒
Department of the Air Force	✓	✓	✓	✓	✓
Department of the Army	✓	✓	✓	✓	✓
Department of Commerce	✓	☒	N/A	✓	✓
Department of Defense – Office of the Secretary	✓	✓	N/A	✓	✓
Department of Education	✓	✓	☒	✓	✓
Department of Energy	✓	✓	☒	✓	✓
Department of Homeland Security	✓	✓	N/A	✓	✓
Department of Housing and Urban Development	☒	✓	N/A	✓	✓
Department of the Interior	✓	✓	N/A	✓	✓
Department of Justice	✓	✓	N/A	✓	✓
Department of Labor	✓	☒	✓	✓	☒
Department of the Navy	✓	✓	✓	✓	✓
Department of State	✓	✓	✓	✓	✓
Department of Transportation	✓	✓	N/A	✓	✓
Department of the Treasury	✓	✓	N/A	✓	✓
Department of Veterans Affairs	✓	✓	☐	✓	✓
Environmental Protection Agency	✓	✓	N/A	✓	☒
General Services Administration	✓	✓	N/A	✓	✓

Table 1. (Continued)

Agency	Demonstrated compliance with section 15(k)				
	15(k): Director experience	15(k)(2): Compensation/ seniority	15(k)(3): Reporting requirement (head of agency or deputy head)[a]	15(k)(7): Supervisory duties	15(k)(15): Collateral duties
National Aeronautics and Space Administration	✓	✓	☐	✓	✓
Office of Personnel Management	✓	☒	N/A	✓	✓
Social Security Administration	✓	☒	☐	✓	☒
U.S. Agency for International Development	✓	✓	N/A	✓	☒

Legend: OSDBU = Office of Small and Disadvantaged Business Utilization, ✓ = demonstrated compliance, ☒ = did not demonstrate compliance, N/A = not assessed Source: GAO. | GAO-18-191T.

Note: The information we collected to make the determinations included survey responses; follow-up responses; and documentation such as policies, position descriptions, organizational charts, and reports. If supporting documentation was not available, we made the determination based solely on the agency's survey response, follow-up with agency officials, or both. See appendix II for more information on 15(k) requirements.

[a]We reviewed compliance with this requirement for 10 agencies (the Departments of Education, Energy, Labor, State, Air Force, Army, Navy, and Veterans Affairs; the National Aeronautics and Space Administration; and the Social Security Administration). "N/A" indicates we did not assess agencies for this requirement.

Table 2. Agencies' Demonstrated Compliance with Section 15(k) Requirements for Select OSDBU Functions as of May 19, 2017

Agency	Demonstrated compliance with section 15(k)							
	15(k)(5): Identify and address bundling of contract requirements	15(k)(6): Provide assistance on payments	15(k)(8): Assign small business technical advisers	15(k)(11): Advise on in-sourcing	15(k)(12): Provide advice to CAO and SPE	15(k)(13): Provide training	15(k)(14): Receive unsolicited proposals and forward them when appropriate	15(k)(17): Respond to notification of an undue restriction on ability of small business to compete
Defense Logistics Agency	✓	✓	✓	☒	✓	✓	✓	☒
Department of Agriculture	✓	✓	✓	✓	✓	✓	✓	☒
Department of the Air Force	✓	✓	✓	✓	✓	✓	✓	✓
Department of the Army	✓	✓	☒	✓	✓	✓	✓	✓
Department of Commerce	✓	✓	☒	☒	✓	✓	✓	☒
Department of Defense – Office of the Secretary	☒	✓	☒	✓	✓	✓	✓	✓
Department of Education	✓	✓	✓	☒	✓	✓	✓	✓
Department of Energy	✓	✓	☒	✓	✓	✓	✓	☒
Department of Homeland Security	✓	✓	✓	✓	✓	✓	✓	✓
Department of Housing and Urban Development	✓	✓	✓	☒	✓	✓	✓	✓
Department of the Interior	✓	✓	✓	☒	✓	✓	✓	☒

Table 2. (Continued)

Agency	Demonstrated compliance with section 15(k)							
	15(k)(5): Identify and address bundling of contract requirements	15(k)(6): Provide assistance on payments	15(k)(8): Assign small business technical advisers	15(k)(11): Advise on in-sourcing	15(k)(12): Provide advice to CAO and SPE	15(k)(13): Provide training	15(k)(14): Receive unsolicited proposals and forward them when appropriate	15(k)(17): Respond to notification of an undue restriction on ability of small business to compete
Department of Justice	✓	✓	✓	✓	✓	✓	✓	✓
Department of Labor	✓	✓	✓	✓	✓	✓	✓	✓
Department of the Navy	✓	✓	☒	✓	✓	✓	✓	✓
Department of State	✓	✓	☒	✓	✓	✓	✓	☒
Department of Transportation	✓	✓	✓	✓	✓	✓	✓	✓
Department of the Treasury	✓	✓	☒	☒	✓	✓	✓	✓
Department of Veterans Affairs	✓	✓	☒	☒	✓	✓	✓	✓
Environmental Protection Agency	✓	✓	✓	✓	✓	✓	✓	✓
General Services Administration	✓	✓	✓	✓	✓	✓	✓	✓
National Aeronautics and Space Administration	✓	✓	✓	✓	✓	✓	✓	☒
Office of Personnel Management	✓	✓	☒	✓	✓	✓	✓	☒

Agency	Demonstrated compliance with section 15(k)							
	15(k)(5): Identify and address bundling of contract requirements	15(k)(6): Provide assistance on payments	15(k)(8): Assign small business technical advisers	15(k)(11): Advise on in-sourcing	15(k)(12): Provide advice to CAO and SPE	15(k)(13): Provide training	15(k)(14): Receive unsolicited proposals and forward them when appropriate	15(k)(17): Respond to notification of an undue restriction on ability of small business to compete
Social Security Administration	✓	☒	☒	☒	✓	✓	✓	✓
U.S. Agency for International Development	✓	✓	✓	✓	✓	✓	✓	☒

Legend: OSDBU = Office of Small and Disadvantaged Business Utilization, ✓ = demonstrated compliance, ☒ = did not demonstrate compliance, CAO = chief acquisition officer, SPE = senior procurement executive.

Source: GAO. | GAO-18-191T.

Note: To obtain information for determinations on OSDBU functions, we surveyed OSDBU directors at 24 agencies about certain OSDBU functions listed in section 15(k) of the Small Business Act. We also reviewed relevant policy documents. We followed up with all 24 OSDBU offices to clarify responses and obtain additional information in instances in which they indicated they did not perform a section 15(k) requirement.

- Twenty-three of the 24 agencies demonstrated compliance related to identifying and addressing significant bundling of contract requirements and providing payment assistance to small businesses.
- Ten and eight of the 24 agencies, respectively, did not demonstrate compliance with requirements for assigning small business technical advisers and providing advice on proposed in-sourcing decisions.[7]
- Nine of the 24 agencies did not demonstrate compliance with the requirement to respond to notification by a small business that a solicitation unduly restricts the ability of the small business to compete for the award.[8]

In our August 2017 report, we made recommendations to 17 agencies to address demonstrated noncompliance with section 15(k) functional requirements (as shown in Table 2).[9] Agency responses to our recommendations varied. For example, some agencies questioned the effectiveness or practicality of performing actions in a certain way. The National Aeronautics and Space Administration (NASA) partially agreed with the part of our recommendation related to section 15(k)(17), responding to notification by a small business that it believes a solicitation unduly restricts the small business's ability to compete. OSDBU directors are required to inform an agency's advocate for competition of such notifications. NASA said that it would do so going forward to comply with the statute. NASA added that it believes that the most practical and effective way to address such notifications is for the OSDBU, in consultation with the contracting officer, to resolve issues at the lowest level possible. In another example, the Department of Veterans Affairs (VA) concurred in principle with the recommendation related to section

[7] In-sourcing refers to converting an activity performed by a small business to an activity performed by a federal employee.

[8] This requirement is triggered when a small business notifies the agency (before contract award) that the small business believes that a solicitation, request for proposal, or request for quotation unduly restricts the ability of the small business to compete for the award.

[9] In GAO-17-675, we made recommendations addressing noncompliance to 19 agencies. The recommendations to some agencies addressed demonstrated noncompliance for both director-related and functional section 15(k) requirements.

15(k)(8), which requires the OSDBU director to assign a small business technical adviser to each office where SBA assigned a procurement center representative. The agency stated that for the OSDBU to select an employee and direct that person's principal work efforts, while that person nominally remains accountable to and on the payroll of the contracting activity, requires an unusual degree of "matrixed" reporting relationships not often found in any workplace. VA said that its OSDBU will seek to collaborate with the cognizant contracting activities through VA's Senior Procurement Council, and develop a clear written understanding of roles and responsibilities in a memorandum of understanding. We maintain our recommendation, as VA's comments do not make it clear if the OSDBU director will assign a small business technical adviser to the procuring activity, or if the assigned staff would be a full-time employee of this activity (as is also required by section 15(k)(8)).

SOME SBPAC REVIEW SCORES WERE NOT CONSISTENT WITH OUR COMPLIANCE DETERMINATIONS

Some SBPAC review scores were inconsistent with our compliance determinations for the section 15(k) requirements we and SBPAC both considered. The SBPAC review panel—comprising OSDBU directors—annually reviews each OSDBU to determine compliance with section 15(k) requirements; it considers seven success factors for achievement of and commitment to small business contracting.[10] The peer reviews are a form of internal control intended to provide some assurance that OSDBUs comply with section 15(k) requirements. Agencies in the most recent review received overall scores (across the seven success factors) of 94- 98 percent.

[10] Some success factors closely mirror requirements and areas of section 15(k), while others are more general and do not align with section 15(k) specifically.

Table 3. Peer Review Scores for Organization Success Factor (FY 2016) Compared with GAO Determinations of Compliance for Related Section 15(k) Requirements (as of May 19, 2017), Selected Agencies

Agency	SBPAC peer review score for organization success factor[a] (FY 2016)	GAO determinations of compliance and associated subsections of section 15(k) (as of May 19, 2017; out of 4 or 5[b])
Department of Agriculture	1.0 (excellent)	Not demonstrated for 2 of 4: (k)(2) and (k)(15)
Department of Energy	0.83 (satisfactory)	Not demonstrated for 2 of 5: (k)(3) and (k)(8)
Department of Justice	0.83 (satisfactory)	Demonstrated for 4 of 4
Department of Labor	0.9 (above average)	Not demonstrated for 2 of 5: (k)(2) and (k)(15)
Department of State	1.0 (excellent)	Not demonstrated for 1 of 5: (k)(8)
Department of Veterans Affairs	0.8 (satisfactory)	Not demonstrated for 2 of 5: (k)(3) and (k)(8)
Environmental Protection Agency	0.93 (above average)	Not demonstrated for 1 of 4: (k)(15)
Office of Personnel Management	0.83 (satisfactory)	Not demonstrated for 2 of 4: (k)(2) and (k)(8)
Social Security Administration	0.8 (satisfactory)	Not demonstrated for 4 of 5: (k)(2), (k)(3), (k)(8), and (k)(15)

Legend: FY = fiscal year; SBPAC = Small Business Procurement Advisory Council Sources: Small Business Administration and GAO. | GAO-18-191T.

Note: This table compares selected agencies for which the SBPAC scores for "organization success factor" were not consistent with our determinations of compliance with similar section 15(k) requirements. We were unable to compare SBPAC scores to our determinations of compliance for the five Department of Defense agencies we reviewed (Office of the Secretary, Defense Logistics Agency, and Departments of the Air Force, Army, and Navy) because SBPAC scores the Department of Defense as a whole rather than by component.

[a]SBA's peer review panel guidance provides the following grading scale for success factor scores: 1.0 (excellent), 0.9 (above average), 0.8 (satisfactory), 0.7 (below average), and 0.6 (unsatisfactory). Individual reviewers provide a score for each success factor, and the scores are then averaged across reviewers to determine an agency's overall score for each success factor. Thus, some agencies' scores fall in between two categories on the grading scale (e.g., between 0.9, above average, and 1.0, excellent). If agencies had scores between two categories, we listed the category to which the score most closely approached.

[b]We reviewed compliance with section 15(k)(3), which generally requires the OSDBU director to report to the head or deputy head of the agency, for 10 of the 24 agencies. Therefore, only some of the agencies listed in the table were assessed on all five section 15(k) requirements considered for this comparison, while other agencies were assessed on the other four requirements: (k)(2), compensation/seniority of the OSDBU director; (k)(7), supervisory duties of the OSDBU director; (k)(8), assigning small business technical advisers; and (k)(15), collateral duties of the OSDBU director.

For several agencies, our compliance determinations for the section 15(k) requirements related to organizational structure did not align with SBPAC's 2016 scores for the "OSDBU organization" success factor (see Table 3).[11] Where our review considered the same section 15(k) requirements as the SBPAC review, we found that several agencies had not demonstrated compliance with multiple requirements.

Other than reviewing documentation agencies choose to provide, SBA's guidance for the review panel does not indicate any other means by which reviewers could obtain or clarify information about agencies' compliance with section 15(k) requirements. In contrast, our review of demonstrated compliance included follow-up discussions with agency officials. According to federal standards for internal control, management should use quality information to make informed decisions. Although SBA has been developing a new review process, preliminary information we reviewed indicates the process will be similar to the current one. Under the new process, the review results will carry twice as much weight in another process that SBA uses to determine an agency's overall grade for small business contracting—underscoring the importance of the SBPAC review results.

We made one recommendation to SBA in our August 2017 report to include more detailed guidance to SBPAC members for the annual reviews. SBA agreed with our recommendation and stated it had begun developing more detailed guidelines that provide more objective criteria for determining compliance that will be used for the fiscal year 2017 review.

In summary, agencies generally demonstrated high levels of compliance with some section 15(k) requirements but less so for others. Some agencies explained they carried out the required activities outside of the OSDBU or by using different processes than those specified in the

[11] To compare SBPAC scores and our determinations, we focused on the organization success factor because it aligned most directly with five requirements—15(k)(2), (k)(3), (k)(7), (k)(8), and (k)(15). Other success factors are less directly related to the additional section 15(k) requirements in our review. The nine members of the peer review panel each provide a score for each success factor, and SBA then calculates an average of each score. SBA's peer review panel guidance provides the following grading scale: 1.0 (excellent), 0.9 (above average), 0.8 (satisfactory), 0.7 (below average), and 0.6 (unsatisfactory).

requirements. But continued noncompliance may undermine the extent to which OSDBUs can advocate for small businesses. If agencies still believe their procedures for certain activities are sufficient to advocate for small business contracts, they should explain their noncompliance to Congress and provide support for their views, including requesting any statutory flexibilities to permit exceptions. The reliability of the SBPAC review will take on greater importance because SBA proposes to make the scores count for more of an agency's scorecard grade. However, the divergence in results between our review and SBPAC scores suggests the review could be enhanced. For instance, improving SBA's guidance can help increase the reliability of the peer review determinations and increase consistency with federal internal control standards.

Chairman Knight, Ranking Member Murphy, and members of the Subcommittee, this concludes my statement. I would be pleased to answer any questions that you may have at this time related to our work on OSDBUs and section 15(k) compliance.

Appendix I: Objectives, Scope, and Methodology

This testimony is based on our August 2017 report (GAO-17-675) on Offices of Small and Disadvantaged Business Utilization (OSDBU) at selected federal agencies.[12] More specifically, the report examined (1) the extent to which selected federal agencies demonstrated compliance with five section 15(k) requirements relating to the OSDBU director; (2) the extent to which selected federal agencies demonstrated compliance with eight section 15(k) requirements on OSDBU functions or activities; and (3) the review by the Small Business Procurement Advisory Council (SBPAC) of OSDBU compliance with section 15(k) requirements.

---

[12] See GAO, Small Business Contracting: Actions Needed to Demonstrate and Better Review Compliance with Select Requirements for Small Business Advocates, GAO-17-675 (Washington, D.C.: Aug. 25, 2017).

To determine how agencies demonstrated compliance with the OSDBU related requirements, we first selected 24 agencies (civilian and military) for review.

- Of the 24 agencies, 23 were selected due to high contracting obligations; each of the 23 procured more than $900 million in goods and services in fiscal year 2015. Together, they accounted for 87 percent of all federal contracting obligations.
- We selected the 24th agency, the Office of the Secretary within the Department of Defense, due to its role as a policy office in the department.

We then selected the following section 15(k) requirements for review (5 requirements relating to OSDBU directors and 8 relating to OSDBU functions):

- 15(k): Director experience
- 15(k)(2): Compensation/seniority
- 15(k)(3): Reporting requirement (head of agency or deputy head)
- 15(k)(5): Identify and address bundling of contract requirements
- 15(k)(6): Provide assistance on payments
- 15(k)(7): Supervisory duties
- 15(k)(8): Assign small business technical advisers
- 15(k)(11): Advise on in-sourcing
- 15(k)(12): Provide advice to chief acquisition officer and senior procurement executive
- 15(k)(13): Provide training[13]
- 15(k)(14): Receive unsolicited proposals and forward them when appropriate
- 15(k)(15): Collateral duties

---

[13] Section 15(k)(13) does not mandate that the OSDBU provide training to small businesses, but we included the permissive training language in 15 U.S.C. § 644(k)(13) in our discussion of "requirements" and reviewed the agencies' training offered under this provision.

- 15(k)(16): Submit training reports to Congress[14]
- 15(k)(17): Respond to notification of an undue restriction on ability of small business to compete

For the section 15(k)(3) requirement relating to OSDBU directors reporting to a head or deputy head of an agency, we reviewed whether 10 agencies demonstrated compliance (Departments of Education, Energy, Labor, State, Air Force, Army, Navy, and Veterans Affairs; the National Aeronautics and Space Administration; and the Social Security Administration). We selected the 10 agencies based on contracting obligations (6 each had more than $10 billion in obligations, and 4 each had fewer) and for variety. Of the 6 agencies with more than $10 billion in obligations, we selected 3 Department of Defense components and 3 other agencies. To determine whether agencies demonstrated compliance, we analyzed documents such as reports, position descriptions, and performance appraisals and interviewed OSDBU directors and other agency officials.

To determine if agencies demonstrated compliance with other provisions of section 15(k)—four that relate to other requirements for OSDBU directors (such as rank and responsibilities) and eight that relate to OSDBU functions or activities—we surveyed OSDBU directors at 24 agencies. The survey questions focused on acquisition planning, solicitation development, proposal evaluation, obtaining payments, training, interaction with SBA, and other functions. The response rate to our survey was 100 percent. We also reviewed agency information such as policy documents and position descriptions and interviewed OSDBU directors and other agency officials.

---

[14] Our review of individual agencies' demonstrated compliance encompasses 13 requirements. As discussed in GAO-17-675, an additional requirement—section 15(k)(16)—directs agencies to submit an annual training and travel report to Congress. During our review, the Small Business Administration established new procedures to submit a consolidated report to Congress, rather than having each agency submit an individual report. Due to the new procedures, we do not include this requirement in the tables about agencies' demonstrated compliance in GAO-17-675 or in this testimony.

We determined if an agency demonstrated compliance with a particular requirement by reviewing agency documentation, survey responses, and responses to follow-up we conducted with agencies (for instance, to clarify survey responses and to obtain additional information in instances in which respondents indicated they did not perform a section 15(k) requirement). In cases in which supporting documentation was not available, we made the determination based solely on the agency's survey response, follow-up with agency officials, or both. See appendix II for more information on the requirements.

To examine the SBPAC review, we reviewed documentation and data related to the Small Business Administration's (SBA) scorecard for small business procurement and SBPAC's peer review process. We also spoke with SBA officials about this program. We compared SBA's "OSDBU organization" success factor scores to the compliance information we obtained from our review to determine whether these scores correlated with our compliance determinations.

APPENDIX II: SELECT STATUTORY REQUIREMENTS FOR OFFICE OF SMALL AND DISADVANTAGED BUSINESS UTILIZATION

Section 15(k) of the Small Business Act, as amended, requires each Office of Small and Disadvantaged Business Utilization (OSDBU) and each OSDBU director to meet certain requirements. We selected 14 requirements from section 15(k) for closer review. This appendix details each requirement and, where appropriate, elaborates on how we determined that agencies demonstrated compliance with each requirement.

Table 4. Requirements of Section 15(k) of the Small Business Act

Requirement	Statutory section[a]	Description
Director experience[b]	15(k)	The management of each OSDBU office must be vested in an officer or employee of the agency with experience serving in any combination of the following roles: • program manager, deputy program manager, or assistant program management for federal acquisition program; • chief engineer, systems engineer, assistant engineer, or product support manager for federal acquisition program; • federal contracting officer; • small business technical adviser; • contracts administrator for federal government contracts; • attorney specializing in federal procurement law; • small business liaison officer; • officer or employee who managed federal contracts for a small business; or • individual whose primary responsibilities were for the functions and duties of section 8, 15, or 44 of the Small Business Act (15 U.S.C. § 637, 644, 657q).
Compensation/seniority[c]	15(k)(2)	The officer or employee in the position of heading the OSDBU office must either: 1. be appointed by the agency's head to a Senior Executive Service position, or 2. only for an agency where the chief acquisition officer and the senior procurement executive are not Senior Executive Service positions, may be appointed to a position compensated not less than the minimum rate for a salary at level 15 of the General Schedule.
Reporting requirement (head of agency or deputy head)	15(k)(3)	The officer or employee in the position of heading the OSDBU office must be responsible only to, and report directly and exclusively to, the head of the agency or to the deputy of the agency, except that the OSDBU for the Office of the Secretary of Defense must be responsible only to and report directly and exclusively to the secretary or the secretary's designee. These requirements include that the OSDBU director's performance appraisals be signed by either the agency head, deputy head, or in the case of the Department of Defense, the secretary or the secretary's designe[e].

Requirement	Statutory section[a]	Description
Identify and address bundling of contract requirements	15(k)(5)	The officer or employee in the position of heading the OSDBU office must (1) identify proposed solicitations that involve significant bundling of contract requirements, and (2) work with the agency acquisition officials and the Small Business Administration to revise the procurement strategies for those proposed solicitations where appropriate to increase the probability of participation by small businesses as prime contractors, or, if the bundled solicitation is issued, to facilitate small business participation as subcontractors and suppliers.
Provide assistance on payments[d]	15(k)(6)	The officer or employee in the position of heading the OSDBU office must assist small businesses in obtaining: (1) payments, (2) required late payment interest penalties, or (3) information regarding payments due to the businesses from an executive agency or a contractor, in conformity with certain statutory provisions, or any other protection for contractors or subcontractors (including suppliers) that is included in the Federal Acquisition Regulations or any individual agency's supplement to the Federal Acquisition Regulations.
Supervisory duties[e]	15(k)(7)	The officer or employee in the position of heading the OSDBU office must have supervisory authority over agency personnel to the extent that the functions and duties of the personnel relate to sections 8 and 15 of the Small Business Act (15 U.S.C. § 637 and 644).
Assign small business technical advisers	15(k)(8)	The officer or employee in the position of heading the OSDBU office must assign a small business technical adviser to each office where the Small Business Administration has assigned a procurement center representative. The technical adviser: 1. must be a full-time employee of the procuring activity and must be well qualified, technically trained, and familiar with the supplies or services purchased at the activity; and 2. must have the principal duty to assist the Small Business Administration procurement center representative in the representative's duties and functions related to sections 8 and 15 of the Small Business Act (15 U.S.C. § 637 and 644).
Advise on in-sourcing	15(k)(11)	The officer or employee in the position of heading the OSDBU office must review and advise the agency on any decision to convert an activity performed by a small business to an activity performed by a federal employee.

Table 4. (Continued)

Requirement	Statutory section[a]	Description
Provide advice to chief acquisition officer and senior procurement executive[f]	15(k)(12)	The officer or employee in the position of heading the OSDBU office must provide the chief acquisition officer and senior procurement executive of the agency with advice and comments on acquisition strategies, market research, and justifications related to consolidation of contract requirements (15 U.S.C. § 657q).
Provide training	15(k)(13)	The officer or employee in the position of heading the OSDBU office may provide training to small businesses and contract specialists, except that the training may only be provided to the extent it does not interfere with the OSDBU director carrying out other responsibilities under section 15(k) (15 U.S.C. § 644(k)).
Receive unsolicited proposals and forward them when appropriate	15(k)(14)	The officer or employee in the position of heading the OSDBU office must receive unsolicited proposals and, when appropriate, forward them to personnel of the activity responsible for reviewing the proposals.
Collateral duties[g]	15(k)(15)	The officer or employee in the position of heading the OSDBU office must carry out exclusively the duties in section 15(k) (15 U.S.C. § 644(k)) and, while director, must not hold any other title, position, or responsibility, except as necessary to carry out the responsibilities of section 15(k).
Submit training report to Congress[h]	15(k)(16)	The officer or employee in the position of heading the OSDBU office each fiscal year must submit a report to the House of Representatives Committee on Small Business and the Senate Committee on Small Business and Entrepreneurship. The report must describe: 1. the training by the director to small businesses and contract specialist completed in the recently completed fiscal year; 2. the percentage of the director's budget used for the training in that fiscal year; and 3. the percentage of the director's budget used for travel in that fiscal year.

Requirement	Statutory section[a]	Description
Respond to notification of an undue restriction on ability of small business to compete	15(k)(17)	When notified by a small business prior to the award of a contract that the small business believes that a solicitation, request for proposal, or request for quotation unduly restricts the ability of the small business to complete, the officer or employee in the position of heading the OSDBU office must: 1. submit the notice to the contracting officer, and if necessary, recommend ways the solicitation, request for proposal, or request for quotation may be altered to increase the opportunity for competition; 2. inform the agency's advocate for competition of the notice; and 3. ensure that the small business is aware of other resources and processes available to address unduly restrictive provisions in a solicitation, request for proposal, or request for quotation, even if the resources and processes are provided by the agency, the Small Business Administration, the Government Accountability Office, or a procurement technical assistance program.

Legend: OSDBU = Office of Small and Disadvantaged Business Utilization Source: GAO. | GAO-18-191T.

Note: The table includes a breakdown of statutory language through 2016, but it does not include language added in the National Defense Authorization Act for Fiscal Year 2017. Pub. L. No. 114-328, 130 Stat. 2000 (2016).

[a]All statutory sections are within 15 U.S.C. § 644(k). These sections all fall within section 15(k) of the Small Business Act and therefore are commonly called section 15(k).

[b]An individual who held one or more of the enumerated list of positions would meet requirements for our review.

[c]In instances in which an agency had an acting OSDBU director, we looked at the seniority of the director who served immediately prior to the acting director.

[d]An OSDBU that provides any assistance would meet requirements for our review.

[e]An OSDBU that supervises personnel within its office to the extent that the functions and duties of the personnel relate to sections 8 and 15 of the Small Business Act (15 U.S.C. § 637 and 644) would meet requirements for our review.

[f]We would not determine that an OSDBU did not demonstrate compliance for failure to provide information to a chief acquisition officer or senior procurement executive if the agency did not have a chief acquisition officer or senior procurement executive. (Continued …)

[g]Acting OSDBU directors may hold other titles or positions while serving as the temporary OSDBU director as long as while so serving they exclusively carry out the duties in section 15(k).

[h]To fulfill this requirement, the Small Business Administration collected the training and travel reports on behalf of individual OSDBUs and submitted them to Congress in June 2017.

In: Small Business Issues
Editor: Andrea Moeller

ISBN: 978-1-53615-870-0

Chapter 3

SMALL BUSINESS CONTRACTING: SBA EFFORTS MAY CLARIFY THE ASSIGNMENT OF INDUSTRY CODES, AND MOST CODE APPEALS WERE DISMISSED*

United States Government Accountability Office

ABBREVIATIONS

DHS	Department of Homeland Security
DOD	Department of Defense
EDWOSB	economically disadvantaged women-owned small business
FAR	Federal Acquisition Regulation
FPDS-NG	Federal Procurement Data System-Next Generation

* This is an edited, reformatted and augmented version of United States Government Accountability Office; Report to the Committee on Small Business, House of Representatives, Publication No. GAO-18-76, dated December 2017.

GSA	General Services Administration
HHS	Department of Health and Human Services
ID/IQ	indefinite delivery/indefinite quantity
NAICS	North American Industry Classification System
NASA	National Aeronautics and Space Administration
OHA	Office of Hearings and Appeals
OMB	Office of Management and Budget
PCR	procurement center representative
SAM	System for Award Management
SBA	Small Business Administration
SDVO	service-disabled veteran-owned
WOSB	women-owned small business

WHY GAO DID THIS STUDY

Federal regulations require that contracting officers assign the NAICS code that best describes the principal purpose of the acquisition. SBA's OHA is responsible for reviewing appeals of NAICS code assignments. Questions have been raised about whether agencies assign the appropriate NAICS codes to ID/IQ contracts with multiple task orders.

GAO was asked to review several issues related to NAICS codes. In this chapter, GAO examines (1) what contracting officers consider when assigning NAICS codes to federal contracts and the status of efforts to clarify code assignment and (2) industry views on NAICS code assignment and the number and outcomes of appeals.

GAO reviewed policies and procedures of the four agencies with the highest ID/IQ obligations from fiscal years 2011–2015: Army, Navy, Department of Homeland Security (DHS), and Department of Health and Human Services (HHS); reviewed one contract and 10 related task orders at each of the selected agencies and interviewed the related contracting officers; analyzed 2016 federal contracting data to identify commonly used NAICS codes and size standards; interviewed three industry groups and five firms that filed appeals for industry views on NAICS code assignment; and analyzed SBA decisions on NAICS code appeals in 2014–2016.

The Department of Defense, DHS, and SBA had no comments on the report. The General Services Administration and HHS had technical comments, which we incorporated as appropriate.

What GAO Found

Agencies' contracting officers consider various factors in assigning North American Industry Classification System (NAICS) codes to federal contracts, and the Small Business Administration (SBA) issued a rule in 2013 intended to clarify NAICS code assignment. NAICS codes are the basis for SBA's size standards; therefore, the code that the contracting officer assigns determines whether a firm is eligible for federal contracting preferences, such as small business set-asides. The contracting officers GAO interviewed cited several factors that affect their assignment of NAICS codes, including information on the work to be performed and input from agency small business specialists. However, they stated that assigning a NAICS code can be challenging when one or more codes could apply to a contract. In the 2013 rule, SBA clarified that under certain circumstances, contracting officers may assign more than one code to multiple-award contracts. Such contracts are awarded to two or more contractors under a single solicitation and include indefinite delivery/indefinite quantity (ID/IQ) contracts used when quantities and timing are not known at the time of the award. However, updates to the Federal Acquisition Regulation (FAR)—the rules governing the federal government's purchasing process—are required to fully implement SBA's final rule. The agencies GAO interviewed plan to implement this rule after it is adopted into the FAR and they can make necessary updates to their information technology for contracting. This FAR rule-making process is ongoing.

Some industry groups and firms GAO interviewed expressed concerns about how contracting officers assign NAICS codes, but SBA's Office of

Hearings and Appeals (OHA) dismissed most appeals and denied more than half of the remaining appeals. Some industry groups and firms GAO interviewed expressed concerns that contracting officers may assign NAICS codes based on the size standard (thereby affecting the number of firms that can compete as a small business) and not the work to be performed. However, some also stated it was difficult to determine how often this practice occurs, and OHA officials noted it is the office's role to review the appropriateness of appealed NAICS codes, not the contracting officer's intention when assigning the code. Of the 62 NAICS code appeals that were filed in calendar years 2014–2016, OHA dismissed 35, denied 15, and granted 12 (see Figure). Appeals were dismissed because, among other things, they were untimely or the contracting officer cancelled the acquisition.

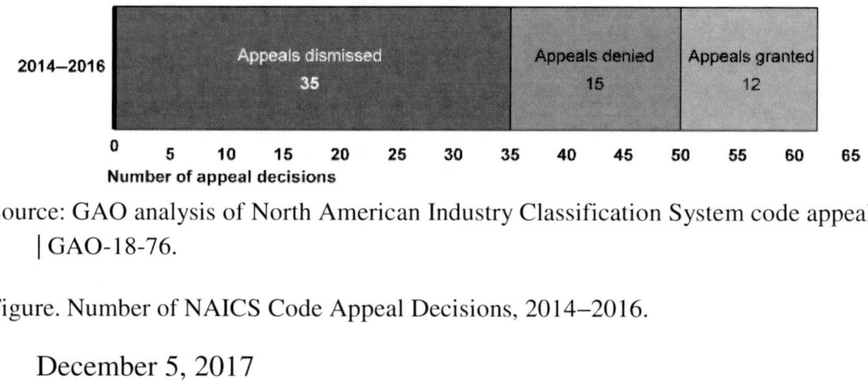

Source: GAO analysis of North American Industry Classification System code appeals. | GAO-18-76.

Figure. Number of NAICS Code Appeal Decisions, 2014–2016.

December 5, 2017

The Honorable Steve Chabot
Chairman

The Honorable Nydia M. Velázquez
Ranking Member
Committee on Small Business
House of Representatives

In fiscal year 2016, about $100 billion in federal contracts were awarded to small businesses. The Small Business Administration (SBA) uses the North American Industry Classification System (NAICS), the federal standard for classifying businesses by industries, as the basis for its small business size standards. Size standards determine eligibility for receiving federal contracting preferences, such as small business set-asides. The Federal Acquisition Regulation (FAR)—the principal set of rules governing the federal acquisition process—requires that contracting officers assign the NAICS code that best describes the principal purpose of the product or service being acquired. The contracting officer's code assignment is final unless SBA or an affected firm files an appeal. SBA's Office of Hearings and Appeals (OHA) reviews appeals of NAICS code assignments.

Questions have been raised about the extent to which contracting officers choose a NAICS code because they want a certain size standard, not because it best describes the principal purpose of the acquisition. Questions have also been raised about the assignment of NAICS codes to indefinite delivery/indefinite quantity (ID/IQ) contracts, which are awarded to one or more firms for the same or similar products or services and are used when the exact times and quantities of future deliveries are not known at the time of award. These contracts may consist of multiple awards and orders, and one concern is that the NAICS code assigned to a contract may not represent the work performed under the majority of the orders.[1]

You asked us to review several issues related to NAICS codes. In this chapter, we examine (1) what contracting officers consider when assigning NAICS codes to federal contracts and the status of efforts to clarify code assignment and (2) industry views on NAICS code assignment and the number and outcomes of appeals filed with SBA OHA.

For our first objective, we reviewed federal laws and regulations related to NAICS code assignment and relevant policies and procedures from the four agencies with the highest ID/IQ obligations from fiscal years 2011– 2015 (the 5 most recent years of data available from the Federal Procurement Data System-Next Generation (FPDS-NG) when we began

---

[1] Multiple-award contracts are contracts awarded to two or more contractors under a single solicitation. An order of supplies, via a delivery order, or an order of services, via a task order, is then placed with one of the contractors pursuant to procedures established in the contract. In this chapter, the term "orders" refers to delivery and task orders.

our review): Army, Navy, Department of Homeland Security (DHS), and Department of Health and Human Services (HHS).[2] To understand how these selected agencies assign NAICS codes to contracts, we reviewed contract documentation, such as acquisition plans and market research documents, for one ID/IQ contract from each of the agencies and interviewed the relevant contracting officers, small business specialists, and SBA procurement center representatives (PCR).[3] We also selected and reviewed 10 orders from each contract and compared the order purposes to the base award purposes. To determine the status of ongoing efforts to clarify code assignment, we reviewed proposed and final regulatory changes and interviewed officials at SBA and the General Services Administration (GSA) (the agency responsible for managing the operation, maintenance, and updating of FPDS-NG). To assess the reliability of the FPDS-NG data we used, we conducted electronic testing for missing data, outliers, and inconsistent coding, and compared the data on selected contracts to contract documentation we obtained. We determined that these data were sufficiently reliable for the purposes of determining ID/IQ obligations and identifying trends in NAICS codes assigned (as discussed below).

For our second objective, we interviewed officials from three industry groups and five firms that filed NAICS code appeals during calendar years 2014–2016 (the 3 most recent years of data available). To identify commonly used NAICS codes and commonly used size standards, we analyzed data from FPDS-NG to identify the top NAICS codes by obligations and by number of contracts awarded in fiscal year 2016. To assess whether contracting officers were more likely to use a NAICS code after the corresponding size standard increased, we analyzed FPDS-NG data on fiscal year 2009–2016 obligations and number of contracts awarded for NAICS codes with size standards that SBA increased in 2012.

---

[2] FPDS-NG is the system used to collect and report data on federal procurements (FAR Subpart 4.6).

[3] SBA PCRs are among the primary staff who implement SBA's prime contracting programs, which are intended to increase contracting opportunities for small businesses and help ensure that small businesses receive a fair and equitable opportunity to participate in federal prime contracts. They are assigned to buying activities at procuring agencies.

To understand SBA OHA's process for reviewing NAICS code appeals, we reviewed federal regulations and interviewed OHA officials. For context, we compared OHA's process for NAICS codes appeals to its processes for other types of appeals. To identify the number and outcomes of NAICS code appeals, we analyzed SBA's OHA decisions on NAICS code appeals filed during calendar years 2014–2016. Appendix I provides additional details on our scope and methodology.

We conducted this performance audit from October 2016 to December 2017 in accordance with generally accepted government auditing standards. Those standards require that we plan and perform the audit to obtain sufficient, appropriate evidence to provide a reasonable basis for our findings and conclusions based in our audit objectives. We believe that the evidence obtained provides a reasonable basis for our findings and conclusions based on our audit objectives.

BACKGROUND

NAICS Codes and SBA's Size Standards

The Economic Classification Policy Committee of the Office of Management and Budget (OMB), Statistics Canada, and Mexico's Instituto Nacional de Estadistica y Geografia developed NAICS codes as a standard for collecting and analyzing data describing the economies of North American countries. The U.S Census Bureau assigns a 6-digit NAICS code to each industry based on its primary activity that generates the most revenue.[4] The Economic Classification Policy Committee reviews NAICS codes every 5 years for potential revisions to ensure the relevance, accuracy, and timeliness of the classifications.

Additionally, SBA uses NAICS codes as the basis for its small business size standards. The Small Business Act authorizes SBA to

---

[4] The first two digits of the NAICS code designate the economic sector, the third digit designates the subsector, the fourth digit designates the industry group, the fifth digit designates the NAICS industry, and the sixth digit designates the national industry.

establish size standards for determining eligibility for federal small business assistance, including contracting preferences. Size standards vary by industry and are generally expressed either as the average number of employees over a 12-month period or the average annual receipts in the previous 3 years.[5] For certain codes, there are more than one size standard. SBA refers to these additional size standards as exceptions. For example, NAICS code 541712 (Research and Development in the Physical, Engineering, and Life Sciences, Except Biotechnology) with a general size standard of 1,000 employees has three exceptions related to aircraft and aircraft engines (1,500 employees), other aircraft parts (1,250 employees), and guided missiles and space vehicles (1,250 employees). The Small Business Jobs Act of 2010 requires SBA to review at least one-third of all size standards during every 18-month period from the date of its enactment and to review all size standards at least every 5 years. SBA has completed the first 5-year review of all size standards.[6]

To help ensure that small businesses receive a share of federal procurement contract dollars, Congress has set an annual government-wide goal of awarding not less than 23 percent of prime contract dollars to small businesses. For firms to compete for government contracts set aside for small businesses, these firms have to meet the small business size standard for the procurement and have the capacity to provide the goods and services.

Indefinite Delivery/Indefinite Quantity (ID/IQ) Contracts

ID/IQ contracts provide flexibility in cases where the government cannot determine the exact quantities and required timing for a product or

---

[5] Businesses provide their average employees and receipts when registering in the System for Award Management (SAM). Businesses must have an active entity registration in SAM to do business with the federal government (FAR Subpart 4.11).

[6] The size standards presented in this chapter are based on 2012 NAICS codes. In April 2017, SBA issued a proposed rule to amend its small business size regulations to incorporate NAICS code revisions for 2017 into its table of small business size standards. 82 Fed. Reg. 18253 (Apr. 18, 2017). In September 2017, SBA finalized its proposed rule, without change, effective October 1, 2017. 82 Fed. Reg. 44886 (Sept. 27, 2017).

service. We found in 2017 that from fiscal years 2011 through 2015, the proportion of spending by federal agencies on ID/IQ contracts remained stable and accounted for about a third (more than $130 billion annually) of total government contract obligations.[7] Contracting officers may award either a single-award or multiple-award ID/IQ contract to meet procurement needs. Single-award ID/IQ contracts refer to situations when only one contract is awarded under a solicitation and are used in certain circumstances such as when only one contractor is capable of providing the product or service. Multiple-award ID/IQ contracts refer to situations when contracts are awarded to two or more contractors under a single solicitation. The FAR contains policies for using multiple-award ID/IQ contracts and states a preference for multiple-award (rather than single-award) ID/IQ contracts.

NAICS Code Assignment and Acquisition Process

Contracting officers have the authority to enter into, administer, or terminate contracts and are responsible for assigning the appropriate NAICS code and corresponding size standard to an acquisition.[8] The FAR requires that contracting officers assign the NAICS code that best describes the principal purpose of the acquisition and states that the contracting officer's assignment of the NAICS code is final unless a person adversely affected by the decision or SBA files an appeal.[9] The FAR states that when selecting the NAICS code, contracting officers are to give primary consideration to the industry descriptions in the NAICS Manual, the product or service description in the solicitation, the relative value and importance of the components of the procurement making up the end item being procured, and the function of the goods or services being

[7] GAO, *Federal Contracts: Agencies Widely Used Indefinite Contracts to Provide Flexibility to Meet Mission Needs*, GAO-17-329 (Washington, D.C.: Apr. 13, 2017).

[8] FAR 19.303.

[9] FAR 19.303(a)(2) and 19.303(c). According to FAR 19.303(a)(1), the contracting officer is to include the appropriate NAICS code and corresponding size standard in solicitations above the micro-purchase threshold. The micro-purchase threshold is $3,500 with some exceptions.

purchased.[10] It also notes that a procurement is usually classified according to the component that accounts for the greatest percentage of contract value.

In addition to the contracting officer, a number of agency officials and offices provide input on the assignment of NAICS codes to federal contracts during different phases of the acquisition process (presolicitation, pre-award, and award) (see Figure 1).

- Presolicitation phase. The program office identifies a need and contacts the contracting officer for guidance on developing and preparing key acquisition documents, such as the market research report and acquisition plan.[11] The contracting officer and program office may also seek advice from the small business specialist and assigned PCR. After the approval of the procurement request, the contracting officer and program office work together to revise planning documents as necessary. Also during the presolicitation phase, the contracting officer coordinates with agency small business specialists and SBA's assigned PCR using a small business coordination form. The contracting officer then publishes the presolicitation notice to summarize proposed contract actions.
- Pre-award phase. After the approval of the NAICS code, the contracting officer publishes the solicitation, which specifies the assigned NAICS code and corresponding size standard.
- Award phase. The agency awards the contract and publishes the award notice. Agencies use their contracting writing systems to execute the acquisition life-cycle from planning to contract award and use FPDS-NG to report contract awards.

---

[10] FAR 19.303(a)(2).

[11] The FAR defines market research as the process used to collect and analyze data about capabilities in the market that could satisfy an agency's procurement needs. Acquisition plans generally discuss the acquisition process, identify the milestones at which decisions should be made, and serve as road maps for implementing these decisions.

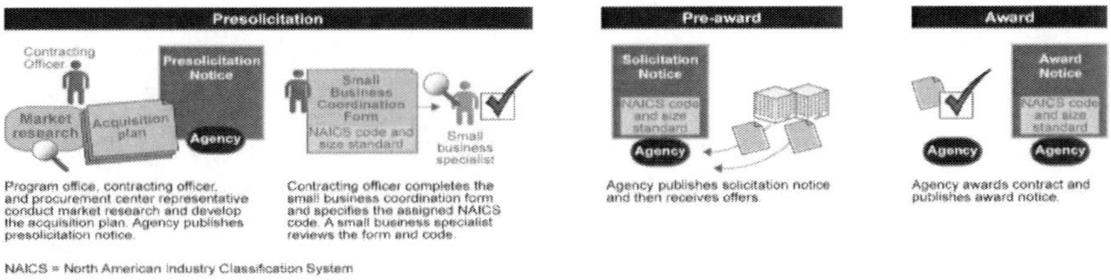

Source: GAO analysis of agency documents. | GAO-18-76.

Figure 1. NAICS Code Assignment and Acquisition Process.

Firms interested in challenging a NAICS code assigned to a solicitation may file an appeal with SBA OHA. OHA was established in 1983 and is responsible for reviewing appeals of NAICS code assignments. OHA also reviews appeals of certain SBA program decisions such as size determinations; eligibility determinations for service-disabled veteran-owned (SDVO) small businesses, women-owned small businesses (WOSB), and economically disadvantaged women-owned small businesses (EDWOSB); and 8(a) business development program eligibility determinations, suspensions, and terminations.[12]

CONTRACTING OFFICERS CONSIDER VARIOUS FACTORS WHEN ASSIGNING NAICS CODES, AND SBA'S 2013 RULE PROVIDES ADDITIONAL GUIDANCE FOR MULTIPLE-AWARD CONTRACTS

Contracting Officers Consider Several Factors When Assigning NAICS Codes

Officials at the Army, the Navy, DHS, and HHS stated that contracting officers refer to the FAR when assigning NAICS codes and consider a

[12] An SDVO small business is a small business concern owned and controlled by one or more service-disabled veterans. A WOSB is a small business that is at least 51 percent owned and controlled by one or more women. An EDWOSB is a small business that meets the ownership and control of a WOSB but is also defined as economically disadvantaged. SBA's 8(a) business development program helps socially and economically disadvantaged small businesses gain access to federal contracting opportunities.

variety of factors. Additionally, in 2010 the Department of Defense (DOD) disseminated a memorandum to its components, which include the Army and the Navy, reiterating the process for determining the size status of contractors, including the requirement that contracting officers determine the appropriate NAICS code and related small business size standard and include them in solicitations. Although these agencies did not have training that specifically focused on NAICS codes, the training for contracting officers included discussion of NAICS code assignment.

Contracting officers at these four agencies cited several factors, including a contract's scope of work, that are involved in determining the NAICS code for a contract solicitation or an order:

- Statements of work and market research reports. The contracting officers we interviewed at all four agencies stated that they review the statements of work and assign the code that represents the majority of the work. One contracting officer stated that she also reviews the market research report when assigning the NAICS code. All of the contracting officers we interviewed at the four agencies stated that the market research reports usually include the relevant NAICS code. We found evidence of market research for two of the four contracts that we reviewed and found that the market research reports included the NAICS codes assigned to the contracts. Navy and HHS contracting officers were unable to provide evidence of market research for the contracts included in our review. Navy officials stated that the contracting team conducted market research but was unable to find copies of the documents.[13] The HHS contracting officer stated that he conducted market research for the contract, but did not document it in a market research report. Instead, he noted in the small business

[13] The Navy acknowledged that the files should have been maintained, but the current Navy contracting officer explained that the market research predated her involvement with the contract and that those market research documents were either not retained or misplaced. She also noted that the Navy now retains documents electronically.

coordination form that he reviewed prior or similar acquisitions as part of efforts to locate small business sources.

- Input from small business specialists. These four agencies' contracting officers consult with their agencies' small business specialists when deciding the NAICS code for a contract. Each of the four agencies we reviewed required their contracting officers to complete small business coordination forms prior to issuing solicitations for their agencies. When completing the forms, contracting officers must include the NAICS code designation and the corresponding size standard. Small business specialists must review the form before the contracting officer can issue the solicitation. All four agencies provided small business coordination forms related to the selected contract we reviewed. Additionally, each form included the signature of the small business specialist and listed the NAICS code and size standard, as required.
- All four of the agencies' small business specialists we interviewed stated that they rarely disagreed with contracting officers on NAICS code assignments. They also noted that they coordinate with contracting officers on the NAICS code early in the acquisition process, for example, during market research. If they are unable to reach agreement on the code assignment, the specialists can elevate their concerns to the SBA PCR assigned to the office. According to SBA officials, the PCR will examine the research and either concur with the decision or file an appeal to the contracting officer.[14] None of the specialists we interviewed had elevated any concerns to their PCR.
- Contract writing system requirements. The contracting officers we interviewed at all four agencies stated that they assign a single NAICS code for each solicitation, including for multiple-award contracts, because their contract writing systems and FPDS-NG do

[14] The PCR also reviews solicitations that are not unilaterally set aside for small business.

not allow them to enter more than one code per contract.[15] While acquisition officials at each agency confirmed that contracting officers can assign only one code per multiple-award contract in their contract writing systems, they noted that contracting officers may list multiple codes for a multiple-award contract in the solicitation.

- Codes assigned to other contracts. Contracting officers we interviewed at all four agencies stated that if the solicitation is for a recurring contract, they refer to the previously assigned code.[16] Two of the four contracting officers also consider the codes assigned to other contracts within their agencies that consisted of similar work.
- The purpose of the order. To issue an order under a contract, the purpose of the order must be within the scope of the underlying base contract. The four contracts we reviewed all had one NAICS code. The contracting officers we interviewed at all four agencies stated that if an order did not relate to the base award's statement of work or NAICS code, they would award the order through another existing contract or award a new contract. We reviewed 10 orders from each of the four selected contracts and found that all 40 of the orders appeared to reflect the purpose of the base award and appeared to relate to the assigned NAICS code.

However, the contracting officers we interviewed at two of the four agencies noted some challenges in assigning NAICS codes. They stated that because NAICS code definitions are broad, sometimes more than one code could be assigned to a solicitation.

---

[15] Agencies' contract writing systems feed into FPDS-NG.

[16] NAICS codes are reviewed every 5 years for potential revisions. When OMB's Economic Classification Policy Committee undertook this review for 2017, OMB published a crosswalk showing how codes that were to be updated in 2017 related to the 2012 codes. *See* 80 Fed. Reg. 46480 (Aug. 4, 2015). If the code assigned to the previous contract is no longer current, a contracting officer can refer to such a crosswalk. OMB adopted the committee's recommendations with one minor exception in 2016. *See* 81 Fed. Reg. 52584 (Aug. 8, 2016).

Table 1. Example of Similar Orders with Different NAICS Codes

Order purpose	NAICS code	Size standard (dollars in millions)	NAICS code definition (2012)
The Architect-Engineer will provide design and documentation, to include specifications and drawings, for a new closed circuit TV (CCTV) System…. The project includes replacing, upgrading, and new installation of: cameras, …, hardware, software, monitors, recording devices, storage devices, equipment rooms, and cables/wires. The new system shall be an I[ternet] P[rotocol]-based system on a dedicated network, and will be replacing an analog system that is stand alone.	541330 – Engineering Services	15	This industry comprises establishments primarily engaged in applying physical laws and principles of engineering in the design, development, and utilization of machines, materials, instruments, structures, processes, and systems. The assignments undertaken by these establishments may involve any of the following activities: provision of advice, preparation of feasibility studies, preparation of preliminary and final plans and designs, provision of technical services during the construction or installation phase, inspection and evaluation of engineering projects, and related services.
This Statement of Work (SOW) addresses the installation of intrusion detection and closed circuit video surveillance for … [several] sites …. This shall include a site visit, mapping of device locations, acquisition, installation, verifying operation, and warranty for IP based cameras. The existing or core system will require additional installation, device hardware, device upgrade, and installed or upgraded software to provide a complete integrated intrusion detection and standardized video surveillance system.	541512 – Computer Systems Design Services	27.5	This U.S. industry comprises establishments primarily engaged in planning and designing computer systems that integrate computer hardware, software, and communication technologies. The hardware and software components of the system may be provided by this establishment or company as part of integrated services or may be provided by third parties or vendors. These establishments often install the system and train and support users of the system.

Source: GAO analysis of a sample of orders from selected agencies. I GAO-18-76.
Note: Bold added by GAO.

In reviewing the 40 orders associated with the four contracts we selected, we noted that in some instances more than one code could appear to apply to a contract. For example, the purpose of one order was to provide recommendations on design, testing, and evaluation in support of engineering activities. We found that this order could relate to the Research and Development in the Physical, Engineering, and Life Sciences (Except Biotechnology) code that was assigned as well as to the Engineering Services code because both include studies and development using engineering sciences. One contracting officer also noted that assigning the NAICS code is subjective and two different contracting officers could review the same contract and find different codes to be appropriate. We also noted this in reviewing our sample of orders. We found that some orders had similar purposes but were assigned different NAICS codes with different corresponding size standards. For example, as shown in Table 1, we found two orders related to the installation of closed-circuit TV systems that had different NAICS codes. Three of the four contracting officers we interviewed stated that there are no unique challenges associated with assigning NAICS codes to ID/IQ contracts compared to other contracts. However, one small business specialist noted that assigning NAICS codes to ID/IQ contracts may be challenging for contracting officers because the statements of work may cover more than one code. One contracting officer we interviewed also stated that it can be challenging to assign NAICS codes to ID/IQ contracts because it is difficult to predict the nature of future orders associated with the base award, especially for research and development contracts.

SBA's 2013 Rule May Clarify NAICS Code Assignments on Multiple-Award Contracts

In 2013, SBA issued a rule on assigning NAICS codes to multiple-award contracts that may further clarify code assignment for contracting officers. The purpose of the rule was to implement the Small Business Jobs Act of 2010, which amended the Small Business Act to allow small business set-asides for parts of multiple-award contracts, for orders placed against multiple-award contracts, and for reserving one or more contract awards for small business concerns.[17] The final rule clarifies that if a multiple-award contract consists of discrete categories, contracting officers may assign a different NAICS code and corresponding size standard to each category. Additionally, under the final rule, contracting officers may issue orders under each category as long as the category's NAICS code matches the order's NAICS code.[18] SBA officials stated that they developed the rule because contracting officers were unclear on how to assign NAICS codes to orders from multiple-award contracts.

Updates to the FAR and FPDS-NG are required to fully implement the portion of SBA's final rule related to NAICS codes. In a 2016 proposed rule to update the FAR, DOD, GSA, and the National Aeronautics and Space Administration (NASA) proposed changes to implement SBA's 2013 rule and stated that enhancements to federal data systems were in process.[19] In June 2017, GSA officials told us that updates to FPDS-NG would be required because the system does not currently allow agencies to assign a NAICS code to an order that differs from the code assigned to the base contract. They also told us that GSA was working on a new version of FPDS-NG that would allow contracting officers to assign NAICS codes to orders that differ from the code assigned to the base contract. SBA officials told us that this planned change would be responsive to their rule. As of mid-November 2017, the final FAR rule had not been issued, and updates to FPDS-NG will depend on the final rule. The four agencies we

[17] In 2011, DOD, GSA, and the National Aeronautics and Space Administration (NASA) issued an interim rule amending the FAR to implement Section 1331 of the Small Business Jobs Act of 2010 and providing guidance to agencies, clarifying their authority to help small businesses through set-asides and reserves under multiple-award contracts. SBA and the Office of Federal Procurement Policy, which were vested under Section 1331 with authority to issue regulations in consultation with GSA, had requested that DOD, GSA, and NASA issue an interim rule. Of the agencies we reviewed, DOD issued guidance on the interim rule. DHS and HHS officials stated that their agencies did not issue guidance on the interim rule, but noted that contracting officers refer to the FAR when setting aside parts of multiple-award contracts.

[18] 78 Fed. Reg. 61114 (Oct. 2, 2013), codified at 13 C.F.R. § 121.402(c).

[19] In its 2013 rule, SBA acknowledged that changes in NAICS code assignments would require a significant planning and implementation effort and stated that it could take years to implement the changes.

interviewed were aware of SBA's 2013 final rule and the 2016 proposed update to the FAR, and stated they would apply the guidance in the rule and update their contract writing systems once the FAR update was finalized.

Some Stakeholders Expressed Concerns about NAICS Code Assignments, but Few Appeals Have Been Filed

Some Industry Groups and Firms Expressed Concern That Contracting Officers Assign NAICS Codes Based on Size Standards

Some of the stakeholders we interviewed—three industry groups and five small businesses that had filed NAICS code appeals (appellants)—expressed concern that some contracting officers assign NAICS codes because they want specific size standards, not because they are the most appropriate codes, but several also stated it was difficult to determine how often this occurs. Specifically, the three industry groups and four of the five appellants we interviewed contended that contracting officers in some instances assign NAICS codes that allow them to make an award to a firm that would not be considered a small business under the "appropriate" code. Conversely, an official of one firm we interviewed told us that contracting officers in some instances assign NAICS codes with smaller size standards to limit competition for a contract. Because agencies have a federal mandate to meet small business contracting goals, contracting officers are required to provide maximum practicable opportunity to award contracts to small businesses in support of those goals.

The following are specific concerns that industry groups and firms expressed:

- Ambiguous and overlapping language. An official from one firm told us that the language in the NAICS Manual can be ambiguous and noted overlap in the descriptions of certain codes with different size standards. For example, NAICS codes 541330 (Engineering Services) and 541712 (Research and Development in the Physical, Engineering and Life Sciences except Biotechnology) both include engineering, but have different size standards ($15 million and 1,000 employees, respectively). An official from another firm stated that the broad NAICS code descriptions result in solicitations that describe identical work having different NAICS codes and size standards. One industry group official stated that the practice of assigning a code based on the size standard and not the principal purpose is particularly a concern for research and development, professional services, and construction contracts. The definitions of the NAICS codes for these industries are broad and there is some overlap. For example, the Professional, Scientific, and Technical Services sector (Sector 54) includes research and development, engineering, legal and accounting, and computer systems design services, among other services. The Construction sector (Sector 23) also includes engineering services in addition to housing construction, water and sewer line construction, and plumbing and heating contractors.
- Preference for incumbent. Officials from two firms we interviewed told us that when recompeting an existing contract, the contracting officer may choose the NAICS code that best positions the incumbent company to compete rather than the code that best represents the work. Officials of one of these firms also stated that they are concerned when the NAICS code assigned to an existing contract that is being recompeted has changed and, in their opinion, the body of work to be performed under the new contract remains the same as the existing contract.[20]

---

[20] SBA regulations once required that contracting officers consider previous government procurement classifications for the same or similar services when making a NAICS code determination. *See*, e.g., 13 C.F.R. § 121.402(b) (2011). The regulations, however, no

- Need to select multiple NAICS codes. In addition, one firm we interviewed stated that it is difficult to predict the code that a contracting officer will use for a procurement. Therefore, the firm selects multiple NAICS codes in its SAM entity registration so contracting officers will consider it for a variety of contracts. The other four firms we interviewed also told us that they selected multiple NAICS codes in SAM. As shown in Table 2, a hypothetical firm that has 450 employees and revenue of $200 million would be a small business under some NAICS codes and large under other codes. Certain NAICS codes such as 541330 (Engineering Services) have exceptions to accommodate military procurement needs.

However, one industry group and some firms stated that it is difficult to determine how often the practice of assigning a code based on the size standard and not the principal purpose occurs. Industry groups and firms also acknowledged that other factors could lead to the assignment of inappropriate NAICS codes. For example, one industry group official stated that human error, not ill intentions, may lead to the assignment of inappropriate codes. In addition, two firms we interviewed cited the inexperience of some contracting officers as a cause. One of these firms also noted that there could be legitimate disagreements about the appropriate NAICS code because individuals can perceive the nature of the work differently, including what is the preponderance of work to be performed. Another industry group official noted that the intended use of NAICS codes is for statistical purposes, not procurement, and as a result, the codes do not always align with procurement needs and the contracting

---

longer include that requirement. 76 Fed. Reg. 5680, 5683 (Feb. 2, 2011). SBA explained its decision to delete the reference to prior government procurement classifications by noting that a "repeated error is not persuasive evidence" and that "[e]ach solicitation should be based on the principal purpose of that particular solicitation, and the contracting officer only needs to make a reasonable choice." 75 Fed. Reg. 9129 (Mar. 1, 2010). Thus, "citations to other procurements . . . do not carry the same weight they would prior to the revision of the [SBA] regulation." *NAICS Appeal of Dellew Corp.,* SBA No. NAICS-5358, 2012 WL 2365474 at *6 (2012).

marketplace.[21] OHA officials acknowledged that assigning codes based on size standards may occur, but noted that it is OHA's role to review the appropriateness of appealed NAICS code assignments, not the contracting officer's intention behind assigning the code. As discussed in more detail later in this chapter, the standard for OHA's review is whether the NAICS code designation was based on clear error of fact or law.

When we shared stakeholders' concerns about the assignment of NAICS codes with officials at the four agencies we reviewed and SBA, officials at three of the five agencies told us that they did not agree with some of the concerns. For example, DHS officials said that some of the observations—particularly the statement that contracting officers may assign the NAICS code that best positions the incumbent company to compete for the contract—were unfair and could be taken out of context. HHS officials told us they did not believe that contracting officers at HHS assign NAICS codes because they want specific size standards. SBA officials also questioned the stakeholders' statements and pointed to the results of NAICS code appeals as an indication that the practice of assigning NAICS codes based on the size standard was not widespread.

In addition, we analyzed the use of NAICS codes from fiscal years 2009– 2016 to determine whether contracting officers used NAICS codes whose size standard increased in 2012 more often than codes whose size standard did not increase. We selected three sectors with size standard increases in 2012 (Sectors 48–49 and 54) for this analysis because these sectors were among the first that SBA reviewed and adjusted.[22] We found that the proportion of obligations and new contracts, respectively, related to NAICS codes with size standards that increased in 2012 remained relatively consistent for Sector 54 and increased for Sectors 48–49 after the size increase. See appendix II for more details.

---

[21] According to the Census website, NAICS was designed for statistical purposes. It notes that although NAICS is frequently used for various contracting and other nonstatistical purposes, the requirements for these nonstatistical purposes played no role in the initial development of NAICS or its later revisions.

[22] Sectors 48–49 are Transportation and Warehousing, and Sector 54 is Professional, Scientific, and Technical Services.

Table 2. Example of Firm That Is Small or Large Depending on the NAICS Code

NAICS code (2012)	Name	Size standard	Small business? (Yes/No)
541330	Engineering Services	$15 million	No
541330 (Exception 1)	Military and Aerospace Equipment and Military Weapons	$38.5 million	No
541330 (Exception 2)	Contracts and Subcontracts For Engineering Services Awarded under the National Energy Policy Act of 1992	$38.5 million	No
541330 (Exception 3)	Marine Engineering and Naval Architecture	$38.5 million	No
336419	Other Guided Missile and Space Vehicle Parts and Auxiliary Equipment Manufacturing	1,000 employees	Yes
541712	Research and Development in the Physical, Engineering, and Life Sciences (Except Biotechnology)	1,000 employees	Yes
541712 (Exception 2)	Other Aircraft Parts and Auxiliary Equipment	1,250 employees	Yes
541712 (Exception 3)	Guided Missiles and Space Vehicles, Their Propulsion Units and Propulsion Parts	1,250 employees	Yes
541712 (Exception 1)	Aircraft, Aircraft Engine and Engine Parts	1,500 employees	Yes

Source: GAO analysis of a hypothetical firm with multiple 2012 NAICS codes matched to different small business size standards. I GAO-18-76.

Note: The hypothetical firm used in this example has 450 employees and revenue of $200 million.

SBA's Process for NAICS Code Appeals Includes Expediting Them

According to OHA officials, OHA expedites NAICS code appeals over other appeals it receives, issuing the decision as soon as practicable because the decision is effectively moot if it is not made before offers are due.[23] They stated that the NAICS code appeal process takes an average of 18 to 30 days to complete, depending on the complexity of the appeal. SBA's process for NAICS code appeals includes (1) determining if appeals are timely and within OHA's jurisdiction, (2) determining if the appellant is adversely affected by the assignment, and (3) expediting NAICS code appeals that are accepted. Interested parties filing a NAICS code appeal do not have to follow a particular format, but the appeal must include the following information: the solicitation or contract number; the name, address, and telephone number of the contracting officer; a full and specific statement as to why the NAICS code designation is alleged to be in error, and argument in support of such allegations; and the name, address, and telephone number of the appellant or its attorney.[24]

Once an appeal is filed, an administrative judge is assigned to adjudicate it. The judge issues a Notice and Order informing the parties of the filing of the appeal petition, establishing the close of record as 15 days after service of the Notice and Order, and informing the parties that OHA must receive any responses to the appeal petition no later than the close of record. Upon receiving notice of the appeal, the contracting officer must place a hold on the solicitation; inform the public about the appeal and the procedures and deadline for interested parties to submit arguments concerning the appeal; and send OHA copies of the solicitation and inform them of any amendments, actions, and developments concerning the procurement in question. When reviewing NAICS code appeals, the judge first considers whether the appeal is timely and within OHA's jurisdiction. SBA regulations define timely appeals as those that are filed within 10 calendar days after issuance of the solicitation or amendment to the solicitation affecting the NAICS code.[25] According to OHA officials, because the office has jurisdiction over small businesses only, large

---

[23] If OHA grants the appeal after the date offers are due, OHA's decision will not apply to the pending procurement, but will apply to future solicitations for the same supplies or services.

[24] An interested party would include a business concern seeking to change the NAICS code designation in order to be considered a small business for the challenged procurement, regardless of whether the procurement is reserved for small businesses or unrestricted.

[25] SBA may file a NAICS code appeal at any time before offers are due. Of the 62 NAICS code appeals filed in 2014–2016, SBA filed three appeals.

businesses cannot file appeals. If the appeal is untimely or outside OHA's jurisdiction, the appeal is dismissed.

If the appeal is not dismissed, OHA officials told us the judge then reviews the NAICS Manual, SBA regulations on size standards, OHA precedent, and the written records to make a final and independent decision. The standard of review is whether the NAICS code designation was based on clear error of fact or law. If there was no clear error of fact or law, OHA will deny the appeal. If it finds a clear error of fact or law, OHA will grant the appeal (see Figure 2).

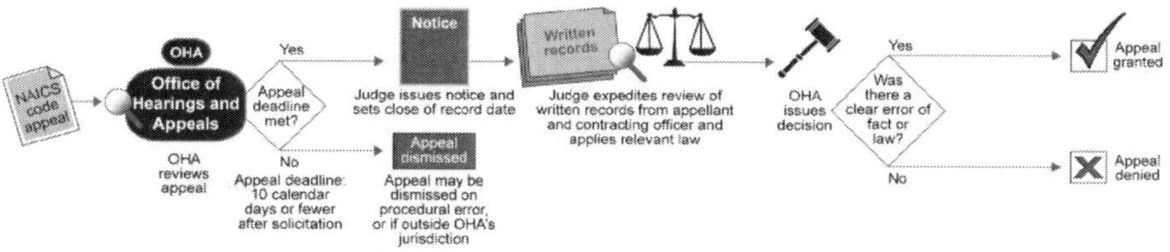

NAICS = North American Industry Classification System
OHA = Office of Hearings and Appeals

Source: GAO analysis of OHA documents. | GAO-18-76.

Figure 2. Process for Reviewing Appeals of NAICS Codes.

We found that OHA's process for reviewing NAICS code appeals is generally similar to other types of OHA appeals (see Table 3). For example, NAICS code appeals and other SBA appeals generally must be filed by an interested party that has been adversely affected. In addition, NAICS code appeals and some other SBA appeals must be filed within 10 calendar or business days.[26] NAICS code appeals are different from other SBA appeals in that OHA is adjudicating an action taken by a contracting agency as opposed to a determination made by an SBA official.

[26] Similarly, bid protests filed with GAO generally must be filed within 10 calendar days after the basis of the protest is known or should have been known (whichever is earlier). A GAO bid protest is a protest of a solicitation or other request by a federal agency for offers for a contract for the procurement of property or services; the cancellation of such a solicitation; an award or proposed award of such a contract; and a termination of such a contract, if the protest alleges that the termination was based on improprieties in the award of the contract.

Table 3. Summary of the NAICS Code Appeal Process and Other Types of Contracting Appeal Processes, 2014–2016

Type of appeal	Decision being appealed	Who can file	Time limit on filing	Number of appeals, 2014–2016
NAICS code appeal process				
NAICS code designation	Appeal of a contracting agency's NAICS code designation	Interested party adversely affected by the code designation or SBA	Within 10 calendar days of issuance of solicitation	62
Other types of contracting appeal processes				
Size determination	Appeal of a formal size determination made by an SBA government contracting area office	Interested party adversely affected by the determination, SBA, or the procuring agency contracting officer	Within 15 calendar days of receiving size determination	219
Service-disabled veteran-owned (SDVO) small business eligibility determination	Appeal of SBA protest determinations related to the status or ownership or control of a SDVO small business concern	Protested concern, the protester, or the contracting officer responsible for the procurement affected by the protest determination	Within 10 business days of receiving protest determination	25
Women-owned small business concern (WOSB) and economically disadvantaged WOSB eligibility determination	Appeal of SBA protest determination related to the status or ownership or control of a WOSB and economically disadvantaged WOSB concern	Protested concern, the protestor, or the contracting officer responsible for the procurement affected by the protest determination	Within 10 business days of receiving the protest determination	2
8(a) business development program determinations	Appeal of SBA determination of eligibility, early graduation, or termination	Applicant or participant firm	Within 45 calendar days of receiving SBA determination being appealed	38

Legend: NAICS = North American Industry Classification System.

Source: GAO analysis of Small Business Administration appeal processes. | GAO-18-76.

Four of the five firms (appellants) that we interviewed to discuss their experience with NAICS code appeals were generally satisfied with the appeals process.[27] Of the five appellants, four used a legal counsel and expressed general satisfaction with the time frames for filing a NAICS code appeal. Four of the five appellants noted that filing within the 10 calendar days was not a challenge, two of them indicating that they had known about the code for some time because it was included in the agency's request for information or proposals. Three of the four firms that used a legal counsel also told us the NAICS code filing process was straightforward. However, the remaining appellant said that 10 calendar days was not enough time. In addition, two appellants noted that firms may not file appeals because they are concerned that filing an appeal will affect their ability to receive future awards from the contracting officer.

Few NAICS Code Appeals Were Filed, and Most Were Dismissed or Denied

Of the 62 NAICS code appeals filed during calendar years 2014–2016, the majority were dismissed or denied. During this same time period, approximately 1.4 million new federal contracts were awarded, and 284 other types of appeals were filed with OHA.

The majority of NAICS code appeals were dismissed, and less than half of the remaining appeals were granted (see Figure 3).

- Thirty-five appeals were dismissed for procedural reasons. For example, OHA dismissed NAICS code appeals that were not filed before the 10 calendar day deadline.[28]

---

[27] The contracting officers we interviewed at four selected agencies did not have any experience with the NAICS code appeal process.

[28] Other reasons for dismissals of NAICS code appeals include: the contracting officer cancelled the solicitation, the appeal was withdrawn, the contracting officer amended the NAICS code, and the appellant was not authorized to file an appeal.

- Fifteen appeals were denied, meaning that OHA determined that the NAICS code designation was not based on a clear error of fact or law.
- Twelve appeals were granted, meaning that OHA determined that the NAICS code designation was based on a clear error of fact or law.

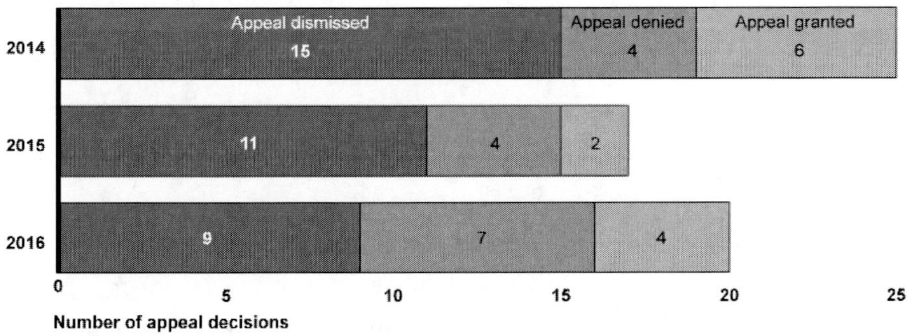

Source: GAO analysis of North American Industry Classification System code appeals. | GAO-18-76.

Figure 3. Number of NAICS Code Appeal Decisions, 2014–2016.

AGENCY COMMENTS

We requested comments from DOD, DHS, GSA, HHS, and SBA on a draft of this chapter. DOD, DHS, and SBA had no comments on the draft report. GSA and HHS provided technical comments, which we incorporated as appropriate.

As agreed with your offices, unless you publicly announce the contents of this chapter earlier, we plan no further distribution until 30 days from the report date. At that time, we will send copies of this chapter to DOD, DHS, GSA, HHS, and SBA and appropriate congressional committees.

William B. Shear
Director, Financial Markets and Community Investment

APPENDIX I: OBJECTIVES, SCOPE, AND METHODOLOGY

This chapter examines (1) what contracting officers consider when assigning North American Industry Classification System (NAICS) codes to federal contracts and the status of efforts to clarify code assignment and (2) stakeholder views on NAICS code assignment and the number and outcomes of appeals filed with the Small Business Administration's (SBA) Office of Hearings and Appeals (OHA).

For our first objective, we reviewed federal laws and regulations related to NAICS code assignment and relevant policies and procedures from the four agencies with the highest indefinite delivery/indefinite quantity (ID/IQ) contract obligations from fiscal years 2011–2015 (the 5 most recent years of Federal Procurement Data System-Next Generation (FPDS-NG) data available when we began our review): Army, Navy, Department of Homeland Security (DHS), and Department of Health and Human Services (HHS).[29] These agencies accounted for approximately $347 billion in obligations and 47 percent of all ID/IQ obligations in fiscal years 2011–2015. To understand how these selected agencies assign NAICS codes to contracts, we reviewed contract documentation, such as acquisition plans and market research documents, for one ID/IQ contract from each of the agencies (see Table 4).

We selected the four contracts we reviewed based on (1) whether they had small business set-asides, (2) the NAICS code, and (3) the number of orders. We selected contracts to obtain a mix of assigned NAICS codes and corresponding size standards. We selected contracts awarded in fiscal years 2014 and 2015 with codes from NAICS industry Sector 54 (Professional, Scientific, and Technical Services) because this sector accounted for half of the 10 NAICS codes with the highest ID/IQ obligations from fiscal years 2011–2015 (see Table 5). We focused on ID/IQ contracts for our contract review because orders for these contracts

---

[29] For the purposes of our review, we considered Department of Defense (DOD) components, such as the Army, the Navy, and the Air Force, to be separate agencies. Within DOD, the Army and the Navy had the most ID/IQ obligations from fiscal years 2011–2015. FPDS-NG is the system used to collect and report on federal procurements.

are ordered after the base contract is awarded, potentially leading to challenges when assigning the NAICS code.

Table 4. Description of Four Selected Contracts Reviewed by GAO, as of September 2015

Agency	Description	Obligations (dollars)	Set-aside type	NAICS code (2012)	Size standard	Number of orders as of September 2015
Army	Development of missile simulation technology	50,552,468	Small business set-aside (total)	541712 –Research and Development in the Physical, Engineering, and Life Sciences (Except Biotechnology)	1,000 employees	132
Navy	Mechanical, electrical, and plumbing design and engineering services	11,198,937	Small business set-aside (total)	541330 – Engineering Services	$14 million	74
Department of Health and Human Services	Installation of closed-circuit television and intrusion detection systems	3,263,822	8(a) sole source	541512 –Computer Systems Design Services	$25.5 million	10
Department of Homeland Security	Strategic operational and technical plans for disaster response	1,472,849	8(a) sole source	541611 – Administrative Management and General Management Consulting Services	$14 million	20

Legend: NAICS = North American Industry Classification System.

Source: GAO analysis of Federal Procurement Data System-Next Generation data and agency documentation. I GAO-18-76.

Table 5. NAICS Codes with Highest Obligations for Indefinite Delivery/Indefinite Quantity (ID/IQ) Contracts, Fiscal Years 2011– 2015

Rank	NAICS code	Description (2012)	ID/IQ obligations for fiscal years 2011–2015 (dollars)
1	541330	Engineering Services	88,237,487,562
2	324110	Petroleum Refineries	40,942,114,343
3	236220	Commercial and Institutional Building Construction	40,371,216,189
4	541712	Research and Development in the Physical, Engineering, and Life Sciences (Except Biotechnology)	36,609,688,536
5	336411	Aircraft Manufacturing	31,478,440,485
6	561210	Facilities Support Services	28,925,203,727
7	541512	Computer Systems Design Services	21,704,097,474
8	541519	Other Computer Related Services	21,586,546,978
9	541611	Administrative Management and General Management Consulting Services	18,654,568,509
10	517110	Wired Telecommunications Carriers	16,521,394,502

Legend: NAICS = North American Industry Classification System.

Source: GAO analysis of Federal Procurement Data System-Next Generation data. I GAO-18-76.

We interviewed contracting officers, small business specialists, and SBA procurement center representatives (PCR) associated with each contract.[30] Of the contracting officers who assigned the NAICS codes to the selected contracts, three no longer worked at the agencies. As such, we interviewed the contracting officer currently assigned to the contract. We also interviewed either the small business specialist who reviewed the NAICS code assignment or the specialist currently responsible for the contract or program office.

To understand how orders relate to the base awards and their NAICS codes, we reviewed 10 orders from each contract and compared each order's purposes to the base award purposes and to the NAICS code

[30] The PCR for the Navy was invited to the meeting we held with the other PCRs, but was unable to attend. SBA PCRs are among the primary staff who implement SBA's prime contracting programs, which are intended to increase contracting opportunities for small businesses and help ensure that small businesses receive a fair and equitable opportunity to participant in federal prime contracts.

definition. We selected a mix of (1) orders that had product and service codes different from the codes assigned to the majority of the contract's orders or did not contain key words contained in the contract's statement of work and (2) orders that were the top orders in terms of obligations.[31] To determine the status of ongoing efforts to clarify code assignment, we reviewed proposed and final regulatory changes to NAICS code assignment and interviewed officials at SBA and the General Services Administration (the agency responsible for managing the operation, maintenance, and updating of FPDS-NG).[32]

For our second objective, to understand stakeholders' views on NAICS code assignment, we interviewed officials from three industry groups and five firms that filed NAICS code appeals during calendar years 2014–2016 (the 3 most recent years of data available). We selected three industry groups to interview that were small business trade associations or contracting interest groups with information on their websites about NAICS codes. We interviewed 5 of the 14 firms that filed appeals in calendar years 2014–2016 of NAICS codes in Sector 54 (the sector with the most appeal decisions). We selected these firms to get a variety of results (granted, denied, or dismissed) and focused on firms that had filed multiple appeals or recent appeals.

To identify commonly used NAICS codes and commonly used size standards, we analyzed data from FPDS-NG to identify the top NAICS codes by obligations and by number of contracts awarded in fiscal year 2016. To assess whether contracting officers were more likely to use a NAICS code when the corresponding size standard increased, we analyzed fiscal year 2009–2016 obligations and number of contracts awarded for NAICS codes in three sectors with size standards that SBA increased in 2012.[33] We assessed the reliability of the FPDS-NG data we used by

[31] Product and service codes are used to describe the products, services, and research and development purchased by the federal government. Because the HHS contract we selected had only 10 orders, we selected all 10 for review.

[32] Specifically, we reviewed 78 Fed. Reg. 61114 (Oct. 2, 2013) and 81 Fed. Reg. 88072 (Dec. 6, 2016).

[33] We selected Sectors 48–49 (Transportation and Warehousing) and 54 (Professional, Scientific, and Technical Services) for this analysis because these sectors were the first to have increased size standards and the increases occurred during the same time period.

electronically testing for missing data, outliers, and inconsistent coding, and by comparing the data on selected contracts to contract documentation we obtained, including the NAICS code and whether or not the contract was an ID/IQ contract. We determined that the data were sufficiently reliable for the purposes of identifying trends in NAICS codes assigned.

To understand SBA OHA's process for reviewing NAICS code appeals, we reviewed federal regulations and interviewed OHA officials. For context, we compared OHA's process for NAICS code appeals to its processes for other types of appeals. To identify the number and outcomes of NAICS code appeals, we obtained and analyzed SBA's OHA decisions on NAICS code appeals filed during calendar years 2014–2016. We summarized the year, agency, outcome, and challenged code for each of the decisions in this time period.

We conducted this performance audit from October 2016 to December 2017 in accordance with generally accepted government auditing standards. Those standards require that we plan and perform the audit to obtain sufficient, appropriate evidence to provide a reasonable basis for our findings and conclusions based in our audit objectives. We believe that the evidence obtained provides a reasonable basis for our findings and conclusions based on our audit objectives.

APPENDIX II: ANALYSIS OF FEDERAL PROCUREMENT DATA SYSTEM-NEXT GENERATION DATA ON NORTH AMERICAN INDUSTRY CLASSIFICATION SYSTEM CODE ASSIGNMENTS

In this appendix, we present analyses of FPDS-NG data on NAICS codes by obligations and number of contracts awarded. Specifically, we analyzed (1) FPDS-NG data for fiscal year 2016 to determine commonly used NAICS codes and size standards and (2) FPDS-NG data for fiscal years 2009 through 2016 to determine whether selected NAICS codes were used more often when the corresponding size standards increased.

Commonly Used NAICS Codes

Tables 6 and 7 contain data on the top 50 NAICS codes by obligations and number of new contracts awarded, respectively, in fiscal year 2016.

Table 6. Top 50 NAICS Codes by Obligations, Fiscal Year 2016

Rank	NAICS code	Description	Obligations (dollars)
1	336411	Aircraft Manufacturing	44,923,652,391
2	541330	Engineering Services	30,893,769,976
3	541712	Research and Development in the Physical, Engineering, and Life Sciences (except Biotechnology)	28,473,115,968
4	561210	Facilities Support Services	21,315,157,389
5	541512	Computer Systems Design Services	17,728,466,597
6	236220	Commercial and Institutional Building Construction	16,168,836,415
7	336611	Ship Building and Repairing	15,890,652,467
8	336414	Guided Missile and Space Vehicle Manufacturing	14,182,990,496
9	541519	Other Computer Related Services	13,255,642,914
10	524114	Direct Health and Medical Insurance Carriers	12,848,976,130
11	336413	Other Aircraft Parts and Auxiliary Equipment Manufacturing	12,839,935,585
12	334511	Search, Detection, Navigation, Guidance, Aeronautical, and Nautical System and Instrument Manufacturing	11,751,497,441
13	541611	Administrative Management and General Management Consulting Services	10,959,866,598
14	325412	Pharmaceutical Preparation Manufacturing	10,025,291,102
15	541710a	Research and Development in the Physical, Engineering, and Life Sciences	8,777,479,755
16	541990	All Other Professional, Scientific, and Technical Services	8,485,253,561
17	336412	Aircraft Engine and Engine Parts Manufacturing	6,316,633,429
18	488190	Other Support Activities for Air Transportation	6,296,296,531
19	324110	Petroleum Refineries	5,219,017,524
20	541511	Custom Computer Programming Services	5,143,283,917
21	562910	Remediation Services	4,303,720,542
22	237990	Other Heavy and Civil Engineering Construction	4,079,203,432
23	336992	Military Armored Vehicle, Tank, and Tank Component Manufacturing	4,034,040,777
24	481212	Nonscheduled Chartered Freight Air Transportation	3,965,730,299

Table 6. (Continued)

Rank	NAICS code	Description	Obligations (dollars)
25	561612	Security Guards and Patrol Services	3,852,769,441
26	332993	Ammunition (except Small Arms) Manufacturing	3,723,012,161
27	325411	Medicinal and Botanical Manufacturing	3,524,153,707
28	517110	Wired Telecommunications Carriers	3,187,389,240
29	334220	Radio and Television Broadcasting and Wireless Communications Equipment Manufacturing	2,925,457,147
30	621111	Offices of Physicians (except Mental Health Specialists)	2,895,364,041
31	541513	Computer Facilities Management Services	2,736,965,226
32	336419	Other Guided Missile and Space Vehicle Parts and Auxiliary Equipment Manufacturing	2,686,065,161
33	334111	Electronic Computer Manufacturing	2,496,191,135
34	511210	Software Publishers	2,290,314,913
35	518210	Data Processing, Hosting, and Related Services	2,229,104,394
36	541690	Other Scientific and Technical Consulting Services	2,089,839,915
37	423940	Jewelry, Watch, Precious Stone, and Precious Metal Merchant Wholesalers	2,068,843,125
38	561990	All Other Support Services	1,983,718,624
39	237310	Highway, Street, and Bridge Construction	1,964,931,838
40	541711	Research and Development in Biotechnology	1,922,008,860
41	562211	Hazardous Waste Treatment and Disposal	1,921,541,169
42	334290	Other Communications Equipment Manufacturing	1,888,859,955
43	483111	Deep Sea Freight Transportation	1,678,399,940
44	443120	Computer and Software Stores	1,652,630,384
45	339113	Surgical Appliance and Supplies Manufacturing	1,571,919,107
46	561720	Janitorial Services	1,557,302,826
47	424210	Drugs and Druggists' Sundries Merchant Wholesalers	1,549,157,640
48	339112	Surgical and Medical Instrument Manufacturing	1,508,392,389
49	423450	Medical, Dental and Hospital Equipment and Supplies Merchant Wholesalers	1,494,824,006
50	332410	Power Boiler and Heat Exchanger Manufacturing	1,445,703,263

Legend: NAICS = North American Industry Classification System.

Source: GAO analysis of Federal Procurement Data System-Next Generation data for fiscal year 2016. I GAO-18-76.

Note: Contracts with obligations totaling about $3.2 billion were missing a NAICS code and therefore were excluded from this analysis.

[a]This code is now obsolete. It was replaced with two codes: 541711 (Research and Development in Biotechnology) and 541712 (Research and Development in the Physical, Engineering, and Life Sciences (Except Biotechnology)).

Table 7. Top 50 NAICS Codes by Number of New Contracts Awarded, Fiscal Year 2016

Rank	NAICS code	Description	Number of new contracts awarded
1	339113	Surgical Appliance and Supplies Manufacturing	38,720
2	336413	Other Aircraft Parts and Auxiliary Equipment Manufacturing	29,128
3	541712	Research and Development in the Physical, Engineering, and Life Sciences (except Biotechnology)	15,887
4	541330	Engineering Services	13,329
5	339112	Surgical and Medical Instrument Manufacturing	13,018
6	334419	Other Electronic Component Manufacturing	11,828
7	236220	Commercial and Institutional Building Construction	11,767
8	332722	Bolt, Nut, Screw, Rivet, and Washer Manufacturing	11,709
9	332510	Hardware Manufacturing	11,618
10	811219	Other Electronic and Precision Equipment Repair and Maintenance	11,157
11	511210	Software Publishers	9,169
12	541611	Administrative Management and General Management Consulting Services	9,081
13	541519	Other Computer Related Services	8,921
14	334516	Analytical Laboratory Instrument Manufacturing	8,762
15	332911	Industrial Valve Manufacturing	8,254
16	541990	All Other Professional, Scientific, and Technical Services	8,190
17	721110	Hotels (except Casino Hotels) and Motels	7,870
18	332999	All Other Miscellaneous Fabricated Metal Product Manufacturing	6,729
19	334220	Radio and Television Broadcasting and Wireless Communications Equipment Manufacturing	6,671
20	332991	Ball and Roller Bearing Manufacturing	6,173
21	332996	Fabricated Pipe and Pipe Fitting Manufacturing	6,024
22	561720	Janitorial Services	5,998
23	334519	Other Measuring and Controlling Device Manufacturing	5,739
24	541511	Custom Computer Programming Services	5,620
25	334511	Search, Detection, Navigation, Guidance, Aeronautical, and Nautical System and Instrument Manufacturing	5,571
26	811310	Commercial and Industrial Machinery and Equipment (except Automotive and Electronic) Repair and Maintenance	5,465

Table 7. (Continued)

Rank	NAICS code	Description	Number of new contracts awarded
27	339991	Gasket, Packing, and Sealing Device Manufacturing	5,134
28	517110	Wired Telecommunications Carriers	5,066
29	332994	Small Arms, Ordnance, and Ordnance Accessories Manufacturing	4,993
30	238220	Plumbing, Heating, and Air-Conditioning Contractors	4,892
31	311999	All Other Miscellaneous Food Manufacturing	4,796
32	115310	Support Activities for Forestry	4,729
33	561210	Facilities Support Services	4,701
34	335999	All Other Miscellaneous Electrical Equipment and Component Manufacturing	4,671
35	611430	Professional and Management Development Training	4,424
36	334417	Electronic Connector Manufacturing	4,378
37	333613	Mechanical Power Transmission Equipment Manufacturing	4,346
38	336390	Other Motor Vehicle Parts Manufacturing	4,287
39	238210	Electrical Contractors and Other Wiring Installation Contractors	4,252
40	333911	Pump and Pumping Equipment Manufacturing	4,235
41	336412	Aircraft Engine and Engine Parts Manufacturing	4,173
42	423430	Computer and Computer Peripheral Equipment and Software Merchant Wholesalers	4,094
43	334111	Electronic Computer Manufacturing	3,859
44	336611	Ship Building and Repairing	3,803
45	541512	Computer System Design Services	3,753
46	333999	All Other Miscellaneous General Purpose Machinery Manufacturing	3,749
47	561612	Security Guards and Patrol Services	3,723
48	332919	Other Metal Valve and Pipe Fitting Manufacturing	3,700
49	337214	Office Furniture (except Wood) Manufacturing	3,700
50	333415	Air-Conditioning and Warm Air Heating Equipment and Commercial and Industrial Refrigeration Equipment Manufacturing	3,569

Legend: NAICS = North American Industry Classification System.

Source: GAO analysis of Federal Procurement Data System-Next Generation data for fiscal year 2016. I GAO-18-76.

Tables 8 and 9 contain data on commonly used revenue-based size standards and employee-based size standards by obligations.

Table 8. Summary of Commonly Used Revenue-Based Size Standards by Obligations, Fiscal Year 2016

2016 size standards (dollars in millions)	Total obligations per size standard for top 50 NAICS codes (dollars)	Number of top 50 NAICS codes with revenue-based size standard
11	4,879,082,665	2
15	43,943,476,489	3
18	1,557,302,826	1
20.5	9,809,120,367	3
27.5	38,864,358,654	4
32.5	8,525,400,925	2
36.5	22,212,971,685	3
38.5	38,375,989,601	4
	168,167,703,212	22

Legend: NAICS = North American Industry Classification System.

Source: GAO analysis of Federal Procurement Data System-Next Generation data for fiscal year 2016. | GAO-18-76.

Table 9. Summary of Commonly Used Employee-Based Size Standards by Obligations, Fiscal Year 2016

2016 size standards (number of employees)	Total obligations per size standard for top 50 NAICS codes (dollars)	Number of top 50 NAICS codes with employee-based size standard
100	2,068,843,125	1
200	1,494,824,006	1
250	1,549,157,640	1
500	18,941,133,256	3
750	4,906,482,325	3
1,000	38,113,736,085	5
1,250	70,112,015,373	7
1,500	71,369,475,821	7
	208,555,667,631	28

Legend: NAICS = North American Industry Classification System.

Source: GAO analysis of Federal Procurement Data System-Next Generation data for fiscal year 2016. I GAO-18-76.

Tables 10 and 11 contain data on commonly used revenue-based size standards and employee-based size standards by new contracts awarded.

Table 10. Summary of Commonly Used Revenue-Based Size Standards by Number of New Contracts Awarded, Fiscal Year 2016

2016 size standards (dollars in millions)	Total number of new contracts awarded per size standard for top 50 NAICS codes	Number of top 50 NAICS codes with revenue-based size standard
7.5	10,194	2
11	4,424	1
15	39,744	5
18	5,998	1
20.5	14,880	2
27.5	18,294	3
32.5	7,870	1
36.5	11,767	1
38.5	13,870	2
	127,041	

Legend: NAICS = North American Industry Classification System.

Source: GAO analysis of Federal Procurement Data System-Next Generation data for fiscal year 2016. | GAO-18-76.

Table 11. Summary of Commonly Used Employee-Based Size Standards by Number of New Contracts Awarded, Fiscal Year 2016

2016 size standards (number of employees)	Total number of new contracts awarded per size standard for top 50 NAICS codes	Number of top 50 NAICS codes with employee-based size standard
250	4,094	1
500	41,822	7
750	89,430	8
1,000	55,025	7
1,250	58,774	7
1,500	9,239	2
	258,384	32

Legend: NAICS = North American Industry Classification System.

Source: GAO analysis of Federal Procurement Data System-Next Generation data for fiscal year 2016. I GAO-18-76.

Use of NAICS Codes with Size Standard Increases in 2012

Industry stakeholders we interviewed stated that contracting officers may assign NAICS codes because they want specific and usually higher size standards, not because they are the most appropriate codes. We analyzed the use of NAICS codes from fiscal years 2009–2016 to determine whether contracting officers used NAICS codes whose size standard increased in 2012 more often than codes whose size standard did not increase. We selected three sectors with size standard increases in 2012 (Sectors 48–49 and 54) for this analysis because these sectors were among the first that the Small Business Administration reviewed and adjusted.[34]

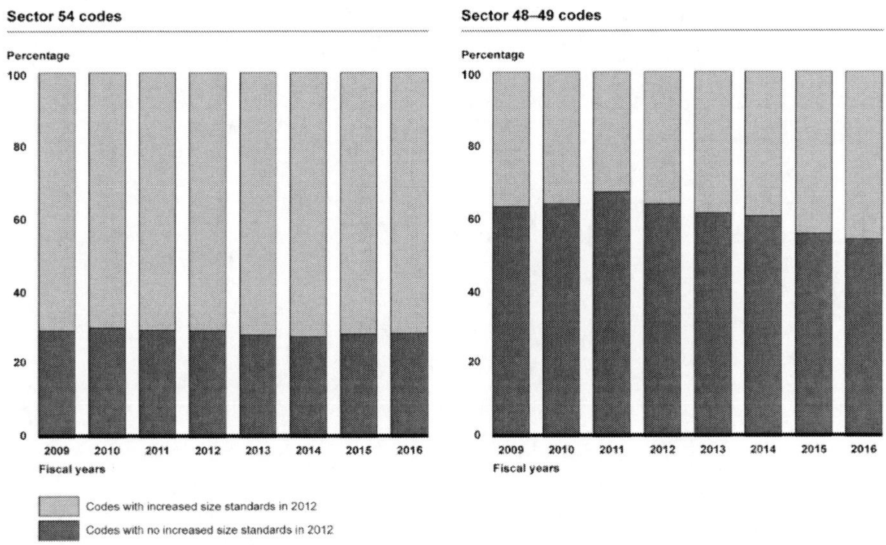

Source: GAO analysis of Federal Procurement Data System-Next Generation data for fiscal years 2009-2016. | GAO-18-76.

Figure 4. Analysis of Fiscal Year 2009–2016 Obligations for NAICS Codes in Sector 54 and Sectors 48–49 with Size Standards That Increased in 2012.

[34] Sectors 48–49 are Transportation and Warehousing, and Sector 54 is Professional, Scientific, and Technical Services.

As shown in Figures 4 and 5, the proportion of obligations and new contracts, respectively, with NAICS codes where size standards increased in 2012 remained relatively consistent for Sector 54 and increased for Sectors 48–49 after the size increase.

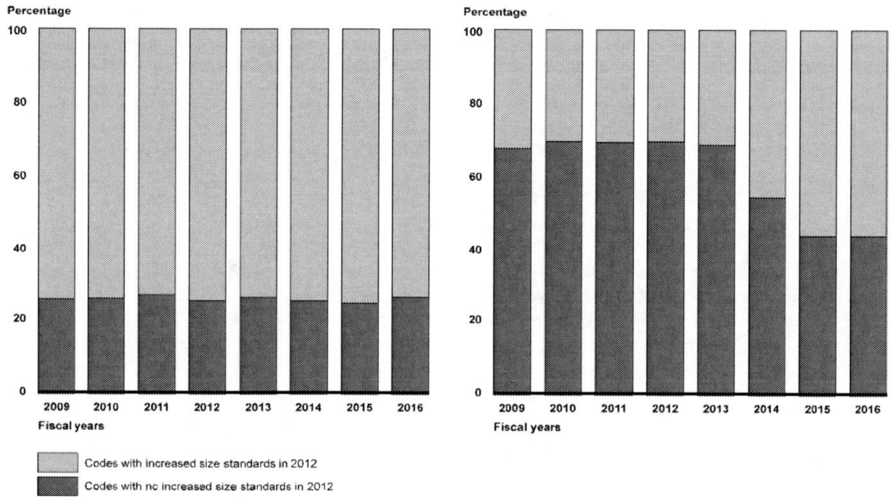

Source: GAO analysis of Federal Procurement Data System-Next Generation data for fiscal years 2009-2016. | GAO-18-76.

Figure 5. Analysis of Fiscal Year 2009–2016 New Awards for NAICS Codes in Sector 54 and Sectors 48–49 with Size Standards That Increased in 2012.

In: Small Business Issues
Editor: Andrea Moeller
ISBN: 978-1-53615-870-0

Chapter 4

SMALL BUSINESS CONTRACTING: SMALL BUSINESS ADMINISTRATION COULD FURTHER STRENGTHEN HUBZONE ELIGIBILITY REVIEWS IN PUERTO RICO AND PROGRAMWIDE*

United States Government Accountability Office

ABBREVIATIONS

HUBZone	Historically Underutilized Business Zone
NAICS	North American Industry Classification System
OIG	Office of Inspector General
PCR	Procurement Center Representative

* This is an edited, reformatted and augmented version of the United States Government Accountability Office Report to Congressional Committees Publication No. GAO-18-666, dated September 2018.

PROMESA	Puerto Rico Oversight, Management, and Economic Stability Act
SBA	Small Business Administration

WHY GAO DID THIS STUDY

The HUBZone program is intended to stimulate economic development in economically distressed areas. Certified HUBZone firms are eligible for federal contracting benefits, including limited competition awards such as set-aside contracts, and are required to be recertified every 3 years. The Puerto Rico Oversight, Management, and Economic Stability Act of 2016 required SBA to develop criteria and guidance for a risk-based approach to verify firm eligibility for the program and included a provision for GAO to review SBA's development and implementation of the required criteria and guidance. This chapter examines, among other objectives, (1) SBA's development of criteria and guidance on using a risk-based approach for certifying and recertifying HUBZone firms, and (2) SBA's implementation of the revised policies and procedures for firms located in Puerto Rico.

GAO analyzed SBA documents and reviewed files of a non-generalizable sample of 12 firms located in Puerto Rico that received certification between March 2017 and March 2018. GAO also interviewed SBA officials, representatives from HUBZone certified firms in Puerto Rico, and local economic development agencies in Puerto Rico.

WHAT GAO RECOMMENDS

GAO recommends that SBA (1) update internal policy manuals to reflect current policies and procedures, and (2) review and document staff compliance with procedures for certification and recertification reviews of firms. SBA generally agreed with GAO's recommendations.

What GAO Found

The Small Business Administration (SBA) adopted criteria and guidance for a risk-based approach to certifying and recertifying firms for the Historically Underutilized Business Zone (HUBZone) program in March 2017, but the extent to which it conducted a risk assessment to inform its approach is unclear. In 2009, in response to GAO's prior recommendations to address weaknesses in the HUBZone certification process, SBA increased documentation requirements for certification, but not recertification (which every 3 years determines continued program eligibility).

- In March 2017, SBA changed its recertification criteria and guidance to require firms with $1 million or more in HUBZone contract awards to provide documentation to support continuing eligibility.
- SBA officials stated they completed a risk assessment of the HUBZone recertification process, but as of July 2018, had not provided GAO with documentation on when they performed the risk assessment, which risks were identified and considered, or what analysis established the $1 million threshold.
- GAO previously found SBA lacked key controls for its recertification process and recommended in 2015 that SBA assess the process.

GAO continues to believe that an assessment of the recertification process would help inform a risk-based approach to reviewing and verifying information from firms that appear to pose the most risk to the program.

Based on GAO's review of case files for a non-generalizable sample of 12 firms in Puerto Rico that received HUBZone certification in March 2017–March 2018, SBA did not consistently document or follow its policies and procedures for certification reviews.

- SBA did not have complete documentation in 9 of 12 cases. SBA officials described alternative procedures they used to determine firms' eligibility, but SBA has not updated its internal policy manuals to reflect these procedures and analysts did not document use of such procedures in the files GAO reviewed.
- In 4 of 12 cases, SBA did not follow its policy to conduct three levels of review (by an analyst, a senior analyst, and the program director or deputy) when determining to approve or deny a firm.
- It is not known to what extent SBA reviewed staff compliance with certification and recertification review procedures. SBA provided an assurance letter stating it evaluated the Office of HUBZone's internal controls and concluded the controls were effective, but the letter did not specify what steps SBA took for the evaluation.

Standards for internal control state management should document its control policies and conduct periodic reviews to ensure controls are effective. Because SBA has not updated its internal policy manuals or conducted a documented review of staff compliance with its quality review procedures, it lacks reasonable assurance that firms are eligible or its review process is effective. In turn, this increases the risk of ineligible firms participating in the HUBZone program and receiving contracting preferences to which they are not entitled.

September 24, 2018

The Honorable James Risch
Chairman

The Honorable Benjamin Cardin
Ranking Member
Committee on Small Business and Entrepreneurship
United States Senate

The Honorable Steve Chabot
Chairman

The Honorable Nydia Velázquez
Ranking Member
Committee on Small Business
House of Representatives

The purpose of the Historically Underutilized Business Zone (HUBZone) program is to provide federal contracting preferences to qualified small businesses located in economically distressed communities (referred to as HUBZones) that employ residents of the areas. The contracting preferences that a certified HUBZone firm (one that meets requirements to participate in the program) can receive include sole-source and set-aside contracts, and the application of a price evaluation preference on awards under full and open competition.

We and the Office of Inspector General (OIG) at the Small Business Administration (SBA) reported over the past 12 years on the need for SBA—which administers the HUBZone program—to strengthen its internal controls and fraud prevention to help ensure that only eligible firms participate in the program.[1] Fraud risks include risks that firms would misrepresent their program eligibility and potentially receive contract awards for which they do not qualify. We identified internal control-related deficiencies in the HUBZone program. For example, in February 2015 we identified problems with the mechanisms that SBA used to certify and

---

[1] See GAO, Small Business Contracting: Opportunities Exist to Further Improve HUBZone Oversight, GAO-15-234 (Washington, D.C.: Feb. 12, 2015); Small Business Administration: Undercover Tests Show HUBZone Program Remains Vulnerable to Fraud and Abuse, GAO-10-759 (Washington, D.C.: June 25, 2010); HUBZone Program: Fraud and Abuse Identified in Four Metropolitan Areas, GAO-09-440 (Washington, D.C.: Mar. 25, 2009); SBA's Control Weaknesses Exposed the Government to Fraud and Abuse, GAO-08-964T (Washington, D.C.: July 17, 2008); and Small Business Administration: Additional Actions Are Needed to Certify and Monitor HUBZone Businesses and Assess Program Results, GAO-08-643 (Washington, D.C.: June 17, 2008). Also see Small Business Administration, Office of Inspector General, Opportunities Exist to Further Improve Quality and Timeliness of HUBZone Certifications, 14-03 (Washington, D.C.: Nov. 19, 2013); and HUBZone Program Examination and Recertification Processes, 6-23 (Washington, D.C.: May 23, 2006).

monitor firms and that SBA was not following its policy of recertifying firms every 3 years (a certified firm can participate in the program as long as it remains eligible and is recertified). In March 2017, we reported that oversight improved but some weaknesses remained.[2]

The Puerto Rico Oversight, Management, and Economic Stability Act (PROMESA) of 2016 mandated that by March 27, 2017, SBA develop and implement criteria and guidance on using a risk-based approach for requesting and verifying information from entities applying to be certified or recertified as a qualified HUBZone small business firm.[3] PROMESA also granted an exemption to a requirement for HUBZone designation that allowed more HUBZones to be established in Puerto Rico.

PROMESA included a provision that we assess SBA's development and implementation of the required criteria and guidance for HUBZone certification and recertification.[4] This chapter (1) examines SBA's development of criteria and guidance on using a risk-based approach for certifying and recertifying HUBZone firms, (2) examines SBA's implementation of the revised policies and procedures for certifying and recertifying firms located in Puerto Rico, and (3) describes any economic impacts of HUBZone expansion and recent trends in federal small business contracting in Puerto Rico.

To examine SBA's development of criteria and guidance for HUBZone certification and recertification, we reviewed prior GAO and SBA OIG reports, applicable statutes and regulations, and SBA documents, including criteria and guidance for certifying and recertifying firms. We compared the process SBA followed to federal internal control standards and GAO's framework for managing fraud risk.[5] To examine SBA's implementation of the criteria and guidance in Puerto Rico, we used SBA's

---

[2] GAO, HUBZone Program: Oversight Has Improved but Some Weaknesses Remain, GAO-17-456T (Washington, D.C.: Mar. 2, 2017).

[3] Pub. L. No. 114-187, § 412(b)(1), 130 Stat. 549, 595 (2016). The mandated risk-based approach and criteria and guidance would be applicable for all firms seeking HUBZone certification or recertification, not just those located in Puerto Rico.

[4] Pub. L. No. 114-187, § 412(b)(2), 130 Stat. 549, 595-96 (2016).

[5] See GAO, *Standards for Internal Control in the Federal Government*, GAO-14-704G (Washington, D.C.: Sept. 10, 2014); and *A Framework for Managing Fraud Risks in Federal Programs*, GAO-15-593SP (Washington, D.C.: July 28, 2015).

Dynamic Small Business Search database to identify HUBZone firms located in Puerto Rico that received HUBZone certification after March 27, 2017. We randomly selected a non-generalizable sample of 12 firms from the total of 47 firms that met those criteria and reviewed case files for the 12 firms' certification applications. We also reviewed the files for two HUBZone firms in Puerto Rico that were subject to recertification during that time.[6] To describe any economic impacts of the expansion of the HUBZone program in Puerto Rico and recent federal contracting trends, we used the Dynamic Small Business Search database and federal procurement data from the Federal Procurement Data System-Next Generation to analyze the number of firms in different HUBZones in Puerto Rico and the dollar amount of federal contract obligations awarded to the firms from fiscal years 2006 through 2018 (June)—that is, from the starting point for the analysis used in our 2017 report to the most recent available data at the time of our current review. We assessed the reliability of the SBA small business database and federal procurement database by reviewing relevant related documentation and determined that they were sufficiently reliable for analyzing trends and for describing economic conditions in HUBZone areas. For all of the objectives, we interviewed SBA officials in Washington, D.C., and Puerto Rico and representatives from the Puerto Rico Chamber of Commerce and the Federal Contracting Center. In addition, we conducted a site visit to San Juan, Puerto Rico, in May 2018 and conducted two discussion groups and one interview with representatives from nine HUBZone firms located there. The views of these representatives are not generalizable to all HUBZone firms. Appendix I describes our scope and methodology in greater detail.

We conducted this performance audit from February 2018 to September 2018 in accordance with generally accepted government

---

[6] According to SBA officials, only two firms in Puerto Rico recertified between March 27, 2017 (when SBA published the new criteria and guidance) and May 30, 2018 (most current data at the time of our review). Neither firm met the threshold to trigger a document review under the March 2017 criteria and guidance. SBA officials said that review processes are essentially the same for certification and recertification. We focused on documentation firms submit to support compliance with the employee residency and primary office location requirements because firms must submit information to demonstrate their compliance with these requirements at certification and recertification.

auditing standards. Those standards require that we plan and perform the audit to obtain sufficient, appropriate evidence to provide a reasonable basis for our findings and conclusions based on our audit objectives. We believe that the evidence obtained provides a reasonable basis for our findings and conclusions based on our audit objectives.

BACKGROUND

The HUBZone Act of 1997 (which established the HUBZone program) identified HUBZones as (1) qualified census tracts, which are determined generally by area poverty rate or household income; (2) qualified nonmetropolitan counties, which are determined generally by area unemployment rate or median household income; and (3) lands meeting certain criteria within the boundaries of an Indian reservation.[7] Congress subsequently expanded the criteria for HUBZones to add former military bases, counties in difficult development areas outside the continental United States, and certain areas affected by disasters.[8] According to SBA officials, 5,306 firms were HUBZone certified as of July 1, 2018. As of that date, there were 20,154 HUBZone qualified census tracts, 834 HUBZone qualified non-metropolitan counties, 125 HUBZone base realignment and closure areas, 593 HUBZone Native American lands

---

[7] HUBZone Act of 1997, Pub. L. No. 105-135. Title VI, 111 Stat. 2592, 2627-2636 (codified in several sections, as amended, in title 15, United States Code). By statute, qualified census tracts are generally those the Secretary of the Department of Housing and Urban Development designates for the Low-Income Housing Tax Credit program.

[8] Difficult development areas have high construction, land, and utility costs relative to area median income, and are designated annually. Consolidated Appropriations Act, 2005, Pub. L. No. 108-447, Div. K, § 152, 118 Stat. 3456-58 (2004), and Safe, Accountable, Flexible, Efficient Transportation Equity Act: A Legacy for Users, Pub. L. No. 109-59, § 10203, 119 Stat. 1933-34 (2005). In addition, Section 866 of the National Defense Authorization Act for Fiscal Year 2016 authorized Native Hawaiian Organizations to own HUBZone "small business concerns"; expanded the definition of "base closure area," and authorized the inclusion of "qualified disaster areas" under the program. In August 2016, SBA issued a final rule to implement these changes. Section 1701 of the National Defense Authorization Act for Fiscal Year 2018 authorized effective January 2020, the inclusion of "Governor-designated covered areas" under the program.

(Indian lands), and 95 HUBZone qualified disaster areas (87 qualified disaster census tracts and 8 qualified disaster non-metropolitan counties).[9]

The HUBZone program provides certified small businesses located in designated areas with contracting opportunities in the form of set-asides, sole-source awards, and price-evaluation preferences. A set-aside restricts competition for a federal contract to specified contractors. For example, competition may be restricted to SBA-certified HUBZone businesses if there is a reasonable expectation of at least two SBA-certified HUBZone bidders and a fair market price. A sole-source award is a federal contract awarded, or proposed for award, without competition. Also, in any full and open competition for a federal contract, the HUBZone price evaluation preference allows the price that a HUBZone firm offers to be deemed lower than the price of another offeror (if the HUBZone firm's offer is not more than 10 percent higher than the other offer and the other offeror is not a small business concern).

HUBZone Certification and Recertification Processes and Related GAO Recommendations

To be certified to participate in the HUBZone program, a firm must meet the following criteria:

- when combined with its affiliates, be small by SBA size standards;[10]
- be at least 51 percent owned and controlled by U.S. citizens, or owned by an Indian Tribal Government, Alaska Native Corporation, Community Development Corporation, or small agricultural cooperative;

---

[9] Different HUBZone area classifications are not mutually exclusive. For example, a qualified census tract may be in a qualified non-metropolitan county.

[10] The firm, with its affiliates, must meet the size standard corresponding to its primary industry classification as defined in 13 C.F.R Part 121. SBA's size standards vary by industry.

- have its principal office—the location where the greatest number of employees perform their work—in a HUBZone;[11] and
- have at least 35 percent of its employees reside in a HUBZone.[12]

In a 2008 report, we found that SBA had relied on information that firms entered into an online application system called the HUBZone Certification Tracking System to indicate they met the size, ownership, location, and employee residence standards.[13] At the time, SBA performed limited verification of the self-reported information. Although agency staff could request additional supporting documentation, SBA did not have specific guidance or criteria for such requests. Thus, we recommended that SBA develop and implement guidance to more routinely and consistently obtain supporting documentation from applicant firms. SBA agreed with the recommendation and changed its certification procedures.

Since fiscal year 2009, SBA has required all firms applying for HUBZone certification to provide supporting documentation about their size, ownership, location, and employees' residence, which the agency then is to review to verify the firm's eligibility for the program. According to SBA officials, the current initial certification process has two components: (1) submission and review of an online application, which is processed by SBA through the HUBZone Certification Tracking System; and (2) submission of corroborative documentation, which SBA processes through a document review. The tracking system contains information on firms that apply to the HUBZone program, as well as on certified firms that apply for recertification. Firms wishing to remain in the program must recertify their continued eligibility to SBA every 3 years. The tracking

[11] While a certified HUBZone firm must have its principal office in a HUBZone area, it can bid on and receive federal contracts for work to be performed anywhere.

[12] SBA defines an employee as an individual employed on a full-time, part-time, or other basis, so long as that individual works a minimum of 40 hours per month. This includes employees obtained from a temporary employee agency or leasing concern, through a union agreement, or co-employed pursuant to a professional employer organization agreement.

[13] See GAO-08-643.

system automatically identifies firms that are due for recertification and sends notifications to those firms.[14]

In 2015, we reported that SBA implemented controls for certification, but generally did not require firms seeking recertification to submit any information to verify continued eligibility. Instead, the agency relied on firms' attestations of continued eligibility.[15] According to SBA officials at the time, they did not believe they needed to request supporting documentation from recertifying firms because all firms in the program had undergone a full document review. We noted that SBA could apply a risk-based approach to its recertification process to review and verify information from firms that appeared to pose the most risk to the program. We concluded that recertification essentially remained a self-certification process. We recommended that SBA reassess its recertification process and add additional controls, such as developing criteria and guidance on using a risk-based approach to requesting and verifying firm information. SBA agreed with our recommendation and noted it would assess the process. In March 2017, we reported that SBA planned to address our recommendation using a technology solution.[16]

GAO's Fraud Risk Framework and Related Legislation

According to federal internal control standards and GAO's fraud risk framework, managers in executive branch agencies are responsible for managing fraud risks and implementing practices for combating those risks.[17] When fraud risks can be identified and mitigated, fraud may be less

---

[14] SBA notifies the firm that it is due to recertify 30 days before the third anniversary of the firm's initial certification or most recent recertification. If the firm does not respond, SBA sends additional notifications on the certification date and 15 days after that date. If the firm has not replied 30 days after it was due to recertify (60 days from the initial notification), SBA sends a notice of proposed decertification. If there is no resolution 30 days later, the program director or deputy sends a notification decertifying the firm.

[15] See GAO-15-234.

[16] GAO-17-456T.

[17] GAO-15-593SP.

likely to occur.[18] Federal internal control standards call for agency management officials to assess the internal and external risks their entities face as they seek to achieve their objectives. The standards state that management should consider the potential for fraud when identifying, analyzing, and responding to risks.[19] Risk management is a formal and disciplined practice for addressing risk and reducing it to an acceptable level.

In July 2015, we issued the fraud risk framework, which provides a comprehensive set of key components and leading practices that serve as a guide for agency managers to use when developing efforts to combat fraud in a strategic, risk-based way.[20] The Fraud Reduction and Data Analytics Act of 2015 required the Office of Management and Budget to establish guidelines for federal agencies to create controls to identify and assess fraud risks and design and implement antifraud control activities.[21] In July 2016, the Office of Management and Budget issued guidelines that, among other things, affirm managers should adhere to the leading practices identified in GAO's fraud risk framework.[22]

National Defense Authorization Act for Fiscal Year 2018

The National Defense Authorization Act for Fiscal Year 2018 includes a number of provisions relating to the HUBZone program.[23] For example,

---

[18] Fraud and "fraud risk" are distinct concepts. Fraud involves obtaining something of value through willful misrepresentation. Fraud risk exists when individuals have an opportunity to engage in fraudulent activity, have an incentive or are under pressure to commit fraud, or are able to rationalize committing fraud. A fraud risk can exist even if fraud has not yet been identified or occurred. When fraud risks can be identified and mitigated, fraud may be less likely to occur. Determining if an act is fraud is beyond management's professional responsibility for assessing risk (such determinations are made through judicial or adjudicative systems). See GAO, *Medicare and Medicaid: CMS Needs to Fully Align Its Antifraud Efforts with the Fraud Risk Framework,* GAO-18-88 (Washington, D.C.: Dec. 5, 2017).

[19] GAO-14-704G.

[20] GAO-15-593SP.

[21] Pub.L. No. 114-186, § 3(a), 130 Stat. 546 (2016).

[22] Office of Management and Budget, *Management's Responsibility for Enterprise Risk Management and Internal Control*, Circular No. A-123 (Washington, D.C.: July 15, 2016).

[23] Pub.L. No. 115-91, § 1701 131 Stat, 1283, 1795 (2017).

the act requires SBA (by January 1, 2020) to verify the accuracy of documentation provided by a HUBZone firm seeking recertification to determine whether the firm remains qualified for HUBZone certification. The act also requires SBA to begin conducting examinations of qualified HUBZone firms by January 1, 2020, using a risk-based analysis to select firms to be examined. According to the act, these risk-based examinations are intended to ensure that each firm examined meets the program requirements for certification. The act also specifies that any small business that SBA determines to have misrepresented its status as a qualified HUBZone firm be subject to liability for fraud.

HUBZone Expansion in Puerto Rico

On June 16, 2016, SBA announced it had revised the definition of qualified census tracts eligible to be designated as HUBZones to provide more opportunities for firms in Puerto Rico. Previously, in addition to poverty rate and income, SBA applied a statutory population cap that limited the number of eligible census tracts.[24] According to the announcement, SBA had determined that the 20 percent population cap was not in keeping with the spirit and intent of the HUBZone program. On June 30, 2016, PROMESA authorized an exemption to the 20 percent cap for HUBZone designations in Puerto Rico for a limited time (10 years or until the date on which the Financial Oversight and Management Board for Puerto Rico ceased to exist, whichever came first). It also required SBA to promulgate regulations to implement the exemption. SBA promulgated the regulations, which became effective December 22, 2017.[25]

By lifting the population cap in June 2016, SBA increased the number of eligible census tracts in Puerto Rico by 516 (from 260 to 776). As a result, nearly all of Puerto Rico now qualifies as a HUBZone (see fig.1).

---

[24] In metropolitan areas in which more than 20 percent of the population qualified, the list of eligible census tracts was ordered from the highest percentage of eligible households to the lowest until the 20 percent limit was exceeded.

[25] 82 Fed. Reg. 48,903 (October 23, 2017) (codified at 13 C.F.R. § 126.103). SBA lifted the population cap in June 2016, before passage of PROMESA.

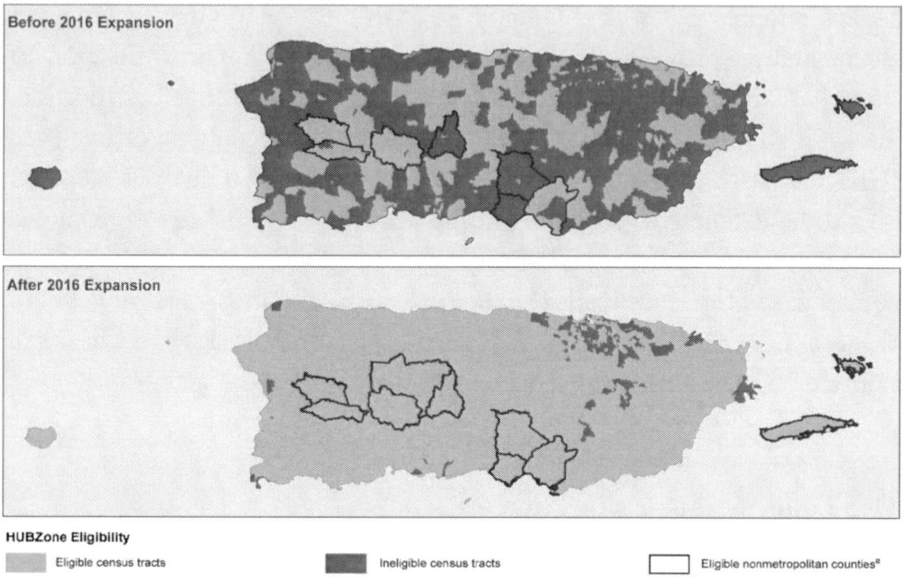

Source: GAO analysis of data provided by the Small Business Administration, MapInfo (map). | GAO-18-666.

Note: SBA's 2016 revision to the definition of qualified census tracts eligible to be designated as HUBZones led to an increase in the number of eligible HUBZone census tracts in Puerto Rico.

[a]In addition to qualified census tracts, HUBZone areas may also be located in certain nonmetropolitan counties.

Figure 1. Historically Underutilized Business Zone (HUBZone) Areas in Puerto Rico, Before and After June 2016 Change to Definition of Qualified Census Tracts.

2017 Hurricanes

In 2017, two major hurricanes (Irma and Maria) hit Puerto Rico. Hurricane Irma skirted Puerto Rico and left more than 1 million people without power. Hurricane Maria, a Category 4 hurricane, made landfall and caused catastrophic damage.[26] For instance, Hurricane Maria wiped

[26] The Saffir-Simpson Hurricane Wind Scale is a 1–5 rating based on a hurricane's sustained wind speed and estimates potential types of property damage in each category. Hurricanes reaching Category 3 and higher are considered major hurricanes because of their potential for significant loss of life and damage. Category 4 hurricanes carry sustained winds of 130–156 miles per hour.

out the power grid, resulting in outages across Puerto Rico that continued for months after the storm. The majority of the island had its power restored by April 4, 2018, according to the Department of Energy. However, the power grid remains fragile. For example, Puerto Rico experienced an island-wide outage on April 18, 2018.

SBA Adopted Criteria and Guidance for a Risk-Based Approach to HUBZone Certification and Recertification but the Extent to Which It Conducted a Risk Assessment of the Recertification Process Is Unclear

SBA Adopted New Documentation Requirements for Recertifying Certain HUBZone Firms

In response to the PROMESA provision to implement a risk-based approach to HUBZone certification and recertification, SBA adopted certification and recertification criteria and guidance on March 27, 2017, for requesting and verifying information.[27] Since 2009 and in response to a prior GAO recommendation, SBA has required and reviewed documentation from all small businesses seeking initial certification to show compliance with HUBZone eligibility requirements.[28] The criteria and guidance adopted by SBA in March 2017 did not change the HUBZone certification process. SBA's internal guidance directs staff to review and confirm the accuracy of all documentation provided by the firms applying for HUBZone certification.

However, the 2017 guidance and criteria introduced some documentation requirements to the recertification process. (Before March 2017, firms seeking HUBZone recertification were not required to submit

---

[27] Pub. L. No. 114-187, § 412(b)(1), 130 Stat. 549, 595 (2016).
[28] GAO-08-643.

documentation to demonstrate continued compliance with eligibility requirements.) Currently, any certified firm seeking recertification that received $1 million or more in HUBZone contract dollars since its last certification or recertification has to demonstrate compliance with the 35 percent HUBZone employee residency and principal office requirements.[29] More specifically, under the March 2017 guidance and criteria, certified HUBZone small business concerns that have received $1 million or more in HUBZone contract dollars since their initial certification or most recent recertification must submit (1) a list of all current employees, identifying the name of the employees, their addresses, the number of hours they worked per month, and the location at which they performed their work; and (2) payroll documentation.[30] HUBZone firms seeking recertification that have not received $1 million in HUBZone contract dollars are not required to submit documentation supporting continual eligibility for the program.

Extent to Which SBA Conducted a Risk Assessment of the Recertification Process Is Unclear

SBA officials stated that they had completed a risk assessment of their HUBZone recertification process to develop the March 2017 guidance and criteria. In our 2015 report, we found SBA did not require firms to submit supporting documentation as part of the recertification process—in effect, firms self-certified.[31] We recommended that SBA conduct an assessment of the recertification process and implement additional controls, such as developing criteria and guidance on using a risk-based approach to requesting and verifying firm information.

---

[29] For purposes of the March 2017 guidance and criteria, SBA officials stated that HUBZone contract dollars are those obtained with a HUBZone contracting preference— that is, a set aside contract, sole-source contract, or price evaluation preference.

[30] SBA's guidance requires that HUBZone firms meeting the $1 million threshold that are seeking recertification retain supporting documentation related to payroll information for individual employees, firm locations, and physical sites of any work performed.

[31] See GAO-15-234.

However, as of July 31, 2018, SBA had not provided documentation of when the risk assessment was performed or of what risks were identified and considered in developing the criteria and guidance. SBA officials stated that out of necessity, given their current information system and staffing resources, they chose the $1 million threshold as the only criterion for their risk-based approach.

As of July 31, 2018, SBA also had not provided documentation of what analysis was performed to establish the $1 million threshold. According to SBA officials, the threshold was determined based on the belief that, when a firm received contract awards over $1 million, it increased opportunity for the firm to fall out of compliance with HUBZone requirements.

SBA officials noted that they plan to review the current threshold at the end of fiscal year 2018 and that the threshold amount will likely decrease because a relatively small number of firms have exceeded the $1 million threshold. Based on our analysis of Federal Procurement Data System-Next Generation data, we estimated that from fiscal year 2015 through fiscal year 2017 about 9 percent of HUBZone firms nationally exceeded the $1 million threshold. SBA officials also noted that the agency has been developing a new information system to replace the current certification tracking system. According to SBA officials, the new system will help simplify the application process and allow firms to submit additional documentation more easily. SBA officials said the 2017 criteria and guidance will be built into the parameters of the new information system, which will allow SBA to expand the review of documentation submitted by firms seeking recertification. Officials have stated that subject to funding and resources, the HUBZone Certification Tracking System is scheduled to be decommissioned in fiscal year 2019.[32]

In the past, SBA has implemented a number of actions to better ensure that only eligible firms participate in the HUBZone program and to address internal control weaknesses that we have identified in previous GAO

---

[32] SBA officials had previously estimated that a new technology-based solution to address some of the ongoing challenges with the recertification process would be available in late 2017. See GAO-17-456T.

reports.[33] However, in 2015, we found that SBA lacked key controls for its recertification process. Specifically, SBA did not require firms to submit supporting documentation as part of the recertification process—in effect, firms self-certified. We reported that by not routinely requiring and reviewing key supporting documentation from recertification applicants, SBA was missing an additional opportunity to reduce the risk that ineligible firms obtain HUBZone contracts. We recommended that SBA conduct an assessment of the recertification process and implement additional controls, such as developing criteria and guidance on using a risk-based approach to requesting and verifying firm information.[34]

Standards for Internal Control in the Federal Government state that management should identify, analyze, and respond to risks related to achieving the defined objectives of the program.[35] Additionally, the standards state that management should use a risk assessment to identify and analyze risks related to achieving the defined objectives to form a basis for designing risk responses. Once identified, management can analyze the identified risks to estimate their significance and design responses to the analyzed risks.[36] Similarly, according to GAO's fraud risk framework, leading practices for managing fraud risk include identifying inherent fraud risks affecting the program, assessing the likelihood and impact of inherent fraud risks, and examining the suitability of existing fraud controls. The Fraud Reduction and Data Analytics Act of 2015 states that agencies shall conduct an evaluation of fraud risks using a risk-based approach, and then design and implement financial and administrative control activities to mitigate identified fraud risks. Additionally, as discussed above, the National Defense Authorization Act for Fiscal Year 2018 requires that SBA perform examinations of HUBZone firms using a risk-based selection process.

---

[33] For more information, see GAO-15-234.

[34] GAO-15-234.

[35] GAO-14-704G.

[36] Significance refers to the effect on achieving a defined objective.

As we reported in 2015, the characteristics of firms and the status of HUBZone areas—the bases for program eligibility—can often change, and need to be monitored. We continue to believe that conducting a risk assessment of the recertification process would help inform a risk-based approach to reviewing and verifying information from firms that appear to pose the most risk to the program. For example, a risk assessment could help inform SBA's planned review of the current threshold for requesting and verifying information from firms seeking HUBZone recertification.

SBA Did Not Consistently Document or Follow Its Policies and Procedures for Certification Reviews for Firms in Puerto Rico That We Reviewed

Our review of 12 case files for Puerto Rican firms that recently received HUBZone certification found incomplete documentation for certification reviews (and by extension, recertification reviews) and undocumented procedures. SBA also did not consistently follow its procedures to complete three distinct levels of review when approving the 12 firms for certification. Representatives of firms in Puerto Rico with whom we spoke said certification was generally straightforward, but identified some challenges, including with providing documentation.

SBA Had Complete Documentation for Office Location but Not Employee Residency for Firms in Puerto Rico We Reviewed and Had Not Updated Its Policies

We found that all 12 cases we reviewed in a non-generalizable sample of Puerto Rican firms that had received HUBZone certification between March 2017 and March 2018 had complete documentation to demonstrate that the primary office was located in a HUBZone.

However, we also found that documents were missing, illegible, or did not corroborate the information claimed regarding employees' residency for 9 of 12 firms that we reviewed. We focused on the document review process for the principal office location and the employee residency requirements because, according to SBA's March 2017 guidance for the certification and recertification processes, firms must corroborate their compliance with these requirements at both certification and recertification.[37] In addition, SBA officials told us that the document review process is essentially the same for firms seeking certification as it is for firms seeing recertification. We also reviewed the files of two HUBZone firms in Puerto Rico that were subject to recertification between March 2017 and March 2018, but neither met the threshold to trigger a document review under the updated criteria and guidance.

SBA's guidance for the certification process requires firms to submit documentation so that SBA can verify that a firm meets the employee residency and principal location requirements. The documentation must show that

- each individual is an employee of the firm (payroll documentation),
- each individual asserted to be a HUBZone resident lives at the address they claim (proof of address, such as a driver's license), and
- the address is in a HUBZone (copy of a HUBZone map indicating the employee and his or her address), and

[37] Under the March 2017 guidance, firms seeking recertification that have received $1 million or more in HUBZone contract dollars since their initial certification or most recent recertification must submit (1) a list of all current employees, identifying the name of the employees, their addresses, the number of hours they worked per month, and the location at which they performed their work; and (2) payroll documentation. Firms seeking initial certification must submit documentation to verify their compliance with all program eligibility requirements.

- the firm's primary office is located in a HUBZone (such as a copy of a lease or rental agreement and list of employees who work there).[38]

Additionally, SBA's internal policy manuals describe procedures that analysts are to follow in reviewing and verifying these documents, including the types of documents that firms may submit to demonstrate eligibility, and scenarios in which analysts should request additional information or clarification from the firm (for example, if a driver's license is expired).

For 9 of 12 cases we reviewed, SBA lacked complete documentation to verify that every employee asserted to be a HUBZone resident lived in a HUBZone. That is, although SBA analysts contacted firms during the certification process to obtain additional documentation, and firms responded to the requests, SBA analysts still had incomplete information for 9 of the 12 cases at the time they approved the firms.

In 5 of these 9 cases, the firm would not be eligible for HUBZone certification if the SBA analyst had not counted employees for which documentation was missing or did not corroborate the information claimed regarding an employee's address. Specifically,

- in 3 cases, the address on the employee's identification for at least one employee did not match the address at which the firm claimed the employee lived.
- in 3 cases, the identification for at least one employee was expired.
- in 1 case, the copies of the HUBZone maps did not indicate to which employees they referred.
- in 1 case, payroll documentation demonstrating that individuals were employees of the firm was missing.[39]

---

[38] Firms seeking recertification and that received $1 million or more in HUBZone contracts must retain this documentation.

[39] For the five cases in question, three had more than one identified discrepancy and two had a single identified discrepancy.

- in the other 4 cases, the firm still would be eligible for HUBZone certification (would meet the 35 percent residency requirement) even if the analyst had not counted the employee for which documentation was missing or illegible (1 case) or for which identification did not match the claimed residency address (4 cases).

We also identified an inconsistency when reviewing the case files for the only Puerto Rican HUBZone firm recertified between June 2017 and May 2018.[40] Specifically, the firm reported on its application that it had zero employees, but also claimed 19 of its employees lived in a HUBZone. The firm did not provide any supporting documentation because it did not meet the threshold in the new recertification criteria to require a document review. SBA officials said this likely resulted from a display error in the online system. SBA officials said that they did not contact the recertifying firm because the firm was not required to submit corroborating documentation. However, without confirmation of the correct total number of employees, SBA analysts would not be able to determine the firm's compliance with the employee residency requirement (35 percent living in a HUBZone) and therefore would not be able to determine the firm's eligibility to continue HUBZone participation.

SBA officials explained how they handled incomplete information provided by firms by describing other procedures that analysts followed in these cases. For example, if any employee's address did not match across the firm's employee list, the employee's identification, or the HUBZone map, the analyst reviewing the firm's application would request clarification and enter the address from the identification into the current HUBZone map. Or if the address could not be plotted, the analyst would presume the employee lived in a HUBZone if the broader geographic area on their identification (such as zip code) was clearly in a HUBZone.

---

[40] SBA decertified the one other firm that was due for recertification because it did not respond to notifications from SBA to recertify. Only two firms in Puerto Rico were due for recertification during this time frame.

SBA officials said this approach is useful for applications from firms in Puerto Rico, because of difficulties with mapping addresses in the territory. SBA officials also said that if a firm did not provide documentation for an employee or SBA could not verify it, but the firm clearly met the 35 percent resident requirement, the analyst would not follow up with additional documentation requests and not count that employee as a HUBZone resident.

However, these procedures are not documented in SBA's internal written policies for certifying HUBZone firms and analysts did not document their use of these procedures in the case files we reviewed. Specifically, the policy manuals do not include certain procedures SBA officials explained to us they used for the document review process, such as assumptions of eligibility for addresses located in a broader geographic area that is clearly a HUBZone. SBA has not updated its three internal policy manuals since 2014, 2010 and 2007, respectively.[41]

According to SBA officials, analysts rely on oral direction from the HUBZone program director or deputy to review and process HUBZone certifications and recertifications to supplement outdated policy documents. Internal control standards state that management should document in policies the internal control responsibilities of the organization.

Because SBA has not updated its internal policy manuals, analysts who review applications for HUBZone certification and recertification may not be consistently following applicable internal policies and procedures. As a result, management does not have reasonable assurance that analysts are following procedures correctly to obtain and review all of the required documents from firms. Without such review, SBA may not have reasonable assurance that firms meet the eligibility criteria for HUBZone participation—which increases the risk of ineligible firms participating in

[41] SBA officials told us they plan to update the standard operating procedures, one of the three internal policy manuals, by December 2018. In 2014, the SBA OIG recommended that SBA update its HUBZone guidance to reflect changes to the certification process. See *Opportunities Exist to Further Improve Quality and Timeliness of HUBZone Certifications,* 14-03. In 2015, we reported that SBA planned to update the standard operating procedures manual in March 2015, but the agency had not updated it as of June 2018. See GAO-15-234.

the program. Because SBA officials told us that firms seeking recertification that meet the threshold for additional document review undergo essentially the same reviews as firms seeking certification, the gaps in certification cases that we observed suggest that gaps are possible in recertification as well.

SBA Did Not Consistently Follow Its Quality Review Procedures When Certifying Firms in Puerto Rico That We Reviewed

SBA did not consistently follow its quality review procedures to complete three distinct levels of review when approving the 12 Puerto Rican firms in our non-generalizable sample for certification. In 4 of 12 cases, one person reviewed the application for two levels of review; in the other 8 cases, three different analysts reviewed the application. We found that SBA notified all 12 firms of their approval in writing, in accordance with its policy.

SBA's internal policy states that the certification process has three levels of review: (1) an analyst reviews the application documents and makes a recommendation to approve or deny the firm, (2) a senior analyst reviews the application and the first analyst's recommendation, and (3) the program director or deputy finalizes the approval or denial and notifies the firm of the decision. The three levels of review are intended to provide quality assurance. For example, the second analyst reviews the case file and the first analyst's recommendation for completeness, accuracy, and consistency with eligibility criteria.

SBA officials told us that, in some cases, one individual's review may count as two of the three levels of reviews in order to make the most efficient use of available analyst capacity. SBA officials said the deputy director reviewed several applications from Puerto Rican firms, including the four cases we identified, as part of work to develop an application screening tool and to engage the Puerto Rico district office when processing applications from firms in Puerto Rico. These reviews were counted as two of the three levels of review. Officials said that in these cases, the program director completes the final review and should annotate the case file notes about the quality assurance actions that were taken. In three of the four cases, the program director noted that she completed the final review and approval but not what quality assurance actions were taken; the deputy director completed both the second and final review in the other case. SBA officials described the third-level review (final approval or denial) as a high-level review to ensure no questions or unresolved matters are outstanding in order to approve or deny the application. Therefore, it is not likely that the program director would be reviewing supporting documents to identify any problems that could be identified if an additional analyst conducted a second-level, quality assurance review.

Internal control standards state that management should design control activities at various levels with a segregation of duties, and periodically review its procedures and associated internal control activities for effectiveness. Management should also monitor its internal control system through ongoing monitoring to assess the quality and effectiveness of the internal control system's performance over time.

SBA provided an assurance letter prepared in response to the Federal Managers Financial Integrity Act that stated the agency evaluated the Office of HUBZone's internal controls and concluded the controls were effective. However, it is not known to what extent SBA reviewed staff's compliance with certification and recertification quality review procedures as part of this assessment, because the letter does not describe what steps SBA took to conduct the evaluation.

Without reviewing staff compliance with certification and recertification procedures, SBA lacks reasonable assurance that analysts follow such procedures and that internal controls function effectively. This increases the risk that ineligible firms could receive HUBZone certification and thus contracting preferences to which they are not entitled.

Representatives of Firms in Puerto Rico We Interviewed Said Certification Process Generally Was Straightforward, but Documentation Requests Presented Some Challenges

Representatives of nine HUBZone firms we interviewed in Puerto Rico were not aware of changes made to the recertification process, but said that the certification process they followed was straightforward and generally easy. However, they reported some challenges, including with documentation.

Representatives of most of the firms said that the most difficult part of the certification process was documenting the address for their primary office location and employees' residences to show they are located in a HUBZone. They said this is time-consuming and tedious, especially for firms with many employees. Although they felt that SBA's HUBZone mapping software had improved, they said the formatting of addresses in Puerto Rico creates a challenge, consistent with what we reported in 2017.[42] One representative described having to pinpoint locations manually in Google Maps to obtain geographic coordinates, and then enter the coordinates into SBA's HUBZone map instead of street addresses. Other representatives noted that some of their employees have informal living arrangements and cannot easily provide proof of address.

Some representatives said that they struggled with the specific time frames that payroll documentation must cover. SBA requires firms to submit payroll documentation for the pay period that includes the date of their application and a sufficient number of preceding payrolls to cover a 4-week period, but firms said it was difficult to submit payroll reports at exactly the right time to meet this requirement.

According to representatives from HUBZone firms and two economic development organizations we interviewed, some challenges with

---

[42] In 2017, we reported that SBA's mapping system could not process certain addresses in Puerto Rico. See GAO, *Puerto Rico: Information on Trends and Challenges to Small Business Federal Contracting,* GAO-17-550 (Washington, D.C.: June 29, 2017). The National Defense Authorization Act for Fiscal Year 2018 requires SBA to update its online mapping tool by January 1, 2020. (Pub. L. No. 115-91 § 1701 (h)(1), (j), 131 Stat. 1283, 1801, 1803 (2017).

certification may be unique to firms in Puerto Rico, including the address format issue described above. Representatives from one firm and the economic development organizations said that some firms in Puerto Rico may face language barriers if Spanish is their primary language, or if they lack formal documentation required for certification, such as not having computerized records. The 2017 hurricanes also created several challenges for firms. For example, some firms did not have electricity and closed for several months. Firms that closed while trying to obtain HUBZone certification could not respond to follow-up requests from SBA immediately or provide documentation of their business operations for the time period in which they were affected.

Representatives from firms we interviewed said they had little contact with SBA other than in relation to compliance. Although some have attended SBA events, representatives said they generally worked with SBA partner organizations, such as the Federal Contracting Center and Small Business and Technology Development Center to obtain assistance with gaining HUBZone certification and applying for federal contracts. Representatives from three firms we interviewed said that officials from SBA visited their offices to provide technical assistance support.

According to SBA officials in Washington, D.C., they have improved their communications with firms and increased outreach for the HUBZone program in recent years. For example, the HUBZone tracking system automatically generates emails to firms, such as reminders that they are due for recertification, which according to SBA officials, has eliminated the backlog of recertifications on which we reported in February 2017.[43] Representatives from the Puerto Rico District Office also said they increased promotion of the HUBZone program in recent years through monthly events and seminars on all SBA programs across Puerto Rico, including a seminar on obtaining HUBZone certification. Representatives from the district office said they are not involved with the certification and recertification processes, but provide support by conducting from three to

---

[43] We reported on this issue in February 2017 and recommended that SBA take steps to eliminate the backlog (see GAO-17-456T).

six site visits to HUBZone firms annually in Puerto Rico and the U.S. Virgin Islands.

HUBZone Set-Aside Contracting Was Minimal in Comparison to Other Small Business Contracting in Puerto Rico; However, Assessment of HUBZone Expansion Impacts Might Be Premature

An increase in HUBZone set-aside contracts could theoretically help deliver economic impact to Puerto Rico, but it is likely too soon to assess larger-scale economic benefits resulting from HUBZone program expansion in Puerto Rico as of June 2018. From fiscal years 2006 through June 2018, the share of HUBZone set-aside contracts as a percentage of small business contracts in Puerto Rico has remained low despite sharp increases in the number of HUBZone firms and overall federal contracting in Puerto Rico. Over this period, small businesses in Puerto Rico have been winning a large and increasing percentage of total federal contracting obligations in Puerto Rico. Firms, economic development organizations, and SBA representatives said any impacts of HUBZone expansion in Puerto Rico may not yet be observable due to hurricane-related setbacks. They also identified longer-standing challenges that Puerto Rican firms have faced in obtaining HUBZone set-aside contracts consistent with those we identified in 2017[44] In 2018, SBA established a procurement center representative (PCR) in Puerto Rico, which the agency expects will help address some of those challenges.

Economic Impacts of HUBZone Expansion in Puerto Rico Not Yet Apparent

Based on our analysis as of June 30, 2018, it appears that larger-scale economic benefits from HUBZone expansion have not been realized (it

---

[44] See GAO-17-550.

may be too early to assess the impact of program expansion). While HUBZone certification alone likely would not have a direct economic impact (such as on job creation) in Puerto Rico, the expansion of HUBZones in Puerto Rico, which now cover nearly the entire island, gives opportunities to more firms to qualify for and pursue preferential contracting opportunities. The number of HUBZone firms has risen since the expansion—from 20 in September 2016 to 101 as of June 30, 2018.

The program could help deliver economic impacts if HUBZone firms received contract awards as a result of contract preferences such as set-aside or sole-source contracts.[45] For instance, employees hired to fulfill HUBZone set-aside contracts could represent jobs created in Puerto Rico (if those contracts otherwise would have been awarded to a firm outside Puerto Rico). However, if the contract otherwise would have been awarded to another Puerto Rican firm, the new jobs would represent an economic transfer, not jobs created.[46]

Our analysis of HUBZone set-aside contracts in Puerto Rico indicated that a few, newly certified HUBZone firms received set-aside contracts, which can be a source of job creation.[47]

- Six of the nine firms that received HUBZone set-aside contracts in fiscal years 2017 and 2018 (through June 2018), totaling $5.1 million, were certified after the 2016 program expansion.[48]

---

[45] Sole-source contracts are awards made without competition and set-aside contracts are awards limited to a designated pool of competing firms.

[46] In our analysis of employment data by month and municipality (Local Area Unemployment Statistics, from the Bureau of Labor Statistics), we did not find a significant relationship between contract awards and employment levels. Even if individual firms experience a significant effect on employment, these effects might not show up in the aggregate municipality level data for various reasons. For example, because these employment data are based on a household survey, the data might not capture small effects given the sample size. Also we did not control for a variety of factors that might affect employment such as other government programs or hurricane damages.

[47] In addition to set-aside and sole-source contracts, certified HUBZone businesses also can receive a price evaluation preference of 10 percent in full and open competition if the apparent successful offering firm is not a small business. There were no cases of awards made using the HUBZone price evaluation preference in our analyses.

[48] The HUBZone set-aside contracts received in fiscal years 2017 and 2018 (through June 2018) by the three previously certified firms totaled more than $400,000.

- One newly certified HUBZone firm that we interviewed said that program expansion resulted in the firm becoming HUBZone-eligible. The firm's representative said that it obtained a 5-year HUBZone set-aside contract for $700,000, which resulted in the firm hiring six employees to fulfill the contract.

But HUBZone set-aside contract obligations have remained largely unchanged in recent years, and firms face both temporary and longer-standing challenges in accessing and winning contract awards, as we discuss later in this section. For a description of contracting trends in Puerto Rico, see appendix II

Federal Contracting to Small Businesses in Puerto Rico More Than Doubled Over the Past 3 Years

Based on our analysis, federal contracts to businesses in Puerto Rico increased from $355 million in fiscal year 2015 to $841 million in fiscal year 2018 (through June 2018). Similarly, federal contracts to small businesses in Puerto Rico increased from $244 million to $688 million in the same period (see fig. 2).[49]

Although HUBZone set-aside contract obligations have remained largely unchanged in recent years, small businesses in Puerto Rico also have been winning a large and increasing percentage of total federal contracting obligations in Puerto Rico. Specifically, federal contract obligations to small businesses located in Puerto Rico as a percentage of total federal contract obligations in Puerto Rico increased from 69 percent in fiscal year 2015 to 82 percent in fiscal year 2018 (through June 2018). A significant portion of the increase in overall contracting and small business contracting to Puerto Rican firms in fiscal year 2018 (through June 2018) was related to hurricane relief. Specifically, we calculated that 55 percent of total federal contracting obligations in Puerto Rico and 64 percent of

---

[49] For a more detailed description of contracting trends in Puerto Rico, see appendix II.

obligations awarded to Puerto Rican small businesses in fiscal 2018 were associated with hurricane relief.

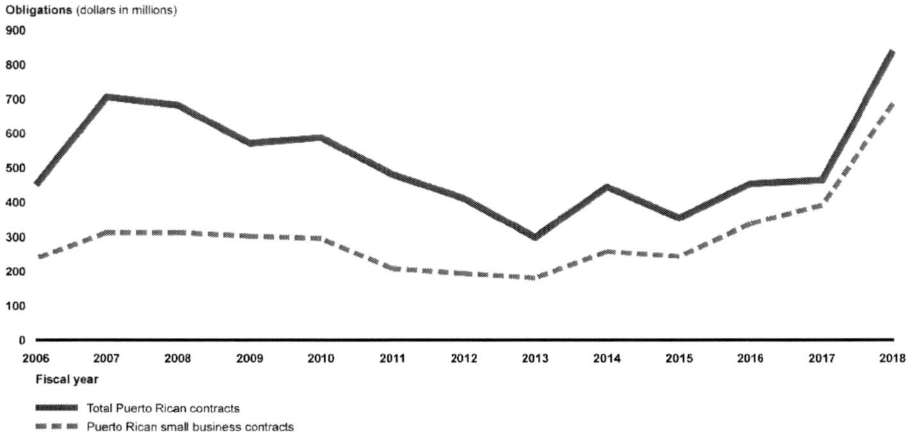

Source: GAO analysis of Federal Procurement Data System-Next Generation data. | GAO-18-666.

Note: We analyzed data for federal prime contracting obligations awarded to all businesses and small businesses in Puerto Rico. The dollar amounts are adjusted for inflation using fiscal year 2017 dollars.

Figure 2. Federal Contracting in Puerto Rico, Fiscal Years 2006–2018 (through June 2018).

HUBZone Set-Aside Contracts as a Share of Federal and Small Business Contracts in Puerto Rico Remained Relatively Low in Recent Years

While the obligations for federal contracting to small businesses in Puerto Rico sharply increased in recent years, as did the number of HUBZone firms, the share of HUBZone set-asides as a percentage of small business contracts in Puerto Rico remained low and relatively unchanged (see fig. 3). HUBZone set-aside contract obligations increased from negative \$20,881 in fiscal year 2016 to \$3.8 million in fiscal year 2017 (1 percent of the total value of small business contracts in Puerto Rico). The set-aside obligations dropped to $1.7 million through June 2018 (0.2 percent of the total value of small business contracts in Puerto Rico).[50]

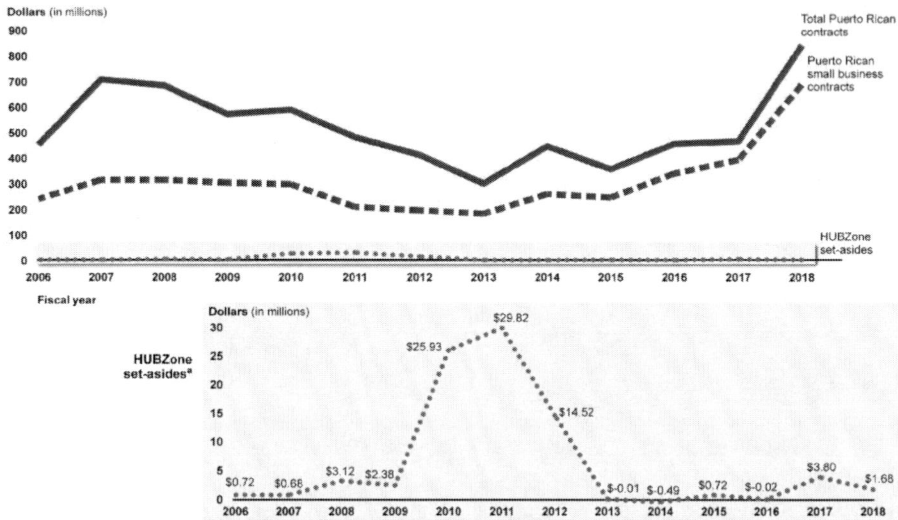

Source: GAO analysis of Federal Procurement Data System-Next Generation data. | GAO-18-666.

Note: We analyzed data for federal prime contracting obligations awarded to all businesses and small businesses in Puerto Rico and those awarded using the HUBZone program. We included HUBZone awards made using sole-source and set-asides, but there were no cases of awards made using the HUBZone price evaluation preference in our analysis. The dollar amounts are adjusted for inflation using fiscal year 2017 dollars.

[a] Negative amounts of obligations for the HUBZone set-asides are a result of de-obligations for prior-year contracts through contract cancellations or other actions.

Figure 3. Federal Contracting and HUBZone Set-Asides in Puerto Rico in Fiscal Years 2006–2018 (through June 2018).

Representatives of two economic development organizations that we interviewed stated that continued low use of HUBZone set-aside contracts by contracting agencies could subsequently decrease firms' willingness to participate in the HUBZone program in Puerto Rico. Representatives of

---

50 Negative amounts of obligations for the HUBZone set-asides are a result of de-obligations for prior-year contracts through contract cancellations or other actions. For a more detailed description of contracting trends in Puerto Rico, see appendix.

firms and two economic development organizations noted that the process of monitoring, identifying, and applying for HUBZone set-aside contracts is time consuming and without the availability of set-aside contracts program participation may not be worthwhile for firms in Puerto Rico.

Temporary Challenges May Hinder Use of HUBZone Set-Aside Contracts in Puerto Rico in the Short Term

Representatives of firms and two economic development organizations and SBA officials in Washington D.C. and the Puerto Rico District Office told us that use of HUBZone set-aside contracts and any resulting economic impacts of HUBZone expansion in Puerto Rico may not yet be observable because of temporary challenges, such as advance contracts and outmigration due to the 2017 hurricanes.

Advance Contracts

One temporary challenge they cited was the use of advance contracts by agencies in response to the 2017 hurricanes. In advance contracts, an agency establishes contracts before a disaster for goods and services typically needed during a disaster response.

Such contracts may prevent contracting officers from establishing a HUBZone set-aside on contracts awarded for disaster response and recovery. For example, a representative from one firm we interviewed said that in the wake of the 2017 hurricanes it had ample supplies of a vaccine in high demand on the island. The firm's representative thought that contracting officers previously established an advance contract with a company in the continental United States to supply the vaccine. Therefore, contracting officers were unable to contract the Puerto Rican HUBZone firm to supply the vaccine to the island. However, SBA officials in the Puerto Rico District Office told us that once advance contracts are completed, the contracting agency can replace the contract with another contract to perform those services, which could be a HUBZone set-aside contract.[51]

Outmigration from 2017 Hurricanes

Representatives of firms and one economic development organization and SBA officials in the Puerto Rico District Office told us that outmigration from Puerto Rico after the 2017 hurricanes reduced the amount of talent and workers available to fulfill contracts. Representatives of one firm said that contracting officers may be concerned that the defection of talent from Puerto Rico could limit firms' abilities to complete contracts, limiting the contracting officers' willingness to set aside contracts.

However, representatives of firms and one economic development organization said that contracts can be fulfilled by multiple Puerto Rican firms if necessary. Also, representatives of firms and one economic development organization said that people who left the island have started returning and replenishing the workforce.

Longer-Standing Challenges Also May Hinder Use of HUBZone Set-Aside Contracts

Representatives of firms and two economic development organizations and SBA officials in Washington D.C. and the Puerto Rico District Office also identified longer-standing challenges to increased use of HUBZone set-aside contracts in Puerto Rico, including difficulty meeting procurement requirements, limited knowledge of the federal contracting process, lack of access to contracting officers, and award of contracts to firms outside Puerto Rico. These concerns are similar to those we

---

[51] For more information on advance contracts, see GAO, *2017 Disaster Contracting: Observations on Federal Contracting for Response and Recovery Efforts,* GAO-18-335 (Washington, D.C.: Feb. 28, 2018).

recognized in our 2017 report on SBA contracting program in Puerto Rico.[52]

Difficulty Meeting Procurement Requirements

Representatives of some firms we interviewed stated that procurement requirements for federal contracts (such as performance history for construction contracts) posed challenges for small businesses in Puerto Rico. Representatives of some firms said that as an island, Puerto Rico faces specific challenges in meeting procurement requirements. For example, one firm's representative said that the construction of a school required a business to demonstrate experience in developing several schools in the past. According to this representative, opportunities to construct schools are limited in Puerto Rico and many Puerto Rican firms would be capable of fulfilling these contracts, but relevant experience constructing similar buildings is not considered as meeting this requirement.

In 2017, we reported that the experience of construction businesses in Puerto Rico does not match procurement requirements, which are often standardized to mainland building standards and do not consider unique conditions in Puerto Rico. As a result, firms and associations that we interviewed in 2017 said that agencies' contracting officers may not consider the experience of Puerto Rican businesses as qualifying. Representatives from four associations that we interviewed in 2017 stated that construction businesses in Puerto Rico demonstrate in their construction plans greater understanding of building requirements in Puerto Rico, such as accounting for tropical climate or the risk of seismic activity, but these factors were not incorporated into federal procurement requirements.

Limited Knowledge of the Federal Contracting Process

Representatives of firms and two economic development organizations and SBA officials in the Puerto Rico District Office said that limited

---

[52] GAO-17-550.

knowledge of the federal contracting process can be a challenge for HUBZone firms in Puerto Rico. One firm's representative explained that responding to agencies' requests for information was important because to create a HUBZone set-aside contract a federal agency must demonstrate that at least two firms could compete for the contract. Another firm's representative said that because it was unaware of the importance of responding to the requests for information, it had not responded to requests for information for any contract opportunities. Firms' representatives also noted that the process of responding to requests for information and requests for proposals is time consuming and often infeasible because they lack the financial and personnel resources of larger businesses.

Firms can obtain information about federal and small business contracting from several sources. Firms' representatives we interviewed said that they generally seek assistance from SBA partner organizations, such as the Federal Contracting Center and Small Business and Technology Development Center, to gain a better understanding of the contracting process. Officials from SBA's Puerto Rico District Office said that they hold regular training on contracting programs and how to navigate the contracting process. The District Office also holds one-on-one appointments with businesses to help them navigate the federal contracting process and has offered training on proposal writing.

Lack of Access to Contracting Officers

Representatives of firms we interviewed said that obtaining HUBZone set-aside contracts was difficult for small businesses in Puerto Rico partially because of a lack of access to contracting officers. Most firms' representatives we interviewed said that, similar to obtaining assistance in navigating the contracting process, they seek assistance from SBA partner organizations, such as the Federal Contracting Center and Small Business and Technology Development Center, to identify HUBZone contract opportunities and connect with contracting officers.

Firms' representatives also said that they attend conferences and matchmaking events at which they meet contracting officers; however, they said that this approach has not yet helped them to obtain increased

HUBZone set-aside contracts in Puerto Rico. One firm's representative said that the advice at networking events is that firms should approach contracting officers, but small businesses do not have the contacts to approach contracting officers. Representatives of some firms said that SBA should act as an advocate or facilitator to provide connections between small businesses and contracting officers. Some of the firms' representatives noted that in the absence of HUBZone set-aside contracts, they tend to pursue subcontracts with companies that have prime federal contracts.

Award of Contracts to Firms Outside of Puerto Rico

Representatives of two economic development organizations we interviewed said that most HUBZone set-aside contracts and most of the hurricane relief-related contracts performed in Puerto Rico were awarded to firms outside Puerto Rico. In 2017, we similarly reported that representatives from four associations stated that challenges such as lack of access to contracting officers and difficulty meeting procurement requirements led to concerns about contracts being awarded to businesses located outside of Puerto Rico for work to be performed in Puerto Rico.

Representatives of firms and one economic development organization also pointed out that for some industries, work does not need to be physically performed at the contract location; therefore, Puerto Rican HUBZone firms could be competitive for contracts located in other states. According to firms and one economic development organization, this is especially true in the technology industry, which is well represented in Puerto Rico with multiple HUBZone firms. However, representatives of the Puerto Rican technology firms we contacted noted that they have experienced great difficulty obtaining HUBZone contracts. One firm's representative suggested that this challenge might be partially due to Puerto Rican firms having less experience than firms outside of Puerto Rico in competing for HUBZone set-aside contracts. To compete for contracts, one firm said that its chief executive officer permanently moved to Washington, D.C., and another firm said its staff travels to Washington, D.C., once a month.

Procurement Center Representative Based in Puerto Rico May Help Address Some Challenges Faced by HUBZone Firms in Puerto Rico

In 2018, SBA established a PCR in Puerto Rico and SBA officials said the agency expects that the PCR will help address some of the challenges discussed previously. SBA PCRs work with federal agencies and small businesses to identify contracting opportunities for small businesses.[53] The Puerto Rico PCR said that she plans to hold events for HUBZone firms to help them better understand and navigate the federal contracting process. For example, she plans to hold a Federal Acquisition Regulation "boot camp," a 40-hour training to educate firms on the federal contracting process. She also stated that through regular interaction with other PCRs and with contracting officers, she can identify and discuss opportunities for HUBZone set-aside contracts for Puerto Rican small businesses. One economic development organization we interviewed said that it is too early to see an effect of the new Puerto Rico PCR, but that they have met with her and have been encouraged by her efforts to date. In 2017, we reported that several stakeholders identified the lack of an SBA PCR in Puerto Rico as a disadvantage for small businesses in Puerto Rico seeking contracts with the federal government.[54] According to a representative from the Federal Contracting Center that we interviewed in 2017, having a PCR in Puerto Rico is important because the PCR can advocate for small businesses there. For example, the PCR can work with contracting officers to determine small business set-asides, make adjustments to procurement requirements, and make agency contracting officers more aware of businesses in Puerto Rico. According to one economic development

---

[53] For more information on the role of PCRs in SBA contracting programs, see GAO, *Improvements Needed to Help Ensure Reliability of SBA's Performance Data on Procurement Center Representatives*, GAO-11-549R (Washington, D.C.: June 15, 2011).

[54] At the time of our 2017 report, a network of PCRs in six SBA area offices was responsible for federal procurement activities nationwide. SBA's Area 1 office (in Boston), was responsible for procurement activities taking place in Puerto Rico. SBA officials stated at the time that while the Area 1 office generally interacted with certain agencies in Puerto Rico, including the General Services Administration and the Department of the Army, PCRs in other area offices also interacted with agencies with contracting activities in Puerto Rico.

organization's representative, the PCR could assist local businesses and promote businesses located in Puerto Rico to federal agencies.

CONCLUSION

Our review of a sample of 12 case files for Puerto Rican firms certified between March 2017 and March 2018 found that SBA lacked complete documentation for one of two requirements we reviewed and did not consistently follow its own procedures for quality control reviews when approving firms. This suggests potential gaps in internal controls for both the certification and recertification processes, as SBA reviews firms' compliance with program requirements at both certification and recertification. Although SBA policy includes documentation reviews and a quality control process, its internal policy manuals do not reflect all document review procedures, and analysts did not always follow procedures for quality control reviews. SBA has not updated its policy manuals and, it is not known to what extent it has reviewed staff compliance with the quality review procedures. Although SBA provided an assurance letter stating its internal controls are effective, the letter did not describe steps taken in the evaluation. Documenting all procedures would help ensure that analysts consistently follow policy when certifying and recertifying firms. Documented reviews of staff compliance also could serve to identify and remediate any noncompliance with certification and recertification processes. Both actions would serve to strengthen the verification function in the HUBZone program, which is necessary to help ensure that only eligible firms participate in the program.

RECOMMENDATIONS FOR EXECUTIVE ACTION

We are making two recommendations to SBA. Specifically:

The Administrator of SBA should update the agency's internal policy manuals for certification and recertification reviews to reflect existing policies and procedures not currently in written guidance. (Recommendation 1)

The Administrator of SBA should conduct and document reviews of staff compliance with procedures associated with HUBZone certification and recertification. (Recommendation 2)

AGENCY COMMENTS AND OUR EVALUATION

We provided a draft of this chapter for review and comment to SBA. In response, SBA provided written comments, which are reproduced in appendix III. SBA also provided technical comments, which we incorporated as appropriate. SBA generally agreed with both of our recommendations. However, SBA disagreed with three of our findings in the draft report.

In the draft report, we stated that SBA's guidance for the certification process requires firms to submit documentation so that SBA can verify that a firm meets the employee residency requirement, including documentation showing that each employee's address is located in a HUBZone, for employees claimed to be HUBZone residents. We noted that documents were missing, illegible, or did not corroborate the information claimed regarding at least one employee's residency for 9 of 12 certifying firms that we reviewed. We also stated that in 5 of these 9 cases, the firm would not be eligible for HUBZone certification if the SBA analyst had not counted such employees. In its comments, SBA stated that it is only required to verify that no fewer than 35 percent of a HUBZone firm's employees reside in a HUBZone. SBA asserted that it had sufficient documentation to conclude that at least 35 percent of each firm's employees resided in a HUBZone for each of the 12 firms we reviewed. While SBA analysts may have addressed insufficient documentation by following additional procedures, which are described in the report, we found that these procedures were not documented in SBA's internal written policies for certifying HUBZone firms and analysts did not document their use of these procedures in the case files we reviewed. Therefore, we were not able to verify that SBA took such steps to verify the employees' addresses.

In the draft report, we identified an inconsistency when reviewing the case files for the only Puerto Rican HUBZone firm recertified between June 2017 and May 2018. Specifically, the firm reported on its application that it had zero employees, but also claimed 19 of its employees lived in a HUBZone. In its comments, SBA stated that these numbers came from a program examination system that is no longer used by the agency and therefore would not have been administratively correct to use in the 2017 recertification process. However, the file we received from SBA's HUBZone Certification Tracking System asks for such information and had a response date noted as December 26, 2017. We recognize and noted that the firm was not required to submit corroborating documentation to verify employee information, because it was under the $1 million threshold. However, SBA policy states that recertifying firms must represent that the circumstances relative to their eligibility at the time of certification have not materially changed. In this instance, SBA recertified the firm when basic information obtained for the firm appeared to be erroneous and did not indicate that the firm was in compliance with the employee residency requirement.

In the draft report, we stated that SBA did not consistently follow its quality review procedures to complete three distinct levels of review when approving the 12 Puerto Rican firms in our non-generalizable sample for certification. In its comments, SBA stated that while its legacy system, the HUBZone Certification Tracking System, requires three levels of review, its internal policies do not require that each level of review be performed by different staff. However, SBA internal policies that we reviewed state that the three levels of review should be conducted by different people, specifically an analyst, a senior analyst, and the program director. Furthermore, internal control standards state that management should design control activities at various levels with a segregation of duties, and periodically review its procedures and associated internal control activities for effectiveness.

We are sending copies of this chapter to congressional committees, the Small Business Administration, and other interested parties.

William B. Shear
Director, Financial Markets and Community Investment

APPENDIX I: OBJECTIVES, SCOPE, AND METHODOLOGY

Our objectives in this chapter were to (1) examine the Small Business Administration's (SBA) development of criteria and guidance on using a risk-based approach for certifying and recertifying Historically Underutilized Business Zone (HUBZone) firms, (2) examine SBA's implementation of the revised policies and procedures for firms located in Puerto Rico, and (3) describe any economic impacts of HUBZone expansion and recent trends in federal small business contracting in Puerto Rico.

To examine SBA's development of its criteria and guidance for HUBZone certification and recertification, we reviewed SBA's policies and procedures for certifying and monitoring HUBZone firms. To learn about SBA's risk-based approach, we interviewed officials at the headquarters level responsible for certifying and recertifying HUBZone firms. We reviewed prior GAO and SBA Office of Inspector General reports, applicable statutes and regulations, and SBA documents. We also compared the development of SBA's certification and recertification processes with federal internal control standards and relevant federal guidance and statutes for managing fraud risk.[55]

---

[55] See GAO, *Standards for Internal Control in the Federal Government*, GAO-14-704G (Washington, D.C.: Sept.10, 2014); and *A Framework for Managing Fraud Risks in Federal Programs*, GAO-15-593SP (Washington, D.C.: July 28, 2015). Also see Office of Management and Budget, *Management's Responsibility for Enterprise Risk Management and Internal Control*, Circular No. A-123 (Washington, D.C.: July 15, 2016); and Pub.L. 114-186 §3,130 Stat. 546. (2016).

To examine SBA's implementation of the revised recertification processes in Puerto Rico, we used SBA's Dynamic Small Business Search database to identify HUBZone firms located in Puerto Rico that received HUBZone certification after March 27, 2017. We examined SBA's document review process for Puerto Rican firms that received HUBZone certification or were due for recertification between March 2017 and March 2018. We reviewed the case files for a non-generalizable sample of 12 firms that received initial certification and two firms that were due for recertification during this time period. We reviewed documents submitted by firms to SBA as part of the initial certification process. But we were unable to examine the document review component of recertification directly. According to SBA officials, only two firms in Puerto Rico recertified between March 27, 2017, and May 30, 2018, when we received the applicant case files from SBA, and neither met the threshold of $1 million in contract awards to trigger a full document review.

From SBA's small business database, we identified 443 firms in Puerto Rico that had had HUBZone certification at any point as of March 12, 2018, and removed 350 firms that exited the program in order to review only currently certified firms (leaving 93 certified firms). From this universe, we identified 47 HUBZone-certified firms located in Puerto Rico with a certification date later than March 27, 2017, after removing duplicates. We chose a judgmental sample of 12 firms that we randomly selected from the total of 47 firms using a random number generator. We checked the city and industry of each of the 12 firms to confirm the firms provided some geographical and industry variation. Results from this sample are not generalizable to all HUBZone-certified firms.

We examined the contents of the case files for each of the 12 firms, which included the application the firm submitted through SBA's HUBZone Certification Tracking System and supporting documents that firms submitted to corroborate their eligibility, including proof of office location, payroll documentation, HUBZone maps, and employees' identification such as driver's licenses.

We compared the case file contents to SBA's guidance on which documents firms must submit and internal guidance for analysts reviewing applications.

- To determine which documents to review, we compared SBA's list of required documents for certification to those required at recertification and identified which are similar. We reviewed SBA analysts' notes, which are recorded in the HUBZone tracking system to verify that they reviewed the documents to determine the firms' eligibility. We also reviewed any emails exchanged between SBA and the applicant to identify cases in which SBA requested follow-up from the firm.
- We reviewed the name of the SBA analyst who completed each level of review, as indicated in the tracking system file, to determine whether SBA followed its policy of completing three levels of review. We also reviewed the tracking system files to verify the final approval and whether SBA sent the certification notice to the firm. We compared these files to SBA's internal policy manuals.

To describe any economic impacts of the expansion of the HUBZone program in Puerto Rico, and to describe recent federal contracting trends, we used SBA's small business database and federal procurement data from the Federal Procurement Data System-Next Generation. We analyzed the number of firms in designated HUBZones in Puerto Rico and the amount of federal contract obligations awarded to the firms from fiscal year 2006 through June of fiscal year 2018—that is, from the starting point for the analysis we used in our 2017 report to the most recent available data at the time of our current review. We assessed the reliability of the two databases by reviewing database guides and prior GAO work, and determined them to be reliable for the purposes of that analysis.

For all of the objectives, we also interviewed SBA officials in Washington, D.C., and Puerto Rico and representatives from the Puerto Rico Chamber of Commerce and the Federal Contracting Center. In addition, we conducted a site visit to San Juan, Puerto Rico, in May 2018. There, we conducted two discussion groups and one interview with representatives from nine HUBZone firms located in Puerto Rico to obtain their perspectives on the HUBZone certification process, federal contracting opportunities, economic impacts of HUBZone expansion in Puerto Rico, and economic impacts of the 2017 hurricanes. We invited every Puerto Rican HUBZone firm to participate in the discussion groups and met with the nine firms that responded to our email. The views of representatives from these firms are not generalizable.

We conducted this performance audit from February 2018 to September 2018 in accordance with generally accepted government auditing standards. Those standards require that we plan and perform the audit to obtain sufficient, appropriate evidence to provide a reasonable basis for our findings and conclusions based on our audit objectives. We believe that the evidence obtained provides a reasonable basis for our findings and conclusions based on our audit objectives.

Appendix II: Federal Contracting Trends and Use of Socioeconomic Set-Asides in Puerto Rico, Fiscal Years 2006–2018

This appendix provides information, based on our analysis of federal procurement data, on small business contracting in Puerto Rico, including the use of socioeconomic set-aside contracts and contracting by sector and agency.

Small Business Contracting in Puerto Rico

Annual federal contract obligations to small businesses in Puerto Rico more than doubled from fiscal year 2015 through June 2018. Small businesses in Puerto Rico also won a larger percentage of total federal contracting obligations in Puerto Rico.

Use of Socioeconomic Set-Asides in Puerto Rico

Although federal contract obligations to small businesses in Puerto Rico sharply increased in recent years, obligations through set-aside contracts for the Historically Underutilized Business Zone (HUBZone), 8(a) Business Development, Women-Owned Small Business, and Service-Disabled Veteran-Owned Small Business programs remained relatively unchanged (see fig. 4). The increases in federal contract obligations to small businesses in fiscal years 2017 and 2018 came mostly through free and open competition and awards reserved for small businesses that excluding those for the 8(a), HUBZone, Women-Owned Small Business, and Service-Disabled Veteran-Owned Small Business programs.

HUBZone set-aside contract obligations increased from negative \$20,881 in fiscal year 2016 to \$3.8 million in fiscal year 2017 (1 percent of the total value of small business contracts in Puerto Rico), but dropped to \$1.7 million through June 2018 (0.2 percent of the total value of small business contracts in Puerto Rico).[56] Furthermore, 17.3 percent of the \$21.9 million in contract obligations awarded to Puerto Rican HUBZone firms in fiscal year 2017 were through HUBZone set-aside contracts, and 3.3 percent of the \$50.5 million awarded in fiscal year 2018 (see fig. 5). Other socioeconomic set-asides accounted for the highest share of obligations awarded (76.6 percent in 2017 and 80.1 percent in 2018) and free and open competition accounted for the rest (6.1 percent in 2017 and 16.6 percent in 2018).

---

[56] Negative obligation amounts are a result of de-obligations for prior-year contracts through contract cancellations or other actions.

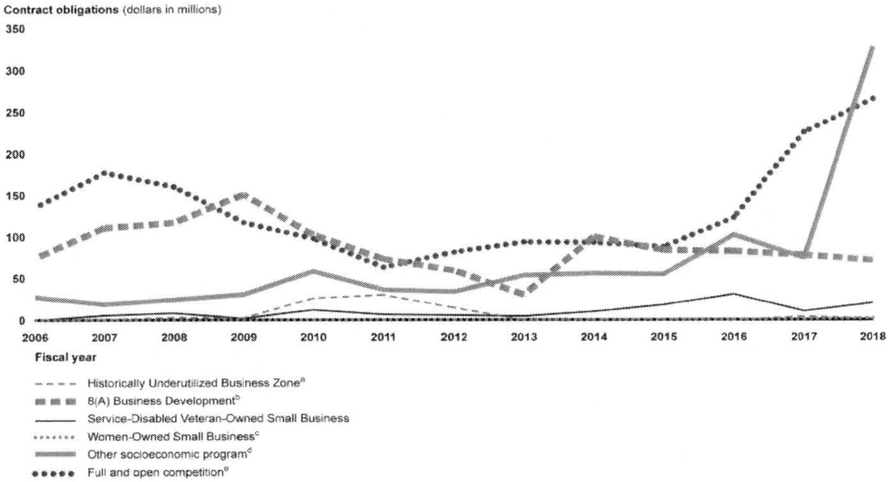

Source: GAO analysis of Federal Procurement Data System-Next Generation data. | GAO-18-666.

Note: For Puerto Rico, we analyzed data for federal prime contracting obligations awarded to small businesses in Puerto Rico. The dollar amounts are adjusted for inflation using fiscal year 2017 dollars.

[a] We included Historically Underutilized Business Zone (HUBZone) awards made using sole-source and set-aside contracts, but no awards were made using price evaluation preference during the time frame of our analysis (fiscal years 2006–2018, through June 2018). For fiscal years 2014 and 2016, the HUBZone program in Puerto Rico had negative amounts of obligations as result of de-obligations for prior-year contracts through contract cancellations or other actions. They were about -$480,000 and -$20,000, respectively.

[b] 8(a) Business Development program included awards given to 8(a) businesses that were also HUBZone businesses. This code was not valid after October 2008.

[c] No obligations were awarded through the Women-Owned Small Business program before fiscal year 2011 (the year in which the program was established). Program obligations include those to economically disadvantaged women-owned small businesses. For Puerto Rico, the percentage of obligations under this program as a share of small business obligations ranged from 0 percent to 0.3 percent in fiscal years 2011–2018 (through June 2018).

[d] Other socioeconomic programs include obligations awarded through other programs, such as those for veterans, small disadvantaged businesses, and other small businesses. Awards reserved for small businesses—excluding those for 8(a), HUBZone, Women-Owned Small Business, and Service-Disabled Veteran-Owned Small Business programs—made up a large portion of these obligations.

[e] Contract awards based on full and open competition consist of awards not identified as awarded through any socioeconomic program and those specifically labeled as having no set-asides.

Figure 4. Federal Contracting and Socioeconomic Set-Asides in Puerto Rico, Fiscal Years 2006–2018 (through June 2018).

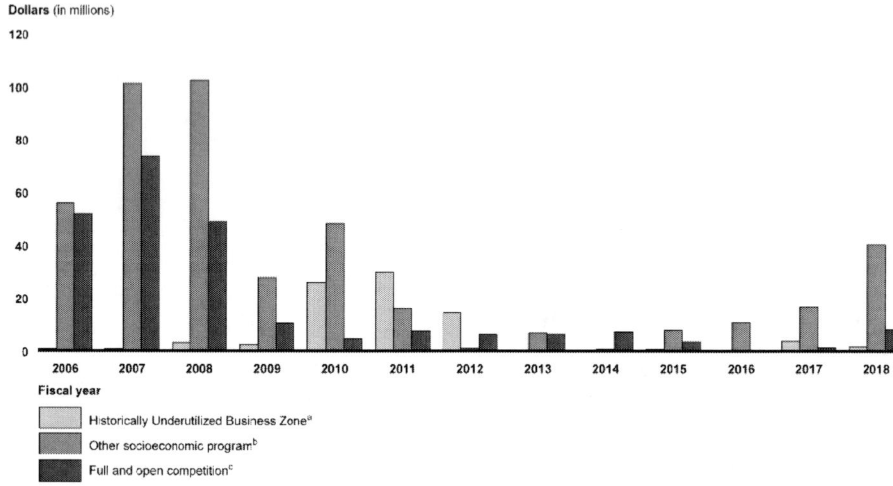

Source: GAO analysis of Federal Procurement Data System-Next Generation data. | GAO-18-666.

Note: We analyzed data for federal prime contracting obligations awarded to small businesses with a HUBZone designation in Puerto Rico. We included HUBZone awards made using sole-source and set-asides but no awards were made using the price evaluation preference in our analysis. The dollar amounts are adjusted for inflation using fiscal year 2017 dollars.

[a] Negative amounts of obligations for the HUBZone set-asides are a result of de-obligations for prior-year contracts through contract cancellations or other actions.

[b] Other socioeconomic programs include obligations awarded through the 8(a) Business Development, Women-Owned Small Business, and Service-Disabled Veteran-Owned Small Business programs as well as other programs, such as those for veterans, small disadvantaged businesses, and other small businesses.

[c] Contract awards based on full and open competition consist of awards not identified as being awarded through any socioeconomic program and those specifically labeled as having no set-asides.

Figure 5. Federal Contracting to HUBZone Firms in Puerto Rico, Fiscal Years 2006–2018 (through June 2018).

The fiscal year 2017 increase in federal contracting obligations in Puerto Rico were not substantially tied to hurricane relief since Hurricane Irma and Hurricane Maria hit Puerto Rico in September, the last month of the fiscal year. One percent of total federal contracting obligations in Puerto Rico and 1 percent of obligations awarded to Puerto Rican small businesses were associated with hurricane relief (see table 1). However, a significant portion of the increase in overall contracting and small business contracting to Puerto Rican firms in fiscal year 2018 (through June 2018) was related to hurricane relief. Specifically, 55.3 percent of total federal contracting obligations in Puerto Rico and 64.3 percent of obligation awarded to Puerto Rican small businesses were associated with hurricane relief. Furthermore, 16.1 percent of HUBZone set-aside contract obligations awarded to Puerto Rican firms were hurricane-related through June 2018.

Table 1. Hurricane-Related Contracting in Puerto Rico, Fiscal Years 2017–2018 (through June 2018)

	FY 2017		**FY 2018**	
	Obligations	Percentage	Obligations	Percentage
Total hurricane-related obligations in Puerto Rico	$4.5	1.0[a]	$465.4	55.3[a]
Hurricane-related small business obligations in Puerto Rico	$3.9	1.0[b]	$442.3	64.3[b]
Hurricane-related HUBZone set-aside obligations in Puerto Rico	$0	0.0[c]	$0.3	16.1[c]

Legend: FY=fiscal year; HUBZone = Historically Underutilized Business Zone.

Source: GAO analysis of Federal Procurement Data System-Next Generation data. | GAO-18-666.

Note: We analyzed data for federal prime contracting obligations awarded to all businesses and small businesses in Puerto Rico and those awarded using the HUBZone program. The dollar amounts are adjusted for inflation using fiscal year 2017 dollars. All dollar amounts are in millions.

[a] This number represents total hurricane-related obligations as a percentage of total obligations in Puerto Rico.

[b] This number represents hurricane-related small business obligations as a percentage of total small business obligations in Puerto Rico.

[c] This number represents hurricane-related HUBZone set-aside obligations as a percentage of total HUBZone set-aside obligations in Puerto Rico.

Contracting in Puerto Rico by Sector

Table 2. Contracting Obligations in Puerto Rico by Sector, Fiscal Years 2017–2018 (through June 2018)

	Sector	FY 2017		FY 2018	
		Obligations	Percentage	Obligations	Percentage
Contracting in Puerto Rico	Construction	$57.5	12.4[a]	$200.5	23.8[a]
	Manufacturing	$284.7	61.3[a]	$165.0	19.6[a]
	Administrative, support, and waste management	$57.5	12.4[a]	$299.2	35.6[a]
	Other sectors	$65.0	14.0[a]	$176.3	21.0[a]
	Total	*$464.8*	*100*	*$841.0*	100
Small business contracting in Puerto Rico	Construction	$61.2	15.6[b]	$175.8	25.6[b]
	Manufacturing	$267.7	68.4[b]	$129.3	18.8[b]
	Administrative, support, and waste management	$22.0	5.6[b]	$251.2	36.5[b]
	Other sectors	$40.7	10.4[b]	$131.3	19.1[b]
	Total	*$391.6*	*100*	*$687.6*	100
HUBZone set-aside contracting in Puerto Rico	Construction	$3.2	83.0[c]	$0.9	52.2[c]
	Information	$0	0.0[c]	$0.2	10.5[c]
	Health care	$0.6	16.6[c]	$0.6	37.0[c]
	Other sectors	$0	0.0[c]	$0	0.0[c]
	Total	*$3.8*	*100*	*$1.7*	100

Legend: FY=fiscal year; HUBZone = Historically Underutilized Business Zone

Source: GAO analysis of Federal Procurement Data System-Next Generation data. | GAO-18-666.

Note: We analyzed data for federal prime contracting obligations awarded to all businesses and small businesses in Puerto Rico and those awarded using the HUBZone program. The contracts include both supply and service contracts. We grouped the economic sectors using the first two digits of the North American Industry Classification System (NAICS) codes. NAICS codes range from two to six digits and increase in specificity of description as the number of digits increase. The dollar amounts are adjusted for inflation using fiscal year 2017 dollars. All dollar amounts are in millions.

[a] This number represents total sector obligations as a percentage of total obligations in Puerto Rico.

[b] This number represents sector small business obligations as a percentage of total small business obligations in Puerto Rico.

[c] This number represents sector HUBZone set-aside obligations as a percentage of total HUBZone set-aside obligations in Puerto Rico.

In fiscal years 2017 and 2018, overall federal prime contracting obligations in Puerto Rico and those awarded to small businesses in Puerto Rico were concentrated in the construction sector (about 25 percent in

2018), the manufacturing sector (about 20 percent in 2018), and the administrative and support and waste management sector (about 36 percent in 2018).[57] For contracts awarded using HUBZone set-asides in Puerto Rico, the construction sector (about 52 percent in 2018), the information sector (about 11 percent in 2018), and the health care sector (about 37 percent in 2018) were most represented (see table 2).[58]

Contracting in Puerto Rico by Agency

Among federal agencies, the Department of Defense has awarded the greatest percentage of overall federal prime contracting obligations, obligations to small businesses, and HUBZone set-aside contract obligations to firms located in Puerto Rico. Specifically, in fiscal year 2018, Department of Defense contract obligations represented 58 percent of total obligations, 64 percent of obligations to small businesses, and 84 percent of HUBZone set-aside obligations to Puerto Rican firms (see table 3). Although, Department of Homeland Security contract obligations in Puerto Rico typically have represented less than 3 percent of total obligations and less than 5 percent of obligations to small businesses in Puerto Rico, those percentages increased to 21 percent and 23 percent, respectively, in fiscal year 2018 due to hurricane-related contracts awarded to Puerto Rican firms.

---

[57] North American Industry Classification System (NAICS) codes range from two to six digits and increase in specificity of description as the number of digits increase. We grouped the economic sectors using the first two digits of the NAICS code. Examples of businesses with construction activities include commercial and institutional building construction and roofing contractors; examples for manufacturing include cut and sew apparel contractors; examples for administrative and support and waste management services include security guard services and waste collection.

[58] Examples of business activities in the information sector include data processing and hosting and in the health care sector, ambulance services.

Table 3. Contracting Obligations in Puerto Rico, Fiscal Years 2017–2018 (through June 2018)

	Agency	FY 2017		FY 2018	
		Obligations	Percentage	Obligations	Percentage
Contracting in Puerto Rico	Department of Defense	$338.3	72.8[a]	$484.1	57.6[a]
	Department of Homeland Security	$8.1	1.7[a]	$178.1	21.2[a]
	Department of State	$34.1	7.3[a]	$43.6	5.2[a]
	Department of Veterans Affairs	$35.9	7.7[a]	$40.9	4.9[a]
	Other agencies	$48.5	10.4[a]	$94.3	11.2[a]
	Total	*$464.8*	*100*	*$841.0*	100
Small business contracting in Puerto Rico	Department of Defense	$324.1	82.8[b]	$442.2	64.3[b]
	Department of Homeland Security	$7.1	1.8[b]	$157.7	22.9[b]
	Department of Veterans Affairs	$31.1	7.9[b]	$31.7	4.6[b]
	Other agencies	$29.4	7.5[b]	$56.0	8.1[b]
	Total	*$391.6*	*100*	*$687.6*	100
HUBZone set-aside contracting in Puerto Rico	Department of Agriculture	$0	0.2[c]	$0.2	10.5[c]
	Department of Defense	$3.3	87.2[c]	$1.4	83.5[c]
	Department of Labor	$0.5	12.6[c]	$0.1	6.0[c]
	Other agencies	$0	0.0[c]	$0	0.0[c]
	Total	*$3.8*	*100*	*$1.7*	100

Legend: FY=fiscal year; HUBZone = Historically Underutilized Business Zone.

Source: GAO analysis of Federal Procurement Data System-Next Generation data. | GAO-18-666.

Note: We analyzed data for federal prime contracting obligations awarded to all businesses and small businesses in Puerto Rico and those awarded using the HUBZone program. The dollar amounts are adjusted for inflation using fiscal year 2017 dollars. All dollar amounts are in millions.

[a] This number represents total agency obligations as a percentage of total obligations in Puerto Rico.

[b] This number represents agency small business obligations as a percentage of total small business obligations in Puerto Rico.

[c] This number represents agency HUBZone set-aside obligations as a percentage of total HUBZone set-aside obligations in Puerto Rico.

APPENDIX III: COMMENTS FROM SBA

U.S. Small Business Administration

September 10, 2018

Mr. William B. Shear, Director
Financial Markets and Community Investment
U.S. Government Accountability Office
Washington, D.C. 20548

Dear Mr. Shear:

Thank you for providing the U.S. Small Business Administration (SBA) with a copy of the U.S. Government Accountability Office (GAO) draft report entitled *Small Business Contracting: Assessing Risks and Fully Documenting Procedures Could Strengthen SBA's Certification and Recertification of HUBZone Firms* (Draft Report).

In this draft report, GAO evaluated (1) SBA's development of criteria and guidance on using a risk-based approach for certifying and recertifying HUBZone firms, and (2) SBA's implementation of the revised policies and procedures for firms located in Puerto Rico. GAO also examined the actions that SBA has taken in response to the two open recommendations it made in February 2015 that SBA should (1) establish a mechanism to better ensure firms are notified of changes that could affect their participation in the program, and (2) assess the recertification process and implement additional controls, such as criteria and guidance for a risk-based approach to requesting and verifying information during recertification.

SBA generally agrees with GAO's two new recommendations described in this draft report:

(1) The Administrator of SBA should update its internal policy manuals for certification and recertification reviews to reflect policies and procedures not currently reflected in written guidance.

(2) The Administrator of SBA should conduct and document reviews of staff compliance with procedures associated with HUBZone certification and recertification.

However, SBA submits the comments below regarding the referenced sections of the draft report.

Pages 13 and 14 of the draft report state that SBA lacked complete documentation to verify that "every employee" resided in a HUBZone. SBA notes that the Small Business Act, which governs the HUBZone Program, requires that "not fewer than 35 percent of its employees reside in a HUBZone." 15 U.S.C. § 632(p)(5)(A)(i)(I)(aa). Likewise, SBA's regulations governing the HUBZone program provide: "At least 35% of the concern's employees must reside in a HUBZone." 13 C.F.R. § 126.200(b)(4). Accordingly, SBA is following the Small Business Act and SBA's implementing regulations by corroborating that at least 35 percent of the employees of the firms undergoing review resided in a HUBZone.

In reviewing the questioned documentation of HUBZone residency for the cases that GAO examined, SBA found that in all cases, it had sufficient documentation to conclude that at least 35 percent of each firm's employees resided in a HUBZone.

On pages 14-15, the report states:

> We also identified an inconsistency when reviewing the case files for the only Puerto Rican HUBZone that was recertified between June 2017 and May 2018. Specifically, the firm reported on its application that it had zero employees, but also claimed 19 of its employees lived in a HUBZone. The firm did not provide any supporting documentation because it did not meet the threshold in the new recertification criteria to require a document review. SBA officials said this likely resulted from a display error in the online system, SBA officials said it did not contact the recertifying firm, because the firm was not required to submit corroborating documentation. However, without confirmation of the correct total number of employees, SBA analysts would not be able to determine the firm's compliance with the 35 percent HUBZone residency requirement and therefore would not be able to determine the firm's eligibility to continue HUBZone participation.

In the 2017 triennial recertification process for this firm, the subject information was not considered by SBA, because it bore no relationship to recertification. That is, this information was captured a number of years back, in a defunct program examination system. To have used this information in the FY 2017 recertification process would have been administratively incorrect.

Page 16 of the draft report states that "SBA's internal policy states that the certification process has three levels of review." SBA believes this statement is inaccurate. SBA notes that its legacy system, the HUBZone Certification Tracking System (HCTS), was developed in the early 2000s with three levels of review. This means that for an application to move through HCTS to a final determination, it must be processed within the system by staff acting in three "roles": Program Analyst (First Level Reviewer), Senior Program Analyst (Second Level Reviewer), and Director/Deputy/designee. That is, HCTS dictates that staff must act in three different capacities to complete the processing of an application, but neither the system nor internal SBA policy requires that each role be performed by a different staff member.

SBA receives approximately 1,500 applications per year. In order to make the most efficient use of staff time, two Team Leaders (Senior Program Analysts) perform First Level reviews on roughly 10% of these applications. In these cases, the other Senior Program Analyst performs a Second Level Review, and "moves" the application to the decision level (Director/Deputy/designee). When this is done, the application is so annotated, to alert the Director/Deputy/designee that additional review should be performed. In this event, the Director/Deputy/designee annotates HCTS with the quality assurance actions taken (i.e., that the Director/Deputy/designee performed the type of review that a Senior Program Analyst (Second Level Reviewer) normally would).

Thank you for giving SBA the opportunity to comment on GAO's draft report, *Small Business Contracting: Assessing Risks and Fully Documenting Procedures Could Strengthen SBA's Certification and Recertification of HUBZone Firms* and for taking SBA's comments into consideration.

Sincerely,

Robb N. Wong
Associate Administrator
Government Contracting and Business Development

In: Small Business Issues
Editor: Andrea Moeller
ISBN: 978-1-53615-870-0

Chapter 5

SMALL BUSINESS RESEARCH PROGRAMS: AGENCIES NEED TO TAKE STEPS TO ASSESS PROGRESS TOWARD COMMERCIALIZING TECHNOLOGIES*

United States Government Accountability Office

ABBREVIATIONS

R&D	research or research and development
SBA	Small Business Administration
SBIR	Small Business Innovation Research
STTR	Small Business Technology Transfer

* This is an edited, reformatted and augmented version of United States Government Accountability Office; Report to the Committee on Science, Space, and Technology, House of Representatives, Publication No. GAO-18-207, dated January 2018.

Why GAO Did This Study

Through the SBIR and STTR programs, federal agencies have awarded about 162,000 contracts and grants totaling $46 billion to small businesses to help them develop and commercialize new technologies. Eleven federal agencies participate in the SBIR program, and 5 agencies also participate in the STTR program. Each program has three phases, which take projects from initial feasibility studies through commercialization activities. SBA oversees both programs.

In response to the 2011 reauthorization of the programs, SBA and the participating agencies developed benchmarks to measure small businesses' progress in developing and commercializing technologies. GAO was asked to review SBA's and the agencies' efforts related to these benchmarks. This chapter examines the extent to which SBA and the participating agencies have implemented these benchmarks, including assessing businesses against them and establishing the consequence of not meeting them. GAO analyzed award data and interviewed officials from SBA and the 11 participating agencies.

What GAO Recommends

GAO is making 11 recommendations to SBA and other agencies to take actions to improve implementation of the benchmarks, including improving the reliability of award data; implementing or revising the Commercialization Benchmark; and updating information about the consequence of not meeting the benchmarks. SBA and these agencies agreed with GAO's recommendations.

What GAO Found

Data challenges have limited the Small Business Administration's (SBA) and the 11 participating federal agencies' efforts to assess businesses against two benchmarks—the Transition Rate Benchmark and the Commercialization Benchmark—of the Small Business Innovation Research (SBIR) and Small Business Technology Transfer (STTR) programs.

- Transition Rate Benchmark. Small businesses that received more than 20 awards for the first phase of the programs in the past 5 fiscal years— excluding the most recent fiscal year—must have received an average of 1 award for the second phase of the programs for every 4 first phase awards. Since 2014, SBA and the agencies participating in the programs have regularly assessed small businesses against this benchmark. From 2014 through 2017, SBA determined that 4 to 7 businesses did not meet the benchmark each year. SBA officials provided GAO guidance on how to enter data into the programs' awards database they said is available to agencies, but GAO found evidence that suggests agencies are not fully utilizing it. For example, GAO found that the database used to perform the assessments contained inaccurate and incomplete data, such as about 2,700 businesses with multiple records with different spellings of their names and more than 1,400 instances in which a unique identification number had errors, such as an incorrect number of digits, all zeros, or hyphens. Thus, it could be difficult to determine which small businesses should be subject to the benchmark.
- Commercialization Benchmark. Small businesses that received more than 15 awards for the second phase of the programs in the past 10 fiscal years— excluding the most recent 2 fiscal years— must have received a certain amount of sales, investments, or patents resulting from their efforts. SBA and participating agencies have assessed small businesses against this benchmark only once, in 2014, and identified 12 businesses that did not meet the benchmark. This is, in part, due to challenges in collecting and verifying the accuracy of the data that small businesses report and that are needed to implement the benchmark, according to

officials from SBA and several agencies. For example, agency officials told GAO that some needed data, such as for reported sales, are not consistently applicable across agencies or projects. The Small Business Act and policy directives provide flexibility in how the agencies can implement the benchmark. Working together to implement it as designed or revise it so that it can be implemented could allow the agencies to fulfill statutory requirements.

SBA and the participating agencies have provided inconsistent information to small businesses about the consequence of not meeting the benchmarks. SBA and the agencies agreed to change how the consequence of not meeting the benchmarks was to be implemented, starting in 2017, from ineligibility to receive certain awards to ineligibility to submit certain proposals. However, as of November 2017, some agencies had not updated this information in their project solicitations. Furthermore, SBA has not updated this information in its policy directives. Without consistent information, businesses may be confused about their eligibility to submit proposals or receive awards and could invest time developing and submitting proposals when they are not eligible to do so.

January 31, 2018

The Honorable Lamar Smith
Chairman

The Honorable Eddie Bernice Johnson
Ranking Member
Committee on Science, Space, and Technology
House of Representatives

Federal agencies support research or research and development (R&D) projects at small businesses through the Small Business Innovation Research (SBIR) and Small Business Technology Transfer (STTR) programs. Federal agencies have awarded about 162,000 contracts and grants, totaling about $46 billion, since the programs' inceptions in 1982 and 1992, respectively. Through the SBIR and STTR programs, federal agencies have sought to help small businesses develop and commercialize innovative technologies. For example, an SBIR award from the Department of Health and Human Services helped a small business develop glasses that allow people with color vision deficiency to see the full color palette, and this business has made more than $20 million in annual sales, according to information on the SBIR website.

Federal agencies with obligations of $100 million or more for extramural R&D are required to participate in the SBIR program, and federal agencies with obligations of $1 billion or more for extramural R&D are required to also participate in the STTR program.[1]

Table 1. Agencies Participating in the Small Business Innovation Research (SBIR) and Small Business Technology Transfer (STTR) Programs

	Program	
Agency	SBIR	STTR
Department of Agriculture	Yes	No
Department of Commerce	Yes	No
Department of Defense	Yes	Yes
Department of Education	Yes	No
Department of Energy	Yes	Yes
Department of Health and Human Services	Yes	Yes
Department of Homeland Security	Yes	No
Department of Transportation	Yes	No
Environmental Protection Agency	Yes	No
National Aeronautics and Space Administration	Yes	Yes
National Science Foundation	Yes	Yes

Source: Small Business Administration. | GAO-18-207.

[1] Agencies' R&D efforts generally include funding for two types of R&D: intramural and extramural. Intramural R&D is conducted by employees of a federal agency in or through government-owned, government-operated facilities. Extramural R&D is generally conducted by nonfederal employees outside of federal facilities.

Currently, 11 agencies participate in the SBIR program, and 5 of these agencies also participate in the STTR program, as shown in Table 1. The Small Business Act authorizes the SBIR and STTR programs, and the Small Business Administration's (SBA) Office of Investment and Innovation is responsible for overseeing and coordinating the participating agencies' efforts for the programs. As part of SBA's oversight and coordination role, the agency issued SBIR and STTR policy directives to explain and outline requirements for agencies' implementation of these programs.[2]

The SBIR and STTR programs each include three phases:

- In phase I, agencies make awards to small businesses to determine the scientific and technical merit and feasibility of ideas that appear to have commercial potential. Phase I awards normally do not exceed $150,000. For SBIR, phase I awards generally last up to 6 months. For STTR, these awards generally last 1 year.
- In phase II, small businesses with phase I projects that demonstrate scientific and technical merit and feasibility, in addition to commercial potential, may compete for awards of up to $1 million to continue the R&D for an additional period, normally not to exceed 2 years.
- In phase III, small businesses pursue commercialization of technology developed in prior phases. Phase III work derives from, extends, or completes an effort made under prior phases, but it is funded by sources other than the SBIR and STTR programs. In this phase, small businesses are expected to raise funds from private investors, the capital markets, or funding sources within the agency that made the initial award other than the agency's SBIR or STTR program. Agencies can also participate in phase III

[2] Small Business Administration, Small Business Innovation Research (SBIR) Program Policy Directive (Washington, D.C.: Feb. 24, 2014), and Small Business Technology Transfer (STTR) Program Policy Directive (Washington, D.C.: Feb. 24, 2014).

by, for example, purchasing the technology developed in prior phases.[3]

The 2011 reauthorization of the SBIR and STTR programs amended the Small Business Act to require participating agencies to establish, and SBA to approve, minimum standards for businesses' progress in developing and commercializing technologies.[4] In response to this requirement, SBA and the participating agencies worked together to develop two "benchmarks" to serve as those minimum standards across all the participating agencies:

- Transition Rate Benchmark: Businesses that received more than 20 phase I awards over the prior 5 fiscal years—excluding the most recent fiscal year—must have received an average of 1 phase II award for every 4 phase I awards during this period. That is, the ratio of phase II to phase I awards must be at least 0.25.[5]
- Commercialization Benchmark: Businesses that received more than 15 phase II awards over the prior 10 fiscal years—excluding the most recent 2 fiscal years—must have received an average of at least $100,000 in sales, investments, or both per phase II award received, or have received a number of patents resulting from the

---

[3] For examples of how one agency has participated in phase III by purchasing technology developed in prior phases, see GAO, *Small Business Innovation Research: DOD's Program Supports Weapon Systems, but Lacks Comprehensive Data on Technology Transition Outcomes,* GAO-14-96 (Washington, D.C.: Dec. 20, 2013).

[4] Legislation enacted in 2011 reauthorized the SBIR and STTR programs for fiscal years 2012 through 2017. SBIR/STTR Reauthorization Act of 2011, Pub. L. No. 112-81, div. E, tit. LI, §§ 5001-5168, 125 Stat. 1298, 1822-62 (codified at 15 U.S.C. §§ 638-638b (2017)). In addition, legislation enacted in 2016 extended the programs for fiscal years 2018 through 2022: National Defense Authorization Act for Fiscal Year 2017. Pub. L. No. 114- 328, § 1834 (2016). The current Transition Rate Benchmark and Commercialization Benchmark were last published respectively at 78 Fed. Reg. 30,951 (May 23, 2013) and 78 Fed. Reg. 48,537 (Aug. 08, 2013).

[5] The SBIR and STTR policy directives refer to this benchmark as either the Phase II Transition Rate Benchmark or the Transition Rate Benchmark, and other agencies' project solicitations refer to it as the Phase I to Phase II Transition Rate Benchmark. For the purpose of this chapter, we refer to this benchmark as the Transition Rate Benchmark.

work equal to or greater than 15 percent of the number of phase II awards received during this period.[6]

The reauthorization act states that, generally, small businesses that do not meet the minimum standards may not participate in phase I of the SBIR or STTR program. The policy directives state that small businesses that do not meet the Transition Rate or Commercialization Benchmarks are ineligible to receive phase I awards starting on June 1, when the consequence period takes effect, through May 31 of the following year.[7]

You asked us to review SBA's and the participating agencies' efforts related to the benchmarks. This chapter examines the extent to which SBA and the participating agencies have implemented the Transition Rate Benchmark and the Commercialization Benchmark, including assessing businesses against them and establishing the consequence of not meeting them.

To accomplish this objective, we reviewed relevant legislation and the SBIR and STTR policy directives to determine the requirements of SBA and the participating agencies for implementing the benchmarks. We reviewed project solicitations and agencies' websites, and we interviewed officials from SBA and each of the 11 participating agencies to obtain information about the agencies' efforts to implement the benchmarks. We reviewed the applicable lists of small businesses that SBA assessed as not having met a benchmark from 2014 through 2017 and analyzed SBIR and STTR program award data.[8] Further, we reviewed *Standards for Internal*

---

[6] The SBIR and STTR policy directives refer to this benchmark as the Commercialization Rate Benchmark, but SBA's website and two agencies' project solicitations refer to it as the Commercialization Benchmark. For the purpose of this chapter, we refer to this benchmark as the Commercialization Benchmark.

[7] Small businesses that did not meet either of the benchmarks would also have been ineligible to receive direct-to-phase II awards under the SBIR program, which are phase II awards to a small business that did not receive a phase I award for that R&D. The Small Business Act states that, from fiscal years 2012 through 2017, the Department of Defense, the National Institutes of Health (within the Department of Health and Human Services), and the Department of Education may issue such direct-to-phase II awards.

[8] SBA and the participating agencies first assessed small businesses against the Transition Rate and Commercialization Benchmarks in 2014, according to SBA officials.

Control in the Federal Government and SBA's data policy and guidelines.[9] We also performed electronic testing of the data to search for missing or incorrect information, and interviewed officials from SBA about the data. We found instances in which the award data were unreliable, which we discuss later in this chapter.

We conducted this performance audit from April 2017 to January 2018 in accordance with generally accepted government auditing standards. Those standards require that we plan and perform the audit to obtain sufficient, appropriate evidence to provide a reasonable basis for our findings and conclusions based on our audit objectives. We believe that the evidence obtained provides a reasonable basis for our findings and conclusions based on our audit objectives.

BACKGROUND

The SBIR program was initiated in 1982 and has four main purposes: (1) use small businesses to meet federal R&D needs, (2) stimulate technological innovation, (3) increase commercialization of innovations derived from federal R&D efforts, and (4) encourage participation in technological innovation by small businesses owned by women and disadvantaged individuals. The STTR program was initiated a decade later, in 1992, and has three main purposes: (1) stimulate technological innovation, (2) foster technology transfer through cooperative R&D between small businesses and research institutions, and (3) increase private-sector commercialization of innovations derived from federal R&D.

The SBIR and STTR programs are similar in that participating agencies identify topics for R&D projects and support small businesses, but the STTR program requires the small business to partner with a

[9] GAO, *Standards for Internal Control in the Federal Government,* GAO-14-704G (Washington, D.C.: September 2014).

nonprofit research institution, such as a college or university or a federally funded research and development center.[10]

Each participating agency must manage its SBIR and STTR programs in accordance with program laws and regulations and the policy directives issued by SBA. In general, the programs are similar across participating agencies. All of the participating agencies follow the same general process to obtain proposals from and make awards to small businesses for both the SBIR and STTR programs. However, each participating agency has considerable flexibility in designing and managing specific aspects of these programs, such as determining research topics, selecting award recipients, and administering funding agreements. At least once a year, each participating agency issues a solicitation requesting proposals for projects in topic areas determined by the agency. Each participating agency uses its own process to review proposals and determine which proposals should receive awards. The agencies that participate in both SBIR and STTR programs usually use the same process for both programs. Also, each participating agency determines whether to provide the funding for awards as grants or contracts.

According to the policy directives, SBA maintains a system that records SBIR and STTR award information—using data submitted by the agencies—as well as commercialization information, such as information about patents, sales, and investments reported by small businesses that received these awards. SBA is to use these data to assess small businesses that received awards against the benchmarks and identify any small businesses that did not meet the benchmarks. SBA is to initially assess the small businesses against the benchmarks and then in April of each year notify those that do not meet the benchmarks so that the businesses can review their award data and work with participating agencies to correct the database if necessary. SBA then is to analyze the award data again to identify, on June 1, those small businesses that still do not meet the

[10] Federally funded research and development centers are government-funded entities operated by nongovernmental organizations to meet long-term research or development needs that cannot be met as effectively by existing governmental or contractor resources. These entities typically assist government agencies with scientific research and analysis, systems development, and system acquisition.

benchmarks. These small businesses are then ineligible for certain awards from that date through May 31 of the following year.

DATA CHALLENGES HAVE LIMITED THE IMPLEMENTATION OF THE BENCHMARKS, AND SBA AND PARTICIPATING AGENCIES HAVE PROVIDED INCONSISTENT INFORMATION ABOUT THE CONSEQUENCE

SBA and Participating Agencies Assessed Small Businesses against the Transition Rate Benchmark, but the Assessments Have Been Based on Inaccurate or Incomplete Data

Data challenges have limited SBA's and the 11 participating agencies' efforts to fully implement the benchmarks. Since 2014, SBA and the participating agencies have regularly assessed small businesses against the Transition Rate Benchmark, but the assessments have been based on inaccurate or incomplete data. SBA and the participating agencies have assessed small businesses against the Commercialization Benchmark only once, in 2014, because of challenges in collecting and verifying the accuracy of data. In addition, SBA and the participating agencies have provided inconsistent information to small businesses about the consequence of not meeting the benchmarks.

Since 2014, SBA and the participating agencies have regularly assessed small businesses against the Transition Rate Benchmark, which, in general, measures the rate at which businesses move projects from phase I to phase II.[11] From 2014 through 2017, SBA determined that 4 to 7 small businesses did not meet the benchmark each year and placed those

[11] As previously stated, the Small Business Act states that, from fiscal years 2012 through 2017, certain agencies may issue phase II awards under the SBIR program to a small business that did not receive a phase I award for that R&D.

businesses on a list of those ineligible to receive certain additional awards.[12]

However, we found instances in which the data used to generate the list were inaccurate or incomplete. For example, we identified an instance in which the data in the awards database changed considerably after SBA's initial assessment, indicating that the data used for that assessment were inaccurate. SBA's list of small businesses subject to the benchmark in 2015 showed that a small business received 297 phase I awards during the assessment period. However, data received from SBA officials in August 2017 showed that this small business received only 1 phase I award. Agencies can update their data in the awards database at any time to, for example, submit additional award data or correct previously submitted award data, which is what an SBA official stated may have caused this change. Because the small business received only 1 award, it would not have been subject to the Transition Rate Benchmark. In this case, the change meant that SBA did not miss identifying a small business that should have been ineligible for an award; however, in other instances, changes to the data may lead SBA to miss identifying a small business that should have been ineligible for awards.

In addition, we identified instances in which the publicly available data on awards were incomplete, including data that were missing or otherwise unusable. For example, based on our review of the award data from 2007 through 2016, we identified more than 2,700 small businesses that had multiple records with different spellings of the same business's name. Furthermore, we identified more than 1,400 instances in which a unique identification number had errors, such as having an incorrect number of digits, all zeros, or hyphens.[13] SBA officials told us that the quality of the award information in the database has been an issue, and that accurate information is important because small businesses may avoid being identified as subject to the benchmark if their business names and identification numbers are different across multiple records. For example,

[12] As discussed below, we identified data problems that prevented us from determining an accurate count of the number of small businesses subject to the benchmark.

[13] We also identified more than 1,100 instances of these unique identification numbers being blank, but small businesses are not required to provide the information.

if the database contains 18 phase I awards made within the assessment period to a small business with a certain unique identification number but also contains 3 other phase I awards within that period with a different or missing unique identification number, the small business may avoid being identified as subject to the benchmark because the data would suggest it did not meet the threshold of receiving more than 20 phase I awards, even if it did. As a result, it could be difficult to determine which small businesses actually received more than 20 awards and should be subject to the benchmark.

Standards for Internal Control in the Federal Government state that management should use quality information to achieve the entity's objectives, and SBA's Information Quality Guidelines state that SBA seeks to ensure the quality, utility, and integrity of the information it shares with the public, among other things.[14] SBA's policy directives for the SBIR and STTR programs state that SBA maintains a system that records SBIR and STTR award information, which is publicly available, and uses this information to calculate small businesses' performance against the benchmark. SBA officials told us they depend on the accuracy of the data received from the participating agencies to perform SBA's assessment. These officials also acknowledged that confirming the accuracy of SBA's annual assessments against the benchmarks has been challenging because agencies can update their data over time. SBA officials stated that they have sought to improve the quality of the data after the data are entered into the database, such as fixing instances in which small businesses' names were spelled differently across multiple records; however, the officials said that correcting the data already entered in the awards database is an ongoing and time-consuming process. SBA officials told us that there are errors in the database, in part because SBA has not worked with participating agencies to ensure that agencies enter high-quality, accurate data into the database. SBA officials provided us guidance on how to enter data that they said is available to agencies, but the errors we found suggest that agencies are not fully utilizing this guidance. As a result, SBA cannot

[14] GAO, *Standards for Internal Control in the Federal Government,* GAO-14-704G.

reasonably ensure the quality and reliability of its award data and therefore cannot reasonably ensure that it has correctly assessed small businesses against the Transition Rate Benchmark.

SBA and the Participating Agencies Assessed Small Businesses against the Commercialization Benchmark Only in 2014

The Small Business Act requires agencies to evaluate whether small businesses have met a minimum performance standard for commercializing their technology. SBA and participating agencies do not know the extent to which small businesses are meeting the Commercialization Benchmark because SBA and the agencies have assessed businesses against the benchmark only once, in 2014, when SBA determined that 12 businesses did not meet the benchmark. This is in part because, according to officials from SBA and several agencies, they cannot collect and verify the accuracy of the data needed to implement the benchmark as written.

For SBA and participating agencies to assess whether small businesses meet the Commercialization Benchmark, these small businesses must provide data on sales, investments, or patents resulting from the awards. However, agency officials told us about challenges related to obtaining the data they need to implement this benchmark. For example, agency officials told us that the needed data are not consistently applicable across agencies or projects. Specifically, these officials said that an agency may purchase the technology developed as a result of the SBIR or STTR award, while another agency may focus on funding technologies that will be sold on the commercial market, leading to different kinds of data on "sales." Additionally, officials from SBA and several of the participating agencies told us they have been unable to collect and verify the accuracy of the information from small businesses to assess them against the Commercialization Benchmark. In addition, officials from 2 agencies told us that small businesses can easily circumvent the benchmark by submitting incorrect data.

The Small Business Act and the policy directives provide agencies flexibility in how they can implement the Commercialization Benchmark. Officials from participating agencies said that they thought the Commercialization Benchmark should be revised, but they provided differing views on how to do it. Officials from SBA and 2 agencies told us that they would consider having individual agencies develop a benchmark or metric tailored to their agency, in part because the definition of successful commercialization could vary across the agencies. However, officials acknowledged that collecting and verifying the accuracy of the data would still be a concern with this approach. Officials from 2 participating agencies told us that collecting and verifying the accuracy of the data is a significant amount of work, and officials from a third agency added that implementing the benchmark independently is impractical because they do not have the capability to track small businesses' commercialization efforts. Officials from 1 agency said they preferred to keep a uniform benchmark across the agencies, in part because having varying benchmarks could lead to a small business being eligible to participate in the programs with one agency but not with another. Although views differed across agencies, working together to find a way to implement the benchmark as designed or revising it so that it can be implemented could allow the agencies to fulfill the requirement in the Small Business Act.

Officials from 3 agencies told us they would prefer to consider businesses' prior commercialization experience as part of their overall evaluation of businesses' proposals, rather than implement the current Commercialization Benchmark. The SBIR and STTR policy directives currently allow agencies to define the benchmark in terms other than revenue or investment, such as using a commercialization scoring system that rates awardees on their past commercialization success. Defining the benchmark in these terms could help agencies to implement the statutory requirement. Officials from SBA said they see the value of allowing reviewers to use professional judgment in determining the commercialization success of applicants, rather than assessing small businesses against standard criteria.

Table 2. Federal Agencies' Use of Prior Commercialization Experience in Selecting Awards for the Small Business Innovation Research (SBIR) and Small Business Technology Transfer (STTR) Programs

Agency	Agency's use of prior commercialization experience in selecting awards
Department of Agriculture	The Department of Agriculture requires small businesses applying for phase I awards that previously received phase II awards under the Department of Agriculture's SBIR program in the preceding 5 fiscal years to document the extent to which they were able to secure phase III funding and commercialize the technology, product, or service funded by the department's SBIR program.
Department of Commerce	The Department of Commerce's National Institute of Standards and Technology and National Oceanic and Atmospheric Administration consider information about applicants' past performance of SBIR awards, which applicants submit with their proposal, as part of their evaluative criteria to select awards.
Department of Defense	The Department of Defense requires applicants for phase I awards to submit a Company Commercialization Report as part of their proposal, even if the small business has not previously received SBIR or STTR awards. This chapter is to include sales revenue from new products and non-research and development services resulting from phase II technology, the number of patents resulting from the small business's participation in the SBIR or STTR program, and growth in the number of employees, among other things. The Department of Defense then compares these results to the historical averages for its SBIR or STTR program to calculate a Commercialization Achievement Index that it uses to rate applicants.
Department of Education	The Department of Education considers the record of research and development, research results, and peer reviewed publications resulting from prior research and commercialization of past SBIR-funded education related products by the applicant, which is included in the proposal.
Department of Energy	The Department of Energy requires applicants for phase I awards who have received SBIR or STTR phase II grants from any federal agency to provide a history of commercialization activity, including sales to private industry and to federal entities, resulting from SBIR and STTR awards. Officials from the Advanced Research Projects Agency-Energy, within the Department of Energy, told us they require that small businesses certify that they have met the Transition Rate Benchmark and Commercialization Benchmark, as applicable.

Agency	Agency's use of prior commercialization experience in selecting awards
Department of Health and Human Services	The Department of Health and Human Services does not consider prior commercialization experience in its evaluation and selection of all SBIR and STTR awards, but officials stated they do consider it for small businesses that have received more than 15 phase II awards.
Department of Homeland Security	The Department of Homeland Security requires that applicants provide a history of previous federal and nonfederal funding and subsequent commercialization of products as part of their phase II proposals and includes this information as part of evaluation criteria for selecting awards.
Department of Transportation	The Department of Transportation considers an applicant's past record of successful commercialization of SBIR or other research included in the proposal as part of its evaluation process.
Environmental Protection Agency	The Environmental Protection Agency requires that applicants provide their commercialization history for phase II SBIR awards from any federal agency, and specifies the template applicants are to use in providing this information.
National Aeronautics and Space Administration	The National Aeronautics and Space Administration uses a survey specific to SBIR/STTR awards, called the Commercialization Metrics Survey, to track small businesses' commercial success with prior SBIR/STTR awards from the agency. As part of the survey, the applicant submits the small business's sales and ownership information, as well as any commercialization success the small business has had as a result of phase II SBIR or STTR awards.
National Science Foundation	The National Science Foundation requires phase II applicants who have received prior phase II awards from any federal agency to submit a commercialization history, which must include percentage of company revenues for each of the past 3 fiscal years from federal SBIR/STTR funding, including phase I and phase II awards.

Source: GAO analysis of agency information. | GAO-18-207.

Officials from 1 agency said that such a change could help achieve the goal of the benchmark without the challenges of collecting data from all small businesses participating in the programs.

Nine of the 11 participating agencies currently consider prior commercialization experience as part of their evaluation when making award selections (see Table 2), which shows that evaluating commercialization experience at individual agencies can be feasible. For example, project solicitations from the Department of Agriculture, the Department of Defense, and the National Science Foundation state that these agencies require applicants to provide sales or revenue information for products resulting from SBIR or STTR awards, and the Department of Homeland Security's solicitation requires applicants to provide a history of previous federal and nonfederal funding and subsequent commercialization of their products. All agencies consider commercialization potential when selecting these awards.

SBA and Participating Agencies Have Provided Inconsistent Information to Small Businesses on the Consequence of Not Meeting the Benchmarks

The consequence for small businesses not meeting the benchmarks is ineligibility to participate in phase I of the SBIR or STTR program for a year, according to the Small Business Act.[15] SBA officials stated that they and the agencies initially interpreted this to mean that small businesses could not receive awards during the ineligibility period of June 1 through May 31 of the following year, and this is how the consequence is described in the SBIR and STTR policy directives. SBA officials told us that they and the participating agencies sought to change how to implement the consequence of businesses not meeting the benchmarks because of SBA's and agencies' difficulties in implementing the benchmarks.[16] Officials from 4 agencies said that they generally evaluate and select awards shortly before SBA releases the list of ineligible companies, leading them to potentially select projects from small businesses that will be on the ineligible list by the time the award period begins. Based on our review of award data from October 2014 to May 2017, we identified 13 phase I awards across 5 small businesses with award start dates during the period that the business was ineligible to receive such awards. According to

[15] Per the Small Business Act, small businesses receiving direct-to-phase II awards would also not be able to receive those awards for a year.

[16] Participating agencies do not have to use a uniform benchmark or implement a benchmark on the same timeline. SBA officials told us they coordinated with the participating agencies to develop a single, uniform benchmark for implementation on one timeline because they thought that it would be easier than having different metrics across agencies.

agency officials, each of these awards was selected before the small business became ineligible to receive the award. SBA and the participating agencies agreed to change how the consequence would be implemented, starting in 2017, so that small businesses that do not meet the benchmarks are ineligible to submit proposals, according to SBA officials.[17]

As of November 2017, however, the information available about this new way to implement the consequence was inconsistent because some of the agencies had not updated their project solicitations. Specifically, information in the most recent project solicitations available at that time for 2 agencies and one subunit of an agency stated that businesses that do not meet the benchmarks are ineligible to submit certain proposals, consistent with the revised approach for how to implement the consequence. However, the most recent project solicitations available at that time for 7 other agencies and the other subunit of the agency mentioned above instead stated that those businesses that do not meet the benchmarks are ineligible to receive certain awards, consistent with the prior approach for how to implement the consequence.[18] One other agency directed users to SBA's website in its solicitation. Table 3 shows the information about the consequence of not meeting the benchmarks that each agency included in its most recent project solicitations as of November 2017.

As of November 2017, the SBIR and STTR policy directives stated that the consequence for not meeting these benchmarks is ineligibility to receive certain awards. SBA officials told us they are in the process of updating the policy directives to reflect this change in how the consequence is implemented, but these officials said that it is a long process and they could not provide a timeframe for when the update would be complete.

---

[17] SBA officials told us that this change is consistent with the consequence mandated in the Small Business Act—that small businesses that do not meet the benchmarks be ineligible to participate in the programs for a year—because they interpret that consequence as meaning that new participation is not allowed.

[18] After we provided a draft of this chapter to the agencies for comment, the Departments of Education and Homeland Security updated their project solicitations to reflect the revised approach for how to implement the consequence of not meeting the benchmarks.

Table 3. Information from Agencies' Project Solicitations on the Consequence of Not Meeting the Benchmarks for the Small Business Innovation Research and Small Business Technology Transfer Programs (as of November 2017)

Agency	Business is ineligible to receive certain awards	Business is ineligible to submit certain proposals	Directs users to Small Business Administration's website
Department of Agriculture	No	Yes	No
Department of Commerce (National Institute of Standards and Technology)	No	Yes	No
Department of Commerce (National Oceanic and Atmospheric Administration)	Yes	No	No
Department of Defense	Yes	No	No
Department of Educationa	Yes	No	No
Department of Energy	Yes	No	No
Department of Health and Human Services	Yes	No	No
Department of Homeland Security[a]	Yes	No	No
Department of Transportation	No	Yes	No
Environmental Protection Agency	Yes	No	No
National Aeronautics and Space Administration	No	No	Yes
National Science Foundation	Yes	No	No

Source: GAO analysis of agency information. | GAO-18-207.

[a]After we provided a draft of this chapter to the agencies for comment, the Departments of Education and Homeland Security updated their project solicitations to reflect the revised approach for how to implement the consequence of not meeting the benchmarks. Specifically, these updated solicitations state that businesses that do not meet the benchmarks are ineligible to submit certain proposals.

As mentioned earlier in this chapter, SBA's Information Quality Guidelines state that SBA seeks to ensure the quality, utility, and integrity of the information it shares with the public, among other things. Until participating agencies update their project solicitations and SBA updates its policy directives to accurately reflect agreed-upon practices about the consequence for small businesses that do not meet the benchmarks, small businesses may be confused about their eligibility to submit proposals and could invest time developing and submitting proposals when they are not eligible to do so.

CONCLUSION

Under the SBIR and STTR programs, federal agencies have awarded billions of dollars to small businesses to help these businesses develop and commercialize innovative technologies. SBA and the participating agencies have assessed these small businesses against the Transition Rate Benchmark, but those assessments have been based on inaccurate or incomplete data. Without ensuring the reliability of its data, SBA cannot reasonably ensure that it has correctly assessed small businesses against the Transition Rate Benchmark.

SBA and the participating agencies developed a Commercialization Benchmark across all the participating agencies but have not fully implemented it, in part because they have been unable to collect information from the small businesses and verify the accuracy of that information. Working together to implement the benchmark as written or revise it so that it can be implemented could allow the agencies to fulfill the requirement in the Small Business Act to evaluate whether small businesses have met a minimum performance standard for commercializing their technology.

Lastly, SBA and the participating agencies have provided inconsistent information to small businesses about the consequence of not meeting the benchmarks. Officials from SBA and the participating agencies had agreed to change how the consequence would be implemented, starting in 2017, because of difficulties implementing the benchmarks. However, as of November 2017, seven agencies, and a subunit of one agency, had not updated their project solicitations and SBA had not updated its policy directives. Without consistent information on the benchmarks, small businesses may be confused about their eligibility to submit proposals and could invest time developing proposals that they are not eligible to submit.

RECOMMENDATIONS FOR EXECUTIVE ACTION

We are making a total of 11 recommendations, including 3 to SBA and 1 each to the Department of Commerce's National Oceanic and Atmospheric Administration; the Departments of Defense, Education, Energy, Health and Human Services, and Homeland Security; the Environmental Protection Agency; and the National Science Foundation. Specifically:

The Director of the Office of Investment and Innovation within SBA should work with participating agencies to improve the reliability of its SBIR and STTR award data (Recommendation 1).

The Director of the Office of Investment and Innovation within SBA should work with participating agencies to implement the Commercialization Benchmark or, if that is not feasible, revise the benchmark so that it can be implemented (Recommendation 2).

The Director of the Office of Investment and Innovation within SBA should update the SBIR and STTR policy directives to accurately reflect how the consequence of the benchmarks is to be implemented (Recommendation 3).

The SBIR Program Manager of the Department of Commerce's National Oceanic and Atmospheric Administration should update the agency's SBIR project solicitation to accurately reflect how the consequence of not meeting the benchmarks is to be implemented (Recommendation 4).

The SBIR Program Administrator within the Department of Defense should update the agency's SBIR and STTR project solicitations to accurately reflect how the consequence of not meeting the benchmarks is to be implemented (Recommendation 5).

The SBIR Program Manager within the Department of Education should update the agency's SBIR project solicitation to accurately reflect how the consequence of not meeting the benchmarks is to be implemented (Recommendation 6).

The SBIR Program Manager within the Department of Energy should update the agency's combined SBIR and STTR project solicitation to accurately reflect how the consequence of not meeting the benchmarks is to be implemented (Recommendation 7).

The SBIR/STTR Program Coordinator within the Department of Health and Human Services should update the agency's SBIR and STTR project solicitations to accurately reflect how the consequence of not meeting the benchmarks is to be implemented (Recommendation 8).

The SBIR Program Director within the Department of Homeland Security should update the agency's SBIR project solicitation to accurately reflect how the consequence of not meeting the benchmarks is to be implemented (Recommendation 9).

The SBIR Program Manager within the Environmental Protection Agency should update the agency's SBIR project solicitation to accurately reflect how the consequence of not meeting the benchmarks is to be implemented (Recommendation 10).

The SBIR and STTR Program Manager within the National Science Foundation should update the agency's SBIR and STTR project solicitations to accurately reflect how the consequence of not meeting the benchmarks is to be implemented (Recommendation 11).

Agency Comments and Our Evaluation

We provided a draft of this chapter to SBA and the 11 participating agencies for review and comment. In written comments, the Department of Commerce's National Oceanic and Atmospheric Administration; the Departments of Defense, Education, Energy, Health and Human Services, and Homeland Security; the Environmental Protection Agency; and SBA agreed with the respective recommendations directed to their agencies.

Agencies' written comments are reproduced in appendixes I through VIII. An official from one agency—the National Science Foundation—stated in an email that the agency concurred with the recommendation and did not have any further comments. Two agencies—the Department of Homeland Security and SBA—also provided technical comments, which we incorporated as appropriate. Three agencies—the Departments of Agriculture and Transportation, and the National Aeronautics and Space Administration—as well as the Department of Commerce's National Institute of Standards and Technology stated via email that they had no technical or written comments.

In its comments, SBA stated that it disagreed with a statement in our draft report that SBA had not worked with agencies to enter high-quality and accurate data into the database and provided us documentation of an instruction guide on entering data that SBA officials said was available to agencies. Based on our review of this information, we clarified the text of the report and modified the draft report's recommendation by removing the suggested example that SBA provide guidance to the agencies to improve SBIR and STTR award data reliability. SBA agreed with the revised recommendation.

After we provided a draft of the report to the agencies for comment, the Departments of Education and Homeland Security took action on their respective recommendations. Specifically, in December 2017, the agencies issued new project solicitations that reflected the updated consequence of not meeting the benchmarks. We agree that these agencies fully implemented the recommendations we made to them in this chapter.

We are sending copies of this chapter to the appropriate congressional committees; the Secretaries of Agriculture, Commerce, Defense, Education, Energy, Health and Human Services, Homeland Security, and Transportation; the Administrators of the Small Business Administration, the Environmental Protection Agency, and the National Aeronautics and Space Administration; the Director of the National Science Foundation; and other interested parties.

John Neumann
Director, Natural Resources and Environment

APPENDIX I: COMMENTS FROM THE SMALL BUSINESS ADMINISTRATION

U.S. SMALL BUSINESS ADMINISTRATION
WASHINGTON, DC 20416

January 5, 2018

Mr. John Neumann
Director
Natural Resources and Environment
U.S. Government Accountability Office
Washington, D.C. 20548

Dear Mr. Neumann:

Thank you for providing the U.S. Small Business Administration (SBA) with a copy of the Government Accountability Office (GAO) draft report titled, *"Small Business Research Programs: Agencies Need to Take Steps to Assess Progress Toward Commercializing Technologies."*

The draft report analyzes SBA and participating agency efforts related to the development of benchmarks to measure Small Business Innovation Research/Small Business Technology Transfer (SBIR/STTR) awardee progress in commercializing technologies. SBA has the following comments on the draft report:

The draft report touches on the costly, time-consuming, and intensive efforts required to correct award data or collect and verify the accuracy of commercialization data. SBA confirms this and agrees that it is important to have consistent and high-quality data. Data to support the Transition Rate Benchmark can be validated and corrected as part of the ongoing effort to ensure data integrity. Data to support the Commercialization Benchmark poses greater challenges, as identified in the draft report on page 9.

The Small Business Act at 15 USC §638 (qq) directs the head of each Federal agency to establish "a minimum performance standard" or "minimum commercialization rate" to demonstrate progress to Phase II success and Phase III success. Establishing a fixed minimum performance standard to be applied across all project and technology types may not be the most effective way to assess commercial progress. It may be more effective for each project evaluation to include consideration of commercialization progress as part of the overall evaluation for an award. GAO indicates that 9 of the 11 participating agencies consider prior commercialization experience as part of their evaluation and that this can be done in an effective way. SBA has convened a working group of participating agency officials to explore the challenges associated with implementing a commercialization rate benchmark and continues to work collaboratively with the agencies on this issue. However, consideration of prior commercialization experience is not typically done by comparing against a single benchmark standard that is administratively determined, but rather incorporated into the technical review performed on a project-by-project basis.

On page 8, the draft report states that, "SBA officials told us that there are errors in the database, in part, because SBA has not worked with participating agencies to ensure that agencies enter high-quality, accurate data into the database." SBA disagrees with the statement that SBA has not worked with participating agencies to ensure that agencies enter high-quality and accurate data into the database. SBA developed and has continuously improved data reporting systems for agencies to submit award information, and provides an instruction guide for the data fields and their attributes, including type of expected data and whether the field is mandatory or optional. The instruction guide is accessible by the agencies when they are logged in to the SBIR.gov system. The award upload instruction guide has been updated multiple times since August 2015 to address data quality issues. In addition, data validation tools have been used to ensure that award data cannot be submitted unless it complies with certain rules. While there continues to be room for improvement in data quality assurance, SBA is actively working with the agencies to improve data integrity.

On page 11, footnote 15 indicates that the single, uniform benchmark was created by participating agencies "because they thought that it would be easier than having different metrics across agencies," and SBA would like to note that the single program-wide benchmark was established to make application of the benchmark easier for small businesses.

SBA generally agrees with the recommendations to SBA. SBA has the following comments related to GAO's recommendations to SBA:

(1) *The Director of the Office of Investment and Innovation within the Small Business Administration should work with participating agencies to improve the reliability of its SBIR and STTR award data.*

    The Director of the Office of Innovation and Technology within the Office of Investment and Innovation of the SBA has been and will continue to provide guidance to participating agencies, and will work with participating agencies to improve the reliability of SBIR and STTR award data.

(2) *The Director of the Office of Investment and Innovation within the Small Business Administration should work with participating agencies to implement the Commercialization Benchmark or, if that is not feasible, revise the benchmark so that it can be implemented.*

    The Director of the Office of Innovation and Technology within the Office of Investment and Innovation of the SBA has convened a working group of participating agency program managers to discuss how best to address the challenges with implementing the Commercialization Benchmark, or revising the benchmark so that it can be implemented.

(3) *The Director of the Office of Investment and Innovation within the Small Business Administration should update the SBIR and STTR policy directives to accurately reflect how the consequences of the benchmarks are to be implemented.*

The Director of the Office of Innovation and Technology within the Office of Investment and Innovation of the SBA has updated the SBIR.gov website description of the performance benchmarks at https://www.sbir.gov/performance-benchmarks and communicated the consequences of the benchmarks to participating agency program managers. SBA intends to update the policy directives to reflect these policy clarifications.

Thank you for allowing SBA the opportunity to comment on GAO's draft report, "Small Business Research Programs: Agencies Need to Take Steps to Assess Progress Toward Commercializing Technologies", and for taking SBA's views into consideration.

Sincerely,

John R. Williams
Director
Office of Innovation and Technology

Appendix II: Comments from the Department of Commerce

UNITED STATES DEPARTMENT OF COMMERCE
The Secretary of Commerce
Washington, D.C. 20230

January 8, 2018

Mr. John Neumann
Director, Natural Resources and Environment
U.S. Government Accountability Office
441 G Street, NW
Washington, DC 20548

Dear Mr. Neumann:

Thank you for the opportunity to review and comment on the Government Accountability Office's (GAO) draft report titled *Small Business Research Programs: Agencies Need to Take Steps to Assess Progress Toward Commercializing Technologies* (GAO-18-207). Enclosed is the National Oceanic and Atmospheric Administration's response to a GAO recommendation in the draft report.

Sincerely,

Wilbur Ross

Wilbur Ross

Department of Commerce
National Oceanic and Atmospheric Administration
Response to the GAO Draft Report Titled
Small Business Research Programs: Agencies Need to Take
Steps to Assess Progress Toward Commercializing Technologies
(GAO-18-207)

General Comments

The Department of Commerce's National Oceanic and Atmospheric Administration (NOAA) appreciates the opportunity to review the Government Accountability Office's (GAO) draft report. Overall, it is informative, thorough, and balanced. Also, it provides a fair illustration of the existing lack of clarity regarding Small Business Innovation Research (SBIR) benchmarks requirements, including how consequences are implemented when benchmark requirements are not met.

NOAA Response to GAO Recommendations

The draft report states, "We are making a total of 11 recommendations," of which one applies to NOAA:

Recommendation 4: "The SBIR Program Manager of Commerce's National Oceanic and Atmospheric Administration should update the agency's SBIR project solicitation to accurately reflect how the consequences of not meeting the benchmarks are to be implemented."

NOAA Response: NOAA agrees with this recommendation. As evident in the draft report, there was previously a lack of clarity and consistency regarding language in solicitations to explain consequences of not meeting SBIR benchmarks. In order to be consistent with other SBIR agencies, NOAA will seek clarification from the Small Business Administration to ensure that the correct language is included in the next solicitation. NOAA will include updated language to accurately reflect the consequences of not meeting the SBIR benchmark qualifications and requirements for the FY 2019 solicitation, which is planned for release in October 2018, since the current (FY 2018) solicitation is already published.

APPENDIX III: COMMENTS FROM THE DEPARTMENT OF DEFENSE

OFFICE OF THE UNDER SECRETARY OF DEFENSE
3000 DEFENSE PENTAGON
WASHINGTON, DC 20301-3000

ACQUISITION, TECHNOLOGY AND LOGISTICS

Mr. John Neumann
Director, Natural Resources and Environment
U.S. Government Accountability Office
441 G Street, N.W.
Washington, DC 20548

Dear Mr. Neumann:

This is the Department of Defense (DoD) response to the Government Accountability Office (GAO) Draft Report, GAO-18-207, "SMALL BUSINESS RESEARCH PROGRAMS: Agencies Need to Take Steps to Assess Progress Toward Commercializing Technologies" dated December 7, 2017 (GAO Code 101978).

The Department is providing official written comments for inclusion in the report.

Sincerely,

James J. Galvin, Jr.
Acting Director, Office of
Small Business Programs

OFFICE OF THE UNDER SECRETARY OF DEFENSE
3000 DEFENSE PENTAGON
WASHINGTON, DC 20301-3000

ACQUISITION, TECHNOLOGY AND LOGISTICS

GAO Draft Report Dated December 7, 2017
GAO-18-207 (GAO CODE 101978)

"SMALL BUSINESS RESEARCH PROGRAMS: Agencies Need to Take Steps to Assess Progress Toward Commercializing Technologies"

DEPARTMENT OF DEFENSE COMMENTS TO THE GAO RECOMMENDATION

RECOMMENDATION: The SBIR Program Administrator within the Department of Defense should update the agency's SBIR and STTR project solicitations to accurately reflect how the consequences of not meeting the benchmarks are to be implemented.

DOD RESPONSE: The DoD position is to concur without comment.

Appendix IV: Comments from the Department of Education

UNITED STATES DEPARTMENT OF EDUCATION
INSTITUTE OF EDUCATION SCIENCES
WASHINGTON, D.C. 20202

Mr. John Neumann
Director
Natural Resources and Environment
U.S. Government Accountability Office
441 G Street, NW
Washington, DC 20548

Dear Mr. Neumann:

I am writing in response to the recommendation made in the U.S. Government Accountability Office (GAO) draft report, "Small Business Research Programs: Agencies Need to Take Steps to Assess Progress Toward Commercializing Technologies" (GAO-18-207). I appreciate the opportunity to comment on the draft report on behalf of the U.S. Department of Education (Department).

We appreciate GAO's review of how participating Federal agencies assess businesses against two benchmarks related to commercialization of the Small Business Innovation Research (SBIR) and Small Business Technology Transfer (STTR) programs. The Department only participates in the SBIR program, which is administered by the Institute of Education Sciences. We provide our response to the recommendation in the report from GAO below:

Recommendation: The SBIR Program Manager within the Department of Education should update the agency's SBIR project solicitation to accurately reflect how the consequences of not meeting the benchmarks are to be implemented.

Response: In response to the recommendation, we have added language to the SBIR program solicitation to clarify that small businesses that do not meet the Department's Transition Benchmark are ineligible to submit a proposal to our SBIR program. On Monday, December 11, 2017, the Department posted the SBIR Phase I solicitation to the Federal Business Opportunities website (Solicitation Number: 91990018R0006, www.fbo.gov).

We appreciate the opportunity to review the draft report and comment on the recommendation. We do not have any technical comments.

Sincerely,

Thomas Brock
Commissioner of the National Center for Education Research, Delegated the Duties of the Director of the Institute of Education Sciences

APPENDIX V: COMMENTS FROM THE DEPARTMENT OF ENERGY

Department of Energy
Washington, DC 20585

January 12, 2018

Mr. John Neumann
Director
Natural Resources and Environment
U.S. Government Accountability Office
441 G Street N.W.
Washington, DC 20548

Dear Mr. Neumann:

We appreciate the opportunity to comment on the draft Government Accountability Office (GAO) report: Small Business Research Programs: Agencies Need to Take Steps to Assess Progress Toward Commercializing Technologies (GAO-18-207).

Recommendation 7: The SBIR Program Manager within the Department of Energy should update the agency's SBIR project solicitation to accurately reflect how the consequences of not meeting the benchmarks are to be implemented.

DOE Response: DOE concurs with the recommendation.

The DOE Small Business Innovation Research/Small Business Technology Transfer (SBIR/STTR) Programs Office issues two Phase I Funding Opportunity Announcements (FOAs) annually, which are referred to as Release 1 and Release 2. For FY 2018, the Release 1 FOA has already closed. The Release 2 FOA closes on February 26, 2018. DOE will modify the language in this and future Phase I FOAs as shown below.

Current language refers to eligibility for award:

> For these companies, the benchmark establishes a minimum number of Phase II awards the company must have received for a given number of Phase I awards received during the five-year time period in order to be eligible to receive a new Phase I award.

Revised language refers to eligibility to submit an application:

> For these companies, the benchmark establishes a minimum number of Phase II awards the company must have received for a given number of Phase I awards received during the five-year time period in order to be eligible to submit a Phase I application.
>
> On June 1 of each year, SBIR/STTR awardees registered on SBIR.gov are assessed to determine if they meet the benchmark requirements. Companies that fail to meet the transition rate benchmark on June 1, 2017 are not eligible to submit a Phase I application during the period June 1, 2017 through May 31, 2018.

Sincerely,

J. Stephen Binkley
Deputy Director for Science Programs
Office of Science

Appendix VI: Comments from the Department of Health and Human Services

DEPARTMENT OF HEALTH & HUMAN SERVICES

OFFICE OF THE SECRETARY

Assistant Secretary for Legislation
Washington, DC 20201

JAN 0 8 2018

John Neumann
Director, Natural Resources and Environment
U.S. Government Accountability Office
441 G Street NW
Washington, DC 20548

Dear Mr. Neumann:

Attached are comments on the U.S. Government Accountability Office's (GAO) report entitled, "*Small Business Research Programs: Agencies Need to Take Steps to Assess Progress Toward Commercializing Technologies*" (GAO-18-207).

The Department appreciates the opportunity to review this report prior to publication.

Sincerely,

Barbara Pisaro Clark
Acting Assistant Secretary for Legislation

GENERAL COMMENTS OF THE DEPARTMENT OF HEALTH AND HUMAN SERVICES (HHS) ON THE GOVERNMENT ACCOUNTABILITY OFFICE'S DRAFT REPORT ENTITLED - SMALL BUSINESS RESEARCH PROGRAMS: AGENCIES NEED TO TAKE STEPS TO ASSESS PROGRESS TOWARD COMMERCIALIZING TECHNOLOGIES (GAO-18-207)

The U.S. Department of Health and Human Services (HHS) appreciates the opportunity from the Government Accountability Office (GAO) to review and comment on this draft report.

Recommendation 8
The Small Business Innovation Research/Small Business Technology Transfer (SBIR/STTR) Program Coordinator within HHS should update the agency's SBIR and STTR project solicitations to accurately reflect how the consequences of not meeting the benchmarks are to be implemented.

HHS Response
HHS concurs with GAO's recommendation.

HHS will update solicitations to include language to adequately reflect how the consequences of not meeting the benchmarks are to be implemented for all new SBIR/STTR solicitations. HHS will include the updated language on new solicitations published after January 1, 2018.

APPENDIX VII: COMMENTS FROM THE DEPARTMENT OF HOMELAND SECURITY

U.S. Department of Homeland Security
Washington, DC 20528

Homeland Security

January 5, 2018

John Neumann
Director, Natural Resources and Environment
U.S. Government Accountability Office
441 G Street, NW
Washington, DC 20548

Re: Managements Response to Draft Report GAO-18-207, "SMALL BUSINESS RESEARCH PROGRAMS: Agencies Need to Take Steps to Assess Progress Toward Commercializing Technologies"

Dear Mr. Neumann:

Thank you for the opportunity to review and comment on this draft report. The U.S. Department of Homeland Security (DHS) appreciates the U.S. Government Accountability Office's (GAO) work in planning and conducting its review and issuing this report.

The Department is pleased to note GAO's recognition of the importance of ensuring that Small Business Innovation Research (SBIR) investments meet minimum transition rate and commercialization benchmarks. DHS remains committed to commercializing promising SBIR technologies and supporting transition benchmarks as a means of ensuring SBIR funds are provided to firms with reasonable intent to transition their technologies. This includes continuing to support strategies to improve the tracking and enforcement activities and ensure that small businesses are aware of the consequences of not meeting benchmarks.

The draft report contained one recommendation for DHS, with which the Department concurs. Attached find our detailed response to the recommendation.

Again, thank you for the opportunity to review and comment on this draft report. Technical comments were previously provided under separate cover. Please feel free to contact me if you have any questions. We look forward to working with you again in the future.

Sincerely,

JIM H. CRUMPACKER, CIA, CFE
Director
Departmental GAO-OIG Liaison Office

Appendix VIII: Comments from the Environmental Protection Agency

UNITED STATES ENVIRONMENTAL PROTECTION AGENCY
WASHINGTON, D.C. 20460

JAN 3 - 2018

OFFICE OF
RESEARCH AND DEVELOPMENT

Mr. John Neumann
Director
Natural Resources and Environment
U.S. Government Accountability Office
Washington, DC 20548

Dear Mr. Neumann:

Thank you for the opportunity to review and comment on GAO's draft report GAO-18-207, "*Small Business Research Programs: Agencies Need to Take Steps to Assess Progress Toward Commercializing Technologies.*

The purpose of this letter is to provide the EPA's response to the report recommendation.

Recommendation: The Small Business Innovation Research (SBIR) Program Manager within the EPA should update the agency's SBIR project solicitation to accurately reflect how the consequences of not meeting the benchmarks are to be implemented.

Response: EPA concurs with this recommendation. EPA will update the next SBIR solicitation (which will be released in 2018) to provide information to small businesses on the consequences of not meeting the benchmarks (i.e., from ineligibility to receive certain awards to ineligibility to submit certain proposals). EPA will also plan on referencing the SBA website on performance benchmarks (https://www.sbir.gov/performance-benchmarks) to ensure consistency with SBA guidance.

Additionally, and as mentioned during interviews with GAO, EPA would like to emphasize our preference to consider businesses' prior commercialization experience as part of our overall evaluation of proposals (allowing reviewers to use professional judgment on commercialization success) rather than implement the current commercialization benchmark which, as noted in the draft report, can be complicated.

Sincerely,

Jennifer Orme-Zavaleta, PhD
Principal Deputy Assistant Administrator

cc: EPA GAO Liaison Team
Mary Ellen Radzikowski, Acting Director, National Center for Environmental Research
James Gentry, Deputy Director, National Center for Environmental Research
April Richards, Program Manager, Small Business Innovation Research (SBIR) Program

In: Small Business Issues
Editor: Andrea Moeller
ISBN: 978-1-53615-870-0

Chapter 6

SMALL BUSINESS TAX BENEFITS: CURRENT LAW AND ARGUMENTS FOR AND AGAINST THEM*

Gary Guenther

SUMMARY

The federal tax burden on small firms and its effects on their formation and growth have long been matters of legislative concern for Congress. This abiding interest has helped pave the way for the enactment of a series of tax laws in recent years that included targeted tax relief for a number of small businesses.

This chapter describes the main federal tax preferences that benefit small firms and examines the main arguments for and against government support for small firms in general and for tax benefits targeted at such firms in particular. It addresses the tax preferences that can be claimed only by small firms in a wide range of industries and excludes those targeted at small firms in specific industries, such as the special deduction for small life insurance companies under Section 806 of the federal tax

* This is an edited, reformatted and augmented version of Congressional Research Service, Publication No. RL32254, dated July 5, 2018.

code. The small business tax preferences discussed here reflect the changes in the tax code under P.L. 115-97.

The following small business tax benefits are examined here:

- Expensing allowance for machinery and equipment under Section 179 of the Internal Revenue Code;
- Cash-basis accounting under Section 446;
- Tax credit for a portion of the costs incurred by small firms in establishing pension funds for employees under Section 45E;
- Tax credit for costs incurred by small firms in complying with the Americans with Disabilities Act under Section 44;
- Full exclusion from the capital gains tax on the sale or exchange of qualified small business stock under Section 1202;
- Exemption from the limitation on the deduction for business interest expenses under Section 163;
- Tax credit for small firms that offer qualified health insurance coverage to employees under Section 45R;
- Simplified dollar-value last-in-last-out accounting under Section 474;
- Deduction for and amortization of business start-up expenses under Section 195;
- Ordinary income treatment of losses on the sale of certain small business stock under Section 1244;
- Treating losses on the sale of Small Business Investment Company stock as ordinary losses under Section 1242;
- Exemption from the uniform capitalization rule under Section 263A; and
- Use of research tax credit to reduce payroll tax for certain small firms under Section 41.

While available information does not allow for an estimate of the federal revenue cost of the small business tax preferences examined here, a recent estimate by the Joint Committee on Taxation suggests that the cost might exceed $17 billion in FY2018.

Tax preferences for small businesses raise several policy issues. For some, a key question is whether they can be justified on economic grounds. In the absence of such a justification, small business tax benefits, while promoting the survival and growth of firms that can take advantage of them, may cause more economic harm than good by distorting the allocation of domestic economic resources.

INTRODUCTION

Small business owners in general have long been praised within the United States for their contributions to the economy, especially their impact on job growth and innovation. Thus, the federal income tax burden on small firms and its effects on their formation and growth have been perennial issues for Congress.

Many regard small firms as a vital source of job creation and technological innovation. Small firms have also been celebrated as effective vehicles for advancing the economic status of minorities, immigrants, and women.

At the same time, some view the federal income tax as an obstacle to the formation and growth of small firms, while others see it as a policy tool for boosting their rates of formation and growth. Going back to the 111th Congress, seven bills have been enacted that established completely new tax preferences for small firms and extended (and in some cases modified) existing ones:

- American Recovery and Reinvestment Act of 2009 (P.L. 111-5),
- Small Business Jobs Act of 2010 (P.L. 111-240),
- Tax Relief, Unemployment Insurance Reauthorization, and Job Creation Act of 2010 (P.L. 111-312),
- American Taxpayer Relief Act of 2012 (P.L. 112-240),
- Tax Increase Prevention Act of 2014 (P.L. 113-295),
- Protecting Americans from Tax Hikes Act of 2015 (Division Q of the Consolidated Appropriations Act, 2016 (P.L. 114-113), and
- P.L. 115-97 (the tax revision act of 2017).

Small business tax benefits (or preferences) raise three potential policy issues for Congress. First, what is the appropriate definition of a small business in the context of public policy? Two considerations seem paramount in finding an answer to that question: (1) choosing the appropriate size measure (e.g., employment, assets, or receipts) and (2) determining whether that measure should apply to all small business tax benefits, as well as other forms of federal assistance for small businesses.

Second, is there a sound economic justification for supporting small firms? If no such rationale can be found, then government support for small businesses may do more harm than good by distorting the allocation of domestic economic resources.

Third, are tax benefits the most cost-effective way for the federal government to assist small firms? Small business tax preferences entail the following economic costs: (1) the foregone revenue and any interest charges from federal borrowing to offset that revenue loss, (2) the resources required to comply with the rules governing the use of the tax benefits and to enforce compliance with those rules, and (3) the opportunity cost of the foregone revenue and the resources devoted to tax compliance and enforcement. Other policy options for assisting small firms entail similar costs.

This chapter is intended to shed light on the first two issues by identifying the main nonagricultural small business tax preferences, determining the foregone revenue associated with them, and examining the economic arguments for and against them. An assessment of the relative cost-effectiveness of existing federal small business tax benefits is beyond the scope of the report. The report begins by exploring the challenges associated with crafting a uniform definition of a small business for public policy purposes. It then describes existing small business tax preferences and reviews what is known about the economic contributions of small firms in general. It concludes with a discussion of the arguments for and against government policies to support small businesses.

Eligibility Criteria: How Small Is Small?

Size Standards and the Small Business Act of 1953

An essential starting point for an assessment of the effects of small business tax benefits is the definition of firms that qualify for the benefits.

And on the question of how to define a small firm for the purpose of federal programs to support small businesses, a necessary starting point is the Small Business Act of 1953 (P.L. 83-163, as amended).

Among other things, the act granted the Administrator of the Small Business Administration (SBA) the authority to establish size standards for federal programs supporting small businesses. A size standard specifies the maximum size a company can attain (whatever the measure) and still qualify for federal assistance. The act also gave the Administrator the authority to determine what those standards should be and how they should be applied. Since the act's passage, Congress has refrained from creating size standards for specific federal programs, with one exception: agricultural enterprises. Other federal agencies may create small business size standards for programs they administer, but they must gain the approval of the Administrator before the new standards can take effect.[1]

While empowering the SBA to select the size standards for federal programs, the act also laid down a basic consideration for identifying small businesses eligible for SBA programs. Paragraph 3(a)(1) stated that "for the purposes of this Act, a small business concern.... shall be deemed to be one which is independently owned and operated and which is not dominant in its field of operation."[2]

In the SBA's view, the act and its legislative history established that two principles should guide the agency in setting size standards for all industries. First, the standards should reflect critical differences among industries. Second, federal programs subject to the standards, including those administered by the SBA, should be designed to help eligible small firms improve their performance within the domestic economy.

For the programs it administers, the SBA has used three criteria to identify eligible firms since the early 1950s: (1) the average number of employees in the past year, (2) the average annual receipts in the previous three years, and (3) the value of assets. Employment and receipt size determine eligibility for the vast majority of industries listed in the North

---

[1] For more information on the historical development of SBA size standards, see CRS Report R40860, *Small Business Size Standards: A Historical Analysis of Contemporary Issues*, by Robert Jay Dilger.

[2] 15 U.S.C. §632(a)(1).

American Industrial Classification System (NAICS). The choice of criterion hinges on an industry's structural features.

The SBA has established three "base" (or "anchor") size standards, which shape its ongoing review of the standard it sets for a particular industry. For manufacturing, mining, and other industries with an employee-based standard, the base standard is 500 employees. For industries with a receipts-based standard, a group that includes most nonmanufacturing industries, the base standard is $7.0 million in average annual receipts. The base standard is 100 employees for firms involved in wholesale trade. For a limited number of industries, the SBA uses other measures of size that are appropriate for their main lines of business. For example, financial assets are used for banking, barrels per calendar-day for petroleum refining, and the share of overall power generation for electric utilities.

In setting or revising a size standard for an industry, the SBA uses its anchor standard as the starting point. Whether a size standard is set below, at, or above that level depends on the results of an evaluation of certain industry characteristics, especially average firm size, start-up costs, entry barriers, degree of competition among firms, and distribution of firms by size. The SBA also takes into consideration the impact of a current or proposed size standard on the access of small firms to federal procurement contracts.

According to the SBA's current table of small business size standards, standards based on receipt size range from $0.75 million to $35.5 million; those based on employment range from 100 to 1,500 employees; those based on financial assets are set at either $7 million or $175 million; those based on power generation are uniformly set at 4 million megawatt hours; and those based on petroleum refining are set at 1,500 employees and 125,000 barrels per calendar day.[3]

The SBA does alter the size standard for particular industries from time to time. Before a proposed change can take effect, however, the agency's Office of Size Standards (OSS) is required to assess the likely

---

[3] See http://www.sba.gov/sites/default/files/files/Size_Standards_Table(1).pdf.

impact of the change on the performance of the affected industry (or industries), focusing on the degree of competition, average firm size, start-up costs, barriers to entry, and distribution of industry sales and employment by firm size. OSS uses the results to make recommendations to SBA's Size Policy Board. If the board agrees with the recommendations, it typically advises the Administrator to approve the proposed change. Approved changes must be published in the *Federal Register* for public comment. The SBA issues no final rule until it has reviewed the comments received from the public, as well as any other new information.[4]

Under the Small Business Jobs Act of 2010 (P.L. 111-240), the SBA has the authority to set alternative size standards based on tangible net worth and average after-tax profits for the 7(a) and the 504/CDC loan programs it administers. Until the SBA does so, the act sets the tangible net worth limit at $15 million and the average after-tax profit limit at $5 million, excluding any net operating losses carried over from previous tax years, in the two fiscal years before the date of a company's loan application. The SBA has not established alternative size standards for those programs as of April 2018.[5]

The act also required the SBA to review at least one-third of NAICS industry size standards every 18 months and to make "appropriate adjustments" to reflect current market conditions. No later than 30 days after a review is completed, the SBA must file a report on its findings to the House Committee on Small Business and the Senate Committee on Small Business and Entrepreneurship. It is also required to publicize its reasons for modifying or retaining each reviewed size standard.

Federal agencies administering programs that reserve a share of procurement contracts for small firms (known as small business set-aside programs) are required to use the SBA size standards. Other federal programs and tax provisions supporting small businesses may use those standards, though they are not required to do so. Agencies are free to

---

[4] Details on current SBA efforts to revise industry size standards can be found at http://www.sba.gov/content/whatsnew-with-size-standards.

[5] CRS Report R40860, *Small Business Size Standards: A Historical Analysis of Contemporary Issues*, by Robert Jay Dilger, p. 23.

develop their own size standards, but they are subjected to a rigorous rulemaking review process overseen by the SBA before the new standards can be applied. An agency must get the approval of the SBA Administrator before a new standard may be used.

The SBA's methodology for selecting size standards for industries continues to stir up concerns among interested lawmakers and analysts.[6] Among the unresolved issues are the following:

- Should there be a fixed range for a size standard (e.g., 100 to 1,500 employees)?
- Should the standards be adjusted for inflation more often than once every five years?
- Should the employment standard be adjusted for productivity gains in an industry?
- Should the SBA lower its size standards for federal contracts in response to recommendations from the private sector?
- Should the size standards be calculated only in dollars to reflect actual structural differences among industries?

How a Small Business Is Defined in the Federal Tax Code

Does the federal tax code use the SBA size standards to determine eligibility for small business tax benefits? Yes, for the most part.

As Table 1 shows, most of these tax preferences use asset, receipt, or employment size to identify eligible firms.[7] The employment and receipt sizes found in the tax code are much smaller than the sizes used by the

[6] See Small Business Administration, Size Standards Division and Office of Contracting & Business Development, *SBA Size Standards Methodology* (Washington: April 2009), pp. 45-48.

[7] According to one source, the Internal Revenue Code contains at least 24 different definitions of a small business. See Douglas K Barney, Chris Bjornson, and Steve Wells, "Just How Small Is Your Business?" *National Public Accountant*, August 2003, pp. 4-6.

SBA to identify small businesses by industry.[8] In addition, a few tax provisions bestow their benefits on small firms not through a size standard but as a consequence of their design, most notably the expensing allowance under Section 179 of the Internal Revenue Code (IRC). Although the statutory language of the provision makes it clear that firms of all sizes may claim the allowance, its limitations effectively confines its benefits to relatively small firms.

There is no explicit rationale in the tax code for the size standards that are used to establish eligibility for small business tax benefits. This lack of a uniform definition of a small business has at least one disadvantage and one advantage. On the one hand, the different IRC size standards can lead to an uneven and seemingly arbitrary distribution of tax benefits among companies that are similar in line of business and employment, receipt, or asset size.[9] On the other hand, the absence of a uniform size standard gives lawmakers greater leeway in designing tax benefits to support specific policy objectives related to small businesses.

MAIN FEDERAL TAX BENEFITS FOR SMALL BUSINESS

In principle, all business income is subject to federal taxation, but the reality is more complicated, as the federal tax code does not treat all business income equally.

---

[8] For instance, as of October 2017, the SBA uses an upper limit of 500 employees for small firms in 98 manufacturing industries and an upper limit of $15.0 million or $20.5 million in average annual sales or receipts for small firms in most administrative and support service industries (see CRS Report R40860, *Small Business Size Standards: A Historical Analysis of Contemporary Issues*, pp. 24-25 for more details). By contrast, only firms with no more than 25 full-time employees earning $50,000 or less in wages or salaries may claim the maximum small employer tax credit for health insurance costs under Section 45, and only corporations and partnerships with less than $5.0 million in average annual gross receipts in the previous three years are eligible to use cash-basis accounting when they otherwise would have to use accrual-basis accounting under Section 446.

[9] For instance, two small companies with the same number of employees engaging in the same lines of business may not be eligible for the same tax preferences because they differ in asset and receipt size.

The tax burden on business income depends on several factors. One is whether or not a firm is organized for tax purposes as a C corporation or as a passthrough entity (i.e., partnerships (including limited liability companies, or LLCs), S corporations, and sole proprietorships). Corporate profits are taxed twice: once at the firm level and a second time at the shareholder level when any profits are distributed as dividends or long-term capital gains. By contrast, the net income of passthrough entities is taxed only at the owner or shareholder level.

Furthermore, the taxation of business income depends on whether or not the owner of a passthrough entity pays the alternative minimum tax (AMT). Corporations were also subject to an AMT from 1987 to 2017; P.L. 115-97 repealed the tax, starting in 2018. Passthrough business owners paying the AMT may or may not be taxed at lower rates than they would be under the regular income tax.

Firm size also plays a role in determining a company's federal tax burden. Some tax provisions offer benefits to smaller firms that are not available to larger firms. There is no formal distinction between the taxation of small and large firms in the tax code. Rather, small business tax benefits are scattered throughout the sections of the code dealing with business taxation. Most come in the form of deductions, exclusions, exemptions, credits, deferrals, and preferential tax rates whose main effect is to reduce the cost of capital for investments and increase a firm's cash flow.

The federal tax benefits targeted at smaller firms with the broadest reach outside agriculture are discussed below. Excluded from the list are subsidies available only to small firms in particular industries, such as life insurance, banking, and energy production or distribution. Nor does the list include tax benefits that may be claimed by many small firms but are available to firms of all sizes, such as the Section 41 research tax credit and the Section 168(k) 100% expensing allowance. Table 1 summarizes the key features of each of these tax benefits.

Table 1. Current Small Business Tax Preferences and Their Estimated Revenue Cost in FY2018

Business Tax Preference	Federal Tax Code Section	Nature of the Benefit	Eligible Firms	Current Status	Revenue Cost in FY2018 Under Current Law[a] ($ billions)
Limited Expensing Allowance	179	Allows firms to deduct as a current expense up to $1 million of their expenditures on qualified depreciable assets placed in service in 2018; begins to phase out when total amount exceeds $2.5 million	No size limit	Permanent	$9.9
Nonagricultural Cash-Basis Accounting	446	Allows eligible partnerships and C corporations (including certain farms) to use the cash method of accounting	C corporations and partnerships with average annual gross receipts of $25 million or less in the previous three tax years	Permanent	5.0
Full Exclusion for Gains from the Sale of Qualified Small Business Stock	1202	Allows noncorporate investors to exclude between 50% and 100% of any gains on the disposition of qualified small business stock held for five or more years	Stock must be issued by C corporations in a qualified business that have $50 million or less in gross assets when the stock is issued	Permanent	1.3
Tax Credit for Employee Health Insurance Costs	45R	Allows eligible small employers to take a nonrefundable tax credit for nonelective contributions that cover 50% or more of the cost of health plans for participating employees	Employers with 25 or fewer employees whose average annual compensation does not exceed $50,000	Permanent	0.6
Simplified Dollar-Value LIFO Accounting Method	474	Allows qualified small firms to use a simpler LIFO method in estimating the base-year value of their inventories	Business taxpayers with average annual gross receipts of $5 million or less in the three previous tax years	Permanent	0.2

Table 1. (Continued)

Business Tax Preference	Federal Tax Code Section	Nature of the Benefit	Eligible Firms	Current Status	Revenue Cost in FY2018 Under Current Law[a] ($ billions)
Deduction and Amortization of Eligible Business Start-Up Expenses	195	Allows start-up businesses to deduct up to $5,000 of eligible start-up expenses in the year they begin to operate, and to amortize the remaining expenses over 180 months; the deduction phases out, dollar for dollar, when total qualified expenses exceed $50,000	Firms in their first year of business	Permanent	0.1
Tax Credit for Expenses Incurred in Improving the Accessibility of a Business for Disabled Individuals	44	Allows qualified small firms to claim a nonrefundable tax credit for qualified expenses they incur in making their facilities more accessible for disabled persons	Employers with gross receipts of $1 million or less in the previous tax year, or with 30 or fewer full-time employees during that year	Permanent	Less than $50 million
Ordinary Income Treatment of Losses on Sales of Certain Small Business Stock	1244	Allows taxpayers to deduct any loss from the sale, exchange, or worthlessness of qualified small business stock as an ordinary loss and not a capital loss	Individuals and partnerships	Permanent	NA
Treating Losses on the Sale of Small Business Investment Company (SBIC) Stock as Ordinary Losses	1242	Allows individual taxpayers who invest in SBICs to deduct from ordinary income all losses from the sale or exchange or worthlessness of SBIC stock	Any individual investing in an operating SBIC	Permanent	NA
Exemption from the Uniform Capitalization Rule	263A	Exempts qualified small firms from the requirement that firms acquiring real or tangible property for resale capitalize or include in the estimated value of their inventory the	Business taxpayers with average annual gross receipts of $25 million or less in the three previous	Permanent	NA

Business Tax Preference	Federal Tax Code Section	Nature of the Benefit	Eligible Firms	Current Status	Revenue Cost in FY2018 Under Current Law[a] ($ billions)
		direct cost of the property included in it, as well as the indirect costs that can be allocated to the property	tax years		
Use of Section 41 research tax credit against payroll tax	41(h) and 3111(f)	Allows qualified firms to claim a payroll tax credit of up to $250,000, using all or a portion of their unused research tax credit for the current tax year	Business taxpayers that have less than $5 million in gross receipts in the current tax year and had no gross receipts in a tax year preceding the previous five years	Permanent	NA
Tax Credit for Pension Plan Start-Up Expenses	45E	Allows qualified small firms to take a nonrefundable tax credit for a portion of the costs they incur in establishing new qualified pension plans for employees	Employers with fewer than 100 employees, each of whom received $5,000 or more in compensation in the previous calendar year, and with one or more highly paid employee participating in the plan	Permanent	NA
Exemption for Qualified Small Firms from the Limitation on the Deduction for Business Interest	Section 163(j)	Allows eligible small firms to deduct business interest without the limits set by P.L. 115-97.	C corporations and passthrough entities with $25 million or less in average annual gross receipts in the three previous tax years.	Permanent	NA

Source: Compiled by the Congressional Research Service; from the following source: Joint Committee on Taxation, *Estimates of Federal Tax Expenditures for Fiscal Years 2017-2021,* JCX-34-18.

[a]. These estimates include the revenue effect from P.L. 115-97.

As a result of the enactment of H.R. 1 (P.L. 115-97) in December 2017, the current lineup of small business tax benefits differs somewhat from the 2017 lineup. Under previous tax law, the graduated corporate income tax (whose rates ranged from 15% to 35%) was considered a small business tax benefit. P.L. 115-97 permanently replaced those rates with a single corporate tax rate of 21%, starting in 2018. The act repealed a second small business tax benefit from 2017: the rollover of gains from the sale of publicly traded securities into specialized small business investment companies under Section 1044. In addition, by repealing the corporate AMT, the act also did away with another small business tax benefit: an exemption under Section 55(e) from the AMT for corporations whose average annual gross receipts did not exceed $5 million in their first three tax years and $7.5 million in each succeeding three-year period.

The current lineup makes no reference to the taxation of passthrough businesses. Some have argued that the tax rates that apply to this income should be considered a small business tax benefit when the returns to passthrough business investment are taxed at lower rates than the returns to corporate business investment. Such a difference existed under the tax law that was in effect in 2017. P.L. 115-97 reversed this difference by setting a corporate tax rate that is 8.6 percentage points lower than the top effective income tax rate for passthrough entities: 29.6%.

There is another reason why it is inadvisable to regard the taxation of passthrough business income in general as a small business tax preference, regardless of the differences between corporate and noncorporate income tax rates. Among C corporations and passthrough entities, there are very small and very large companies, and they differ in their economic roles. According to data from the Internal Revenue Service, in 2014, for example, relatively small companies (those with $500,000 or less in receipts) accounted for 68% of C corporation tax returns, 70% of S corporation returns, 89% of partnership returns, and 98% of sole proprietorship returns.[10] By contrast, relatively large companies (those with more than $50 million in receipts) represented 91% of total C corporation receipts, 40% of S corporation receipts, and 71% of partnership receipts in

[10] See U.S. Congress, Joint Committee on Taxation, *Present Law and Background Regarding the Federal Income Taxation of Small Businesses*, JCX-32-17 (Washington, DC: July 11, 2017), Tables 1 to 4, pp. 24-28.

2014; large firms made only a small contribution to total sole proprietorship receipts. These figures show that not all passthrough firms are small and not all C corporations are large, regardless of the size standard.

It is not known how much revenue is lost because of tax benefits shown in Table 1. Nevertheless, a recent estimate by the Joint Committee on Taxation (JCT) indicates that their revenue cost could exceed $17 billion in FY2018 (see Table 1).[11] To put this amount in the proper context, the budget for the SBA in FY2018 totals $887 million.

Expensing Allowance for Certain Depreciable Business Assets

Expensing is the most accelerated form of depreciation. It treats the cost of acquiring a depreciable asset (e.g., a machine tool or building) as a current expense rather than a capital expense. As a result, the full cost of the asset is deducted in the year when it is placed into service. In the absence of expensing, companies have to recover capital costs over longer periods by using the appropriate depreciation method and schedule.

Under IRC Section 179, a company may expense (or deduct) up to $1 million of the cost of qualified property—mainly machinery, equipment, standardized computer software, and improvements to nonresidential buildings—placed into service in 2018 and write off any remaining cost using the appropriate depreciation schedule under the Modified Accelerated Cost Recovery System (MACRS).[12] The maximum allowance is permanently fixed at $1 million and is indexed for inflation, starting in 2019.

Use of the allowance is subject to several limitations, the most important of which is the dollar limitation. Under this limitation, the maximum allowance is reduced (dollar for dollar) by the amount (if any)

---

[11] U.S. Congress, Joint Committee on Taxation, *Estimates for Federal Tax Expenditures for Fiscal Years 2017-2021*, JCX-34-18 (Washington, DC: May 25, 2018).

[12] For more details on the current expensing allowance and its economic effects, see CRS Report RL31852, *The Section 179 and Section 168(k) Expensing Allowances: Current Law and Economic Effects*, by Gary Guenther.

by which the aggregate cost of qualified property a firm places in service during a tax year exceeds a phaseout threshold. In 2018, the threshold is set at $2.5 million; it too is indexed for inflation starting in 2019. This means that a firm may expense as much as $1 million of its spending on qualified assets in the 2018, provided its total spending for this purpose during the year remains below $2.5 million. Once the firm's total spending surpasses that amount, the amount that can be expensed drops until total spending reaches $3.5 million, at which point none of that cost may be deducted under Section 179.

Congress established the expensing allowance mainly to serve two related purposes. One was to lower the cost of capital for relatively small companies. The other purpose was to stimulate increased business investment during periods of weak or negative economic growth.

There is no size limit on the companies that may avail themselves of Section 179. It is the phaseout threshold that makes the expensing allowance a benefit for small firms. Large firms such as GM, Microsoft, or Intel typically spend far more on assets that qualify for the allowance than the threshold for being ineligible for the allowance.

In theory, the allowance can stimulate business investment in two ways. First, it lowers the user cost of capital for investment in qualified assets, all other things being equal. This is because expensing produces a zero marginal effective tax rate on the returns to investment in those assets under the standard economic model for determining the user cost of capital.[13] Second, the allowance increases the cash flow of firms using it, all other things being equal. For firms whose cost of internal funds is lower than their cost of external funds such as debt or equity, a rise in cash flow may be critical to their ability to undertake new investments.

---

[13] See Jane G. Gravelle, "Effects of the 1981 Depreciation Revisions on the Taxation of Income From Business Capital," *National Tax Journal*, vol. 35, no. 1, March 1982, pp. 2-6. In effect, under expensing, the after-tax rate of return on an investment becomes equal to the pretax rate of return. This happens because expensing reduces costs and after-tax returns by the same proportion, which is determined by the tax rate.

Economist Douglas Holtz-Eakin illustrated the impact of the allowance on the cost of capital in a 1995 article.[14] Table 2 summarizes his results. The first column shows the corporate tax rate; the second gives the required pretax rate of return if the entire cost of the investment is expensed; the third column provides the required pretax rate of return if the entire cost is recovered through the depreciation deductions allowed under federal tax law in the early 1990s; and the final column presents the effective tax subsidy from expensing, which is expressed as the difference (in percentage points) between the required rates of return shown in columns two and three.

At least two conclusions can be drawn from the results. First, expensing offered a significant investment subsidy that increased with a firm's marginal tax rate, as one would expect with a deduction. For example, at a tax rate of 15%, expensing lowered the user cost of capital by 11.3%; but at a rate of 35%, the reduction rose to 27.9%. Second, the user cost of capital under expensing declined as the tax rate increased because tax deductions were worth more at higher tax rates.

Table 2. Estimated User Cost of Capital Under-Expensing (%)

Corporate Tax Rate	Expensing	Regular Depreciation	Absolute Size of the Subsidy
15%	17.95%	20.23%	2.28a
25	17.05	21.13	4.08
35	16.15	22.40	6.25

Source: Douglas Holtz-Eakin, "Should Small Business Be Tax-Favored?" National Tax Journal, September 1995.

Note: The calculations assume an interest rate of 9%, an inflation rate of 3%, and a rate of economic depreciation of 13.3%. The following formula is used to compute the user cost of capital: $c/q = [(p - \pi - d)/(1 - t)]\ (1 - tz)$.

c is the annual value of revenue from the investment, q is the purchase price of the capital good, p is the after-tax financial cost of capital, ii is the rate of inflation, d is the rate of geometric depreciation, t is the marginal tax rate, and z is the present value of depreciation allowances per dollar of investment. In the case of expensing, z = 1.0; and in the case of regular depreciation, z = 0.2814.

a. Percentage points, not percent.

---

[14] Douglas Holtz-Eakin, "Should Small Businesses Be Tax-Favored?" *Tax Notes*, vol. 48, No. 3, September 1995, p. 389. (Dr. Holtz-Eakin served as Director, Congressional Budget Office, from 2003 to 2005).

In FY2018, according to the Joint Committee on Taxation, the allowance may produce a revenue loss of $50.4 billion (see Table 1). But the allowance does not necessarily produce a revenue loss. Its revenue effect generally hinges on the aggregate amount of U.S. investment in qualified assets in a particular tax year. In periods of rising business investment, the allowance is likely to generate substantial revenue losses because a share of the total cost of that investment is expensed. But the reverse is likely to happen in periods of declining investment, when the revenue gains from recent claims for the allowance exceed the revenue loss from new uses of it. Any shift from revenue loss to gain simply reflects the timing of depreciation deductions under current law. Firms that write off the entire cost of an asset in the year when it is placed in service under Section 179 can claim no additional depreciation allowances against future profits. In effect, they exchange a lower tax liability in the present for larger tax liabilities in the future. But companies making this tradeoff come out ahead, particularly in the case of relatively long-lived assets, since the present value of all depreciation deductions is greater with expensing than it is with less accelerated methods of depreciation. In other words, a company is better off with expensing than without it because one dollar of tax savings in the present is worth more than one dollar of tax savings in a future year.

Amortization of Business Start-Up Costs

A key concept underlying the federal income tax is that business taxable income should exclude all costs incurred in earning it. Consequently, companies are allowed to deduct as current expenses all ordinary and necessary costs paid or incurred in conducting a trade or business in determining their taxable income. The concept also implies that costs paid or incurred in starting or organizing a business should not be treated as current expenses, as they are not directly related to the generation of income. Rather, because these expenses are incurred in an attempt to create a capital asset (namely, the business) with a useful life that is likely to extend beyond a single tax year, they should be capitalized, added to the owner's basis in the business, and recovered when the business is sold or ceases to exist.

IRC Section 195 (as amended by the American Jobs Creation Act of 2004 or AJCA, P.L. 108-357) deviates from this principle by permitting individuals who incur business start-up and organizational costs after October 22, 2004, to deduct up to $5,000 of those costs in the year when the new trade or business begins to operate. This deduction is reduced, dollar for dollar (but not below zero), by the amount by which eligible expenditures exceed $50,000. Expenditures that cannot be deducted may be amortized over 15 years, beginning in the first month the new trade or business earns income. In order to claim the $5,000 deduction, a taxpayer must have an equity interest in the trade or business and actively participate in its management.

The Small Business Job Creation Act of 2010 (P.L. 111-240) raised the deduction to $10,000 and the phaseout threshold to $60,000 for qualified start-up and organizational expenses incurred or paid in 2010 only. These higher amounts have not been extended.

To qualify for the deduction, start-up and organizational costs must meet two requirements. First, they must be paid or incurred as part of an investigation into creating or acquiring an active trade or business, as part of starting a new trade or business, or as part of an effort to produce income or profit before starting a trade or business with the aim of converting the effort into an active trade or business. Second, the costs must be similar in kind to costs that would be deductible if they were paid or incurred in connection with the expansion of an active trade or business in the same industry.

Businesses that incurred or paid business start-up and organizational costs and then entered a trade or business on or before October 22, 2004, were allowed to amortize (or deduct in equal annual amounts) those expenditures over five or more years, beginning in the month when the new trade or business commenced.

The option to deduct as much as $5,000 in business start-up and organizational costs in the first year of operation permits the owner of a new firm to deduct expenses in the year when the business begins. Without such a provision, the expenses could not be recovered until the owner sells his or her interest in the business or five years after the business started, whichever comes first. As a result, the option accelerates the recovery of certain business expenses, and this acceleration can aid the growth of small start-up firms by reducing their cost of capital and increasing their cash flow at a time when their access to financial capital may be restricted. For firms that lose money in their first year of operation, the deduction adds to their net operating losses, which may be carried forward up to 20 years and used to offset future taxes paid or owed.[15]

Cash-Basis Accounting

IRC Section 446 requires firms to compute their taxable income using the same method of accounting they regularly employ in keeping their books, as long as that method clearly reflects income for tax purposes. A business taxpayer's method of accounting clearly reflects income if it treats items of income and deductions consistently from one tax year to the next. Permissible methods of accounting include the cash-receipts method, the accrual method, the installment method, the long-term-contract method, the crop method, the special methods for research and development expenditures, and the method for soil and water conservation expenditures.

Two methods of financial accounting are widely used in the private sector: cash-basis and accrual-basis. Under the former, which is the preferred method for self-employed individuals, income generally is recorded when it is received in the form of cash or its equivalent, and expenses generally are recorded when they are paid, regardless of when the income is actually earned or the expenses are actually incurred.

---

[15] Under the American Recovery and Reinvestment Act of 2009 (P.L. 111-5), eligible firms with net operating losses in the 2008 tax year may carry them back up to five years. Only firms with average annual gross receipts in the past three tax years of less than $15 million may take advantage of this expanded carryback.

Under accrual-basis accounting, income and expenses generally are recorded when the transactions giving rise to them are completed or nearly completed, regardless of when cash or its equivalent is received or paid. More specifically, a firm using accrual-basis accounting records income when its right to receive it is established and records expenses when the amounts are fixed and its liability for them established.

Each accounting method has its advantages. Cash-basis accounting is much simpler to administer and allows firms that employ it to control the timing of the recognition of items of income or deductions. In contrast, accrual-basis accounting often yields a more accurate measure of a firm's economic income because it matches income with expenses with greater precision and rigor.

Under certain circumstances, the accrual method must be used for tax purposes. For instance, when keeping an inventory is necessary to the operation of a business, a taxpayer must use the accrual method in computing taxable income—unless the IRS determines that another method clearly reflects income and may be used instead. Inventories are considered necessary when a firm earns income from the production, purchase, or sale of merchandise. In addition, C corporations, partnerships with C corporations as partners, trusts that earn unrelated business income, and authorized tax shelters generally are required to use the accrual method of accounting.

But there are some exceptions to these rules. Beginning in 2018, any partnership or C corporation with average annual gross receipts of $25 million or less in the three previous tax years may use the cash method of accounting. Individuals, S corporations, and qualifying partnerships and personal service corporations also have the option of using the method. This dollar threshold is indexed for inflation, starting in 2019.

As these exceptions show, many of the eligible firms are relatively small in receipt size. In effect, the cash method offers the same benefit to small firms as the expensing allowance under Section 179 does: the deferral of income tax payments. The federal tax code operates in part on the principle that a firm receives income when it gains the legal right to be paid for something it has provided. But under the cash method, firms have greater control over the timing of receipts and payments for expenses than they do under the accrual method. As a result, firms using the cash method have the option of deferring the payment of taxes, or taking advantage of lower tax rates by shifting deductions and the recognition of income from one tax year to the next.

Despite the potential benefits to eligible small firms from using the cash method, it may not always be in their self-interest to do so. A case in point: a small business might be better off using accrual-basis accounting if it needs to periodically issue accurate and reliable financial reports. Cash-basis accounting can distort a firm's financial position in at least two ways.[16] First, because it records transactions involving only cash or its equivalent, the method excludes transactions involving exchanges of assets or liabilities. Second, the determination of net income under cash-basis accounting can be manipulated by recording revenues or expenses long before or after goods and services are produced or sold.

Exemption from Limitation on the Deduction for Business Interest Expenses

Before the enactment of P.L. 115-97, interest and other borrowing expenses incurred in the pursuit of a trade or business were generally deductible from a company's gross income in the year when the expenses were paid or incurred under Section 163. No deduction was allowed for interest paid on tax-exempt bonds, interest from unregistered obligations, interest paid on insurance contracts, and interest paid on original discount, high-yield obligations.

The act placed a limit on the amount of business interest a company can deduct; this limit applies to all legal forms of business organization. Under Section 163(j) as amended by the 2017 act, the deduction for business interest expenses in any tax year is limited to the sum of a firm's interest income, 30% of its adjusted taxable income, and any floor-plan

[16] See Robert Libby, Patricia A. Libby, and Daniel G. Short, *Financial Accounting* (Chicago: Irwin, 1996), p. 111.

financing interest it paid or incurred. Interest that cannot be deducted may be carried forward indefinitely, subject to certain restrictions for partnerships and S corporations.

Adjusted taxable income is defined as a company's regular taxable income calculated without (1) any item of income, gain, deduction, or loss not allocated to a trade or business, (2) any business interest or business interest income, (3) a deduction for net operating losses, (4) the 20% deduction for qualified passthrough business income under Section 199A, and (5) any allowable deduction for depreciation, depletion, or amortization in the years before 2022. Floor-plan financing interest is the interest paid or accrued on debt used to finance the acquisition of motor vehicles held for sale or lease to customers and secured by seller's inventory.

Companies with average annual gross receipts in the previous three tax years of $25 million or less are exempt from this limitation. There is no estimate of the revenue forgone because of this exclusion.

Tax Incentives for Equity Investment in Small Firms

Several tax provisions benefit smaller enterprises by encouraging equity investment in qualified small firms that otherwise may have trouble raising needed funds. The provisions, which are described below, do so by increasing the potential after-tax returns or reducing the potential after-tax losses on such investment, relative to alternative investment options. The same tax benefits are not available to individuals investing in larger firms.

Full Exclusion of Capital Gains on Eligible Small Business Stock

Two key considerations in determining the income tax liability for many individuals are the recognition of income as ordinary or capital gain, and the difference between long-term and short-term capital gains or losses.

A capital gain or loss arises when a capital asset such as a stock or bond is sold or exchanged. If the selling price is greater than the acquisition or purchase price, the transaction produces a capital gain. Conversely, a capital loss results when the reverse is true.

Capital assets held longer than 12 months and then sold or exchanged give rise to what are known as long-term capital gains or losses, whereas sales or exchanges of capital assets held one year or less generate short-term capital gains or losses. Short-term capital gains are considered ordinary income and taxed at regular income tax rates. By contrast, long-term capital gains are considered capital income and taxed in 2018 at 20% for single filers with taxable incomes of $425,800 or more and joint filers with taxable incomes of $479,000 or more; 15% for single filers with taxable incomes between $38,600 and $425,800 and joint filers with taxable incomes between $77,200 and $479,000, and 0% for single filers with taxable incomes below $38,600 and joint filers with taxable incomes below $77,200.

IRC Section 1202 allows noncorporate taxpayers (including partnerships, LLCs, and S corporations) to permanently exclude from gross income the entire gain from the sale or exchange of qualified small business stock (QSBS) that has been held for a minimum of five years and a day. More precisely, the exclusion is 100% for QSBS acquired after September 27, 2010. For QSBS acquired between August 11, 1993, and February 17, 2009, 50% of any gain on its sale or exchange may be excluded. The exclusion is 75% for QSBS acquired between February 18, 2009, and September 27, 2010.

There is a total limit on the gain from stock issued by an eligible corporation that a taxpayer may exclude. In any tax year, the gain cannot exceed the greater of 10 times the taxpayer's adjusted basis in all QSBS issued by that firm and sold or exchanged by the taxpayer during that year, or $10 million—reduced by any excluded gains from sales of the same stock in previous years. This means that the amount a taxpayer may exclude over time from the sale of a firm's QSBS cannot exceed $10 million. Any remaining gain is taxed at a fixed rate of 28%.

To qualify for the partial exclusion, small business stock must satisfy several requirements. First, it must be issued after August 10, 1993, and acquired by the taxpayer at its original issue, either directly or through an underwriter, in exchange for money, property, or as compensation for services rendered to the issuing corporation. Second, the stock must be issued by a domestic C corporation whose gross assets do not exceed $50 million before the stock is issued. Third, at least 80% of an eligible corporation's assets must be deployed in the active conduct of one or more qualified trades or businesses during "substantially all" of the requisite five-year holding period. Assets used for working capital, start-up activities, and research and development meet the active business test, even if they are devoted mainly to the development of future lines of business. Specialized small business investment companies licensed under the Small Business Investment Act of 1958 also meet the active business test, making their stock eligible for the gain exclusion.

Stock issued by C corporations with less than $50 million in gross assets is eligible for the exclusion if the issuing corporation is primarily engaged in an eligible trade or business. All trades and lines of business are eligible except the following: health care, law, engineering, architecture, hospitality, farming, insurance, finance, and mineral extraction. Stock issued by the following small C corporations is also ineligible for the exclusion: current or former domestic international sales corporations (DISCs), regulated investment companies (RICs), real estate investment trusts (REITs), real estate mortgage investment conduits (REMICs), financial asset securitization investment trusts (FASITs), cooperatives, or C corporations that have claimed the possessions tax credit under IRC Section 936.

The full exclusion for QSBS is intended to improve the access of small start-up firms in manufacturing and certain other industries to what might be called patient equity capital. It accomplishes this by increasing the potential after-tax returns an investor can earn on purchases of QSBS, relative to the potential after-tax returns on other investment opportunities, over five years. Under current law, the maximum capital gains rate is 20% and the exclusion is 100% of realized gains from QSBS acquired after September 27, 2010. A full exclusion yields an effective capital gains tax rate of 0% for QSBS. Supporters of the 100% exclusion say it is needed to compensate for the uncertainty and asymmetric information that surrounds the growth prospects of new start-up firms in industries where sizable upfront investments in activities such as research and development are critical to their survival and expansion.

There is some evidence that the exclusion reduces the cost of capital for eligible C corporations issuing QSBS. In a 1999 study of the issue prices for such stock just before and after the enactment of Section 1202, David Guenther and Michael Willenborg found that the prices of QSBS issued by a sample of eligible firms after the tax change were "significantly higher than the issue prices before the change.[17] Meanwhile, there were no significant differences in the issue prices for a sample of firms that were ineligible to issue QSBS. They concluded that nearly all the future benefits from the capital gains rate reduction were being passed on to issuing corporations in the form of higher stock prices, instead of being captured by investors. All other things being equal, rising stock prices lower a firm's cost of capital.

Still, not everyone thinks the gains exclusion is a good idea. Alan Viard of the American Enterprise Institute, while recognizing the efficiency gains from using equity instead of debt to finance new investments, has argued that the exclusion is undesirable because it distorts the allocation of investment capital. As he noted in a 2012 article, the tax preference encourages equity investment in very small companies in certain industries only and may be claimed by certain investors only, not by all investors.[18] In his view, the rules governing the use of the exclusion dampen its economic impact.

Losses on Small Business Investment Company Stock Treated as Ordinary Losses without Limitation

Generally, losses on investments in stock are treated as capital losses for tax purposes. They may be used to offset any capital gains a taxpayer has in the same tax year. Individuals may also use any combination of

---

[17] David A. Guenther and Michael Willenborg, "Capital Gains Tax Rates and the Cost of Capital for Small Business: Evidence from the IPO Market," *Journal of Financial Economics*, v. 53, 1999, p. 401.

[18] Alan D. Viard, "The Misdirected Debate and the Small Business Stock Exclusion," *Tax Notes*, February 6, 2012, p. 741.

short-term and long-term capital losses to offset up to $3,000 in ordinary income in a tax year.

Under IRC Section 1242, however, individuals who invest in small business investment companies (SBICs) are permitted to deduct from their ordinary income all losses from the sale or exchange or worthlessness of stock they hold in these companies. This exception from the general rule is intended to foster equity investment in these companies by lowering the potential after-tax loss on an investment in an SBIC, relative to the potential after-tax loss on other investments.

SBICs are private regulated investment corporations that are licensed under the Small Business Investment Act of 1958 to provide equity capital, long-term loans, and managerial guidance to firms with a net worth of less than $18 million and an average net income of less than $6 million in the previous two years. SBICs use their own capital and funds borrowed at favorable rates as a result of SBA loan guarantees to make equity and debt investments in qualified firms. For tax purposes, most SBICs are treated as C corporations.

Ordinary Income Treatment of Losses on Sales of Small Business Stock

IRC Section 1244 allows taxpayers to treat any loss from the sale, exchange, or worthlessness of qualified small business stock as an ordinary loss rather than a capital loss. For business taxpayers, ordinary losses are treated as business losses in computing a net operating loss.

To qualify for this treatment, stock must meet four requirements. First, it must be issued by a small business corporation after November 6, 1978. A small business corporation is defined as a domestic C corporation whose cash and property received as a contribution to capital and paid-in surplus totals less than $1 million at the time the stock is issued. Second, the stock must be acquired by an individual investor or a partnership in exchange for money or other property (but not stock and securities). Third, during the five tax years before a loss on the stock is recognized, the small business corporation must derive more than 50% of its gross receipts from sources other than royalties, rents, dividends, interest, annuities, and stock or security transactions. The amount that may be deducted as an ordinary loss in a tax year is capped at $50,000 for single filers and $100,000 for married couples filing jointly.

Uniform Capitalization of Inventory Costs

Firms that earn income from the production, purchase, or sale of merchandise are required to maintain inventories in order to account for the cost of goods sold during a tax year. This cost is subtracted from gross receipts in the computation of taxable income. In most cases, the cost of goods sold is determined by adding the value of a firm's inventory at the beginning of the year to purchases of inventory items made during the year and subtracting that amount from the value of the firm's inventory at the end of the year.

IRC Section 263A requires business taxpayers engaged in the production of real or tangible property, or in the purchase of real or tangible and intangible property for resale, to "capitalize" (i.e., include in the estimated value of their inventories) both the direct costs of the property included in inventory and the indirect costs that can be allocated to it. This rule is known as the uniform capitalization rule and was added to the tax code by the Tax Reform Act of 1986. In general, direct costs are considered the material and labor costs related to the production or acquisition of goods, and indirect costs refer to all other costs incurred through the production or acquisition of goods (e.g., repair and maintenance of equipment and facilities, utilities, insurance, rental of equipment, land, or facilities, and certain administrative costs). Taxpayers have some discretion in assigning indirect costs to production or resale activities, but the methods used to allocate the costs should yield reasonable and defensible results for the trade or business.

Some small firms, however, are exempt from the uniform capitalization rule. Specifically, it does not apply to firms with average annual gross receipts of $25 million or less in the last three tax years that acquire tangible or intangible property for resale. This exemption is beneficial because eligible firms have lower administrative costs, face less complexity in complying with income tax laws, and can exercise more control over the timing of business expense deductions, opening up opportunities for the deferral of income tax liabilities.[19]

Simplified Dollar-Value LIFO Accounting Method for Small Firms

Businesses that maintain inventories to account for the cost of goods sold are required to estimate the value of their inventories at the beginning and at the end of each tax year. Since doing this item by item is time-consuming and costly, many taxpayers use estimation methods that assume certain item or cost flows.

One such method is known as "last-in-first-out" (or LIFO). LIFO operates on the assumption that the most recently acquired goods are sold before all other goods. Consequently, LIFO assigns the most recent unit costs to the cost of goods sold and the oldest unit costs to the remaining inventory at the end of the year. The method can be advantageous during periods when the cost of many inventory items is rising, since it yields a lower taxable income and inventory valuation than other methods. There are various ways to apply LIFO. A widely used application is known as the dollar-value method. Under it, a taxpayer accounts for the value of its inventories on the basis of a pool of dollars rather than a pool of specific items. Each dollar pool includes the value of a variety of inventory items and is measured by the dollar value of the items in their base year, which is the year when they were first added to the inventory. Use of the dollar-value method is complicated and costly and thus beyond the reach of most small firms.[20]

---

[19] See Paul G. Schloemer, "Simplifying the Uniform Inventory Capitalization Rules," *Tax Notes*, vol. 53, no. 9, December 2, 1991, pp. 1065-1069.

[20] For more details on this method, see U.S. Congress, Joint Committee on Taxation, *Impact on Small Business of Replacing the Federal Income Tax*, JCS-3-96 (Washington, April 23, 1996), pp. 18-19.

But IRC Section 474, which was added to the tax code by the Tax Reform Act of 1986, allows certain small firms to use a simplified dollar-value LIFO method. It differs from the regular dollar-value method in how the inventory items are pooled and how the base-year value of the pooled items is estimated. Firms with average annual gross receipts of $5 million or less in the three previous tax years are allowed to use the simplified method.

Nonrefundable Tax Credit for Pension Plan Start-Up Costs of Small Firms

Under IRC Section 45E, certain small firms may claim a nonrefundable tax credit for a portion of the start-up costs incurred in setting up new retirement plans for employees. The credit, which was enacted as part of the Economic Growth and Tax Relief Reconciliation Act of 2001, began in 2002 and originally was scheduled to expire (or "sunset") at the end of 2010. But a provision of the Pension Protection Act of 2006 permanently extended the credit. It is a component of the general business credit under IRC Section 38 and thus subject to its dollar limitations and rules for carryover.

The credit is equal to 50% of the first $1,000 in eligible costs paid or incurred in each of the first three years a qualified pension plan is operative. Eligible costs consist of the ordinary and necessary expenses associated with administering the plan and informing employees about the plan's benefits and requirements. Any new defined benefit or defined contribution plan, savings incentive match plan for employees, or simplified employee pension plan qualifies for the credit. Only firms with fewer than 100 employees, each of whom received at least $5,000 in compensation in the previous year, are allowed to claim the credit if at least one highly compensated employee participates in the plan. The maximum credit an eligible firm can claim is $1,500 (.5 x $3,000).

In effect, the credit gives owners of small firms an incentive to establish pension plans for employees by lowering the after-tax cost of setting up and administering these plans over the first three years they are available. Supporters of the credit say the reduced cost should spur increased plan sponsorship among small employers. As a 2010 report issued by the SBA made clear, startup costs can be considerable on a per-employee basis for companies with relatively few employees.[21] Yet available data on pension benefits by employer size offer no clear evidence that the credit has had its intended effect on the share of small employers offering pension plans. According to figures published by the Employee Benefit Research Institute (EBRI), the percentage of firms with fewer than 100 employees sponsoring pension plans was lower in 2013 (the most recent year for which survey results are available) than it was in 2002, the first year the credit was available.[22]

Nonrefundable Tax Credit for Expenses Paid or Incurred in Making a Business More Accessible for Disabled Persons

Under IRC Section 44, an eligible small firm may claim a nonrefundable tax credit for expenses incurred in making its business facilities more accessible for disabled employees. The credit is equal to 50% of eligible expenditures in a tax year above $250 but not greater than $10,250; it is capped at $5,000 for a firm in a tax year.

---

[21] See Kathryn Kobe, *Small Business Retirement Plan Availability and Worker Participation* SBA Office of Advocacy, contract no. SBA-HQ-06M0477 (Washington: March 2010), p. 22.

[22] In 2013, according to an EBRI report, 10.3% of firms with fewer than 10 employees sponsored pension plans; the share in 2002 was 16.5%; for firms with 10 to 49 employees, the 2013 share was 24.0%, and the 2002 share 31.4%; and for firms with 50 to 99 employees, the 2013 share was 36.1%, and the 2002 share 46.9%. See Employee Benefit research Institute, "Employment-Based Retirement Plan Participation: Geographic Differences and Trends, 2013," *Issue Brief*, no. 405 (Washington, Oct., 2014), Figure 2, p. 11; and "Employment-Based Retirement and Pension Plan Participation: Declining Levels and Geographic Differences," *Issue Brief*, no. 262 (Washington: October 2003), Figure 2, p. 7.

In the case of a partnership and S corporation, this upper limit applies separately at the entity level, and at the partner or shareholder level. The disabled-access credit is a component of the general business credit under IRC Section 38 and thus subject to its dollar limitations and rules for carry-forward and carry-back.

A firm may claim the credit if, during its previous tax year, its gross receipts (less any returns and allowances) totaled no more than $1 million, or its full-time equivalent (FTE) work force did not exceed 30 persons.

Any amount an eligible small firm pays or incurs to bring its business into compliance with the Americans with Disabilities Act of 1990 (ADA) qualifies for the credit. The expenses must be reasonable in amount and required by law. Eligible expenses include the cost of removing architectural, communication, transportation, or physical barriers to making a business accessible to or usable by disabled individuals; providing interpreters or other effective methods of making materials understandable to hearing-impaired individuals; and supplying qualified readers, taped texts, and other effective methods of making materials understandable to visually impaired individuals.

The credit is intended to lower the net cost to smaller firms of complying with the mandates of the ADA and to encourage them to hire more disabled persons. Although the credit has been available for over two decades, it remains unclear how effective it has been in stimulating business investment in making workplaces more accommodative to the special needs of disabled persons seeking employment. In a 2002 report, the then-named General Accounting Office (GAO) noted that it could find no studies of the effectiveness of the credit and that few businesses were even aware of it.[23] It appears that no such studies have been done since 2002.

---

[23] U.S. General Accounting Office, *Incentives to Employ Workers with Disabilities Receive Limited Use and Have an Uncertain Impact*, GAO-03-39 (Washington: December 2002), p. 19.

Nonrefundable Tax Credit for Employee Health Insurance Expenses

The Patient Protection and Affordable Care Act (ACA, P.L. 111-148) added a provision to the federal tax code (IRC Section 45R) that grants certain small employers a tax credit for nonelective contributions to health plans that cover at least 50% of the cost for participating employees. An employer's contribution is considered nonelective if it does not involve a reduction in participating employees' salaries or wages.

Eligible employers have been able to take the credit since the 2010 tax year. From 2010 through 2013, the maximum credit was equal to 35% of the *lesser* of the total amount of an employer's nonelective contributions during a tax year for the payment of qualified health insurance for its employees through a "contribution arrangement," or the total amount of nonelective contributions that would have been made if each employee had enrolled in a qualified health plan with a premium equal to the average premium for the small-group market in the state where the employer is located. Under such a scheme, an employer may not claim the credit for the portion of employer-paid premiums above the average premium for the small-group market where the employer is located.

Employers with up to 25 or fewer full-time employees who earn an average annual compensation of $50,000 or less can benefit from the credit, but the full credit may be claimed only by employers with 10 or fewer full-time employees with an average annual compensation of $25,000 or less. The credit phases out by 6.667% for each full-time employee above 10, and by 4% for every $1,000 in average annual compensation above $25,000.

For tax years beginning in 2014, an eligible employer may claim the credit no more than two consecutive tax years (e.g., 2014 and 2015) if it offers one or more qualified health plans through a state-based health insurance exchange. Each state was required to establish such an exchange by 2014. The maximum credit for tax years after 2013 will be equal to 50% of the *lesser* of the total amount of employer contributions for qualified health plans offered through an exchange, or the total amount of employer contributions that would have been made that year if each employee had enrolled in a qualified health plan with a premium equal to the average premium for the small-group market in the rating area where the employees receive coverage. The credit does not apply to premiums deemed excessive.

Several rules governing the use of the credit affect its effective rate. The credit is a component of the general business credit (GBC), and thus subject to its limitations. Unused GBCs may be carried back one year or forward up to 20 years. Any credit not used by the end of the 20-year carry-forward period may be deducted in its entirety for the next tax year. Since 2011, employers have been able to take the credit against both the regular income and alternative minimum taxes. But to prevent employers from deriving two tax benefits from the same expenditures, any employer taking the credit must reduce its deduction for employer-paid health insurance premiums by the amount of the credit.

The credit is intended to increase the share of employers with 25 or fewer low-wage employees that offer health insurance to employees. It does so by lowering the after-tax cost of coverage by as much as 35% from 2010 to 2013 and by as much as 50% in any two consecutive years starting in 2014 for firms with sufficient tax liability.

Congress added the credit to the ACA in part to address a longstanding concern about gaps in the domestic web of employer-provided health insurance. While the vast majority of large employers offer health benefits to employees, a much smaller share of small employers have done so, and the share is even smaller for small employers with mostly low-wage workers. According to the latest survey of employer health benefits by the Henry J. Kaiser Family Foundation (KFF) and the Health Research and Educational Trust (HRET), 96% of employers with 100 or more employees offered health benefits in 2017, compared with 90% of employers with 50 to 99 employees and 50% of employers with 3 to 49 employees. Among all the employers surveyed, regardless of their employment size, 64% of those with relatively low ratio of low-wage workers (defined as those earning

$24,000 or less) to total workers offered health benefits in 2017, whereas 44% of those with a relatively high ratio did so.[24]

MAIN ARGUMENTS FOR AND AGAINST FEDERAL SUPPORT FOR SMALL BUSINESS

Available data indicate that small firms play a major role, on the whole, in domestic economic activity. For example, according to figures published by the SBA, firms with fewer than 500 employees accounted for 99.9% of all domestic firms, 99.7% of firms with paid employees, and 48.0% of private-sector employment in 2013.[25] These indicators of economic importance raise the question of why government assistance is needed when small firms typically account for substantial shares of employment and output and make important contributions to technological innovation over time.

The answer to this question is no trivial matter. Small firms could receive more than $17 billion in federal tax benefits in FY2018[26]—in addition to the subsidies they obtain through other federal programs targeted at small businesses. As with any public expenditure, this support carries an opportunity cost in the form of alternative uses of these funds and their potential economic effects. If it turns out that there is no sound economic justification for existing federal government support for small business, then one could argue that the U.S. economy would be better off using the funds going to small firms for other purposes with significant economic effects, such as investing in infrastructure expansion and modernization, research and development, or deficit reduction.

This section describes the chief arguments for and against government support (including tax preferences) for small businesses.

---

[24] Henry J. Kaiser Family Foundation and Health Research & Educational Trust, *Employer Health Benefits 2017 Annual Survey*, (Washington, DC: Sept. 19, 2017), pp. 10 and 60, http://files.kff.org/attachment/Report-EmployerHealth-Benefits-Annual-Survey-2017.

[25] See U.S. Small Business Administration, Office of Advocacy, *Frequently Asked Questions*, June 2016, https://www.sba.gov/sites/default/files/advocacy/SB-FAQ-2016_WEB.pdf.

[26] See **Table 1** beginning on p. 6.

Arguments in Favor of Government Support

Proponents of government support for small business generally cite four reasons why they believe it is justified: (1) the special economic role played by small firms; (2) the financial barriers to their formation and growth; (3) the impact of relatively high marginal tax rates on the formation and growth of small entrepreneurial firms; and (4) the unique opportunities for individual economic advancement created by small business ownership.

Special Economic Role of Small Firms

Many lawmakers cite the economic importance of small firms as a primary reason to support them through government programs and other subsidies. For example, in remarks made on the floor of the Senate in 2003, Senator Olympia Snowe urged her colleagues to back the creation of more tax benefits for small firms by noting that "they represent 99% of all employers, employ 51% of private-sector workforce, provide about 75% of the net new jobs, contribute 51% of the private-sector output, and represent 96% of all exporters of goods."[27] Statements such as this suggest that small firms in general deserve federal support, not because they are prone to some kind of market failure, but because they play an important role in economic activity.

Some proponents of government support for small businesses take this line of reasoning a step further by arguing that small firms generate uniquely valuable economic benefits. These benefits, they say, can be seen in the multitude of jobs and new technologies small firms create over time, their innumerable and ever-changing linkages to larger firms in supply chains, and their unique contributions to economic renewal and growth. Proponents maintain that the net effect of these activities is to accelerate the growth of the U.S. economy in ways that large firms cannot.

---

[27] Sen. Olympia Snowe, remarks in the Senate, *Congressional Record*, daily edition, vol. 149, no. 6, January 14, 2003, p. S299.

Job Creation

On the issue of job creation, those who favor government support for small firms note that SBA data show that firms with fewer than 500 employees accounted for 63.3% of net job creation from 1992 to 2013.[28] The data also indicate that, though many small firms fail within five years of starting up, the survivors, especially firms known as gazelles because of their rapid growth starting at a young age, typically create enough jobs to more than offset those lost because of firms going out of business.

Technological Innovation

On the issue of technological innovation, proponents of government support for small firms cite several findings from the literature on firm size and technological innovation. One study found that the contributions of small firms to innovation varied by industry, and that their contributions tended to be most important in industries where no firm had established substantial market power.[29]

Another study concluded that in certain industries, small start-up firms were more adept than large established ones at identifying promising commercial applications for new technologies and exploiting them. More specifically, the study provided evidence that during the 1980s and 1990s, there were many instances in which small start-up firms gained temporary competitive advantages over larger established rivals in the commercial development of new technologies in biotechnology, microelectronics, computer software, and electronic commerce.[30]

A 2003 study by CHI Research, Inc. uncovered further evidence that small firms have made important contributions over time to the commercial development of new technologies. The researchers found that firms with fewer than 500 employees held 41% of all patents filed by U.S. corporations from 1996 to 2000. The study also found that those firms

---

[28] SBA, Office of Advocacy, *Frequently Asked Questions*, June 2016.

[29] Joshua Lerner, "Small Business, Innovation, and Public Policy," in *Are Small Firms Important? Their Role and Impact*, Zoltan Acs ed., Kluwer (Academic Publishers: 1999), p. 160.

[30] Ibid., p. 160.

received 13 to 14 times as many patents per employee as larger firms did.[31] Furthermore, the results showed that small firms filed 25% of the patents related to biotechnology, 19% of the patents related to pharmaceuticals, 11% of the patents related to medical equipment and electronics, and 9% of the patents related to chemicals other than pharmaceuticals.[32]

According to a 2011 study of small business innovation in "green" technologies, among all firms awarded 15 or more patents between 2005 and 2009; small firms were 16 times more prolific than other firms. In this case, productivity was measured on the basis of the number of patent awards per employee. Innovative firms with fewer than 500 employees acquired an average of 27 patents per employee, compared to an average of 1.6 patents per employee for larger firms.[33]

Industrial Supply Chains

Proponents of government support for small business also contend that such support is needed because of the special roles many small firms play in industrial supply chains involving large companies in a variety of industries. To substantiate this claim, they point to evidence that small firms have tended to supply certain goods and services more efficiently than larger ones. For instance, economist Bo Carlsson noted in a 1999 study that such an efficiency edge was apparent in industries where economies of scale in production were the main drivers of competition and success. Foremost among the industries exhibiting this linkage were computers, automobiles, and steel.[34] In industries such as these, small and large firms specialized in providing specific products or services. The two groups ended up interacting more as partners or suppliers than as competitors. In Carlsson's view, the dramatic rise in foreign outsourcing among large U.S. manufacturing firms in the 1990s reinforced this pattern

---

31 CHI Research, Inc., *Small Serial Innovators: The Small Firm Contribution to Technical Change*, report for the Small Business Administration (Washington: 2003), p 3.

32 Ibid., p. 17.

33 Small Business Administration, Office of Advocacy, *Analysis of Small Business Innovation in Green Technologies*, no. 389, summary of findings (Washington: October 2011).

34 Bo Carlsson, "Small Business, Entrepreneurship, and Industrial Dynamics," in *Are Small Firms Important? Their Role and Impact*, Zoltan J. Acs, ed. (Boston: Kluwer Academic Publishers, 1999), p. 100.

of specialization between large and small firms. His findings led him to conclude that small firms in general possessed at least one significant advantage over larger firms in the supply chains that underpinned the U.S. economy: small firms could act with greater flexibility and speed in responding to new market opportunities and emerging competitive threats.

Opportunities for the Economic Advancement of Immigrants, Women, and Members of Minority Groups

Proponents of government support for small business also cite the financial (and social) benefits of small business ownership for women, minority groups, and immigrants and the communities where they live as another reason to provide such support.

They argue that owning and managing a small business gives these individuals opportunities to increase their income and independence and to move into the economic mainstream of the United States. According to data from the American Community Survey conducted by the U.S. Bureau of the Census, 18% of small business owners in 2010 were immigrants, and they employed 14% of all people working for small businesses that year.[35]

In addition, according to proponents, there is evidence that women-, minority-, and immigrant-owned small firms generate benefits for their communities that go beyond job and wealth creation. For example, female small business owners have done more than their male counterparts to encourage openness in workplace communication and decisionmaking, hire a diverse workforce, establish desirable child-care programs, and pay full benefits to employees. In addition, families with self-employed women who work out of their homes seem more stable than the average family.[36] And among minority and immigrant groups, small business ownership

---

[35] David Dyssegaard Kallick, *Immigrant Small Business Owners*, Fiscal Policy Institute (New York: June 2012), p. 1.

[36] See Candida Brush and Robert D. Hisrich, "Women-Owned Businesses: Why Do They Matter?," in *Are Small Firms Important? Their Role and Impact*, pp. 111-127.

encourages the emergence of tight-knit social networks, provides critical job and skills training, and establishes informal local capital markets.[37]

Imperfections in Capital Markets

Another argument made in favor of government support for small businesses concerns the difficulties many younger small firms (especially new small entrepreneurial firms) encounter in raising the financial capital needed to start and grow a business. In their view, government intervention can lessen or offset these difficulties, paving the way to faster rates of domestic business formation, especially businesses given over to commercializing new technologies.

If capital markets were truly efficient, every investment opportunity offering an after-tax rate of return greater than the cost of capital would be funded, regardless of the profitability, cash flow, size, or age of a firm. But proponents of government support for small business say that such a condition applies to relatively few new small firms. In their view, owners of such firms typically experience considerable difficulty in borrowing from lending institutions or attracting equity capital, mainly because lenders and investors lack the information they require to evaluate the profit potential of the proposed venture. As a consequence, aspiring small business owners often are forced to finance projects out of their own resources (e.g., savings accounts, retirement funds, and credit cards) or the resources of friends and family members, or, lacking access to those resources, to abandon the ambition of owning their own business.

Proponents also note that the problem of limited access to capital markets does not affect start-up companies only. Established small business owners may also have difficulty raising capital through borrowing or equity investment.

In light of these difficulties, proponents maintain that government support, especially loan guarantees and tax incentives for equity

[37] See John Sibley Butler and Patricia Gene Greene, "Don't Call Me Small: The Contribution of Ethnic Enterprises to the Economic and Social Well-Being of America," in *Are Small Firms Important? Their Role and Impact* (Boston: Kluwer Academic Publishers, 1999), pp. 129-145.

investment, is needed to enable cash-starved small firms to obtain the funds they need to survive and grow.

Cost of Tax Compliance

Proponents of government support for small firms point to the relatively high tax compliance costs borne by small firms as another reason to grant them some kind preferential treatment through the tax code, at least until the code can be simplified in ways that benefit small business owners. To substantiate this argument, they cite the results of a 2007 study that estimated federal tax compliance costs by various measures of the size of business. Among other things, the researchers found that the compliance burden, as measured by the time and money devoted to tax compliance per employee, was inversely proportional to the size of a business. Specifically, for the 2002 tax year, the estimated financial burden per employee ranged from $8,435 for firms with 1 to 5 employees down to $348 for firms with more than 50 employees.[38] Proponents maintain that large differences between the tax compliance costs for small firms and larger firms could exacerbate any competitive disadvantages the former face in vying with latter for sales or contracts.

Arguments against Government Support for Small Firms

Not everyone agrees that government support for small business is justified on economic grounds. Critics of such support cite the findings of several recent studies as grounds for questioning the economic arguments made by proponents.

A key element of standard economic analysis is that government intervention in the economy is warranted mainly to remedy a market

---

[38] The financial burden is the per-employee sum of the monetized time and money spent on complying with federal taxes. Much of the time burden was given over to recordkeeping, while most of the monetary cost stemmed from hiring paid tax professionals. See DeLuca, Donald, John Guyton, Wu-Lang Lee, John O'Hare, and Scott Stilmar, "Estimates of U.S. Federal Income Tax Compliance Burden for Small Businesses," in *Proceedings of the 100th Annual Conference on Taxation*, Columbus, OH, 2007 (Washington: 2007), table 9, p. 80.

failure. In general, such a failure represents a condition that prevents or hinders the emergence of economically efficient outcomes. Foremost among the market failures identified by economists as justifications for government intervention are the following:

- Lack of perfect competition,
- Presence of public goods,
- Positive or negative external effects (or externalities),
- Incomplete markets, and
- Imperfect or asymmetric information on the part of key economic agents.[39]

Critics of government support for small businesses say there is no evidence that a market failure is affecting (or has affected) trends in small business formation, growth, investment, and failure. More specifically, they can find no evidence that imperfections in financial markets are leading to the formation of too few or the failure of too many small firms, or that small firms in general generate uniquely valuable positive externalities. Therefore, say critics, in the absence of a verifiable market failure, government support (including tax subsidies) for small business seems unwarranted on economic grounds.

Equity Concerns

Proponents of government support for small businesses generally ignore their equity effects in defending them on economic grounds.

But to critics, those effects are one of several reasons to reduce or end such support through the federal tax code. In their view, small business tax preferences undercut the progressivity of the federal individual income tax. Under a progressive income tax, an individual's tax liability depends critically on his or her taxable income. Taxpayers with higher taxable incomes pay a greater share of their income in taxes than do taxpayers with

---

[39] For more information on market failures, see Joseph E. Stiglitz and Jay K. Rosengard, *Economics of the Public Sector*, 4th Edition (New York: W.W. Norton & Co., 2015), pp. 81-98.

lower taxable incomes. Small business tax preferences, however, weaken the link between tax liability and income by lowering the tax burden on the earnings of small firms, the vast share of which are organized as passthrough entities. The earnings of such a business pass through to the owner(s) and are taxed at his/her/their individual income tax rates. A substantial share of those earnings goes to individuals subject to the highest income tax rates. According to an estimate by the Tax Policy Center, passthrough business income represented 31.9% of total adjusted gross income (AGI) for taxpayers in the 39.6% tax bracket in 2017; for taxpayers subject to the 35% and 33% tax brackets, the AGI shares were 27.9% and 17.1%, respectively; the average share for all tax brackets was 8.8% in 2017.[40]

Among public finance economists, it is assumed that individuals, not firms, ultimately bear the burden of business income taxes or reap the benefits of business tax subsidies. Critics of government support for small business argue that these benefits ultimately increase the after-tax earnings of small firms. As a result, small business owners may have lower tax burdens than individuals whose taxable income comes primarily from wages and salaries. In this case, small business tax preferences may interfere with the achievement of horizontal equity in the taxation of household income. Horizontal equity involves taxing individuals with similar taxable incomes in the same manner. Differences in the taxation of key sources of income tend to undermine horizontal equity.

Efficiency Concerns

Some also oppose small business tax subsidies on efficiency grounds. In theory, income taxes reduce economic welfare by driving a wedge between the costs and benefits of the available choices for consumption and production facing consumers and firms, respectively. Standard economic analysis holds that the best possible tax system is one that raises needed revenue without distorting the allocation of economic resources

---

[40] See Urban-Brookings Tax Policy Center, Table T17-0075, Mar. 20, 2017, https://www.taxpolicycenter.org/modelestimates/distribution-business-income-march-2017/distribution-business-income-statutory.

among investment and consumption choices. The only tax that meets such a requirement is a lump-sum tax, since it would impose the same tax on all individuals, regardless of their income or wealth.

Such a view has several notable implications for tax policy:

- The returns to all investments should be taxed at the same rate;
- Any tax that is not uniform across businesses (regardless of size or organizational form) is likely to diminish social welfare;[41] and
- Taxes should not distort a firm's choice of inputs or its investment or production decisions.

Small business tax preferences, say critics, conflict with each of these principles. In their view, an efficient allocation of resources is possible only if the tax code is neutral with regard to business investments and the natural growth and decline of firms.[42] A departure from the neutral taxation of capital income to assist small firms might be warranted if there were something uniquely or extraordinarily valuable about their economic role and if the majority of small firms can play that role only with government support. Proponents of such support contend that small firms, on the whole, demonstrate their unique value by consistently creating more jobs and generating more technological innovations than larger firms. They also claim that those contributions would be placed in jeopardy if the federal government were to stop supporting small firms. Critics call into question the empirical evidence for this argument.

Special Economic Role of Small Firms

Critics disagree with the view that small firms as a whole deserve government support because they make valuable economic contributions that larger firms cannot readily match or duplicate. According to critics, however, there is no evidence that small firms in general have a decisive long-term edge over larger firms in such important economic activities

---

[41] Stiglitz, *Economics of the Public Sector*, pp. 567-569.

[42] Douglas Holtz-Eakin, "Should Small Businesses be Tax-Favored?," *National Tax Journal*, vol. 48, no. 3, September 1995, p. 390.

such as creating jobs, developing new marketable goods and services, improving the efficiency and productivity of supply chains, and promoting beneficial economic change and renewal. They also argue that there is a lack of evidence to substantiate the claim that too few small firms are created over time owing to systematic failures by private lenders and investors to provide adequate financing for start-up firms. Each of these issues tied to the claim that small businesses play a special role in the U.S. economy is examined below.

Small Firms and Job Creation

Critics and proponents of government support for small business largely agree that small firms are responsible for most job growth over time. According to the SBA, firms with 500 or fewer workers created 63.3% of all net new U.S. jobs from 1992 to 2013.[43]

But the two sides differ on the economic significance and policy implications of this contribution. On the one hand, proponents see the large share of net new jobs attributed to small firms as a reason for the federal government to support such firms. Critics, on the other hand, say that the share of net new jobs attributed to small firms does not prove what proponents claim it does. To back their case, they cite certain findings from the academic literature on firm size and job growth.

According to critics, small firms are not consistently better at creating jobs than large firms. To substantiate this claim, they cite a 1994 study by David Birch and James Medoff of U.S. job creation. Birch and Medoff estimated that the share of the total number of net new jobs generated in the late 1980s and early 1990s by firms employing 100 or fewer workers varied from 40% to 140%, depending on the stage of the business cycle.[44]

---

[43] U.S. Small Business Administration, Office of Advocacy, *Frequently Asked Questions*, (Washington: June 2016).

[44] See David Birch and James Medoff, "Gazelles," in *Labor Markets, Employment Policy, and Job Creation*, Lewis C. Solomon and Alec R. Levenson, eds. (Boulder, CO: Westview Press, 1994), p. 162. The share of net new jobs created by firms with 100 or fewer workers can exceed 100% in a year if these firms create more jobs than they destroy, all other firms destroy more jobs than they create, and the net job gain arising from the former exceeds the net job loss arising from the latter. For example, if firms with 100 or fewer employees account for a net job gain of 100 and all other firms generate a net job loss of 25, then the

Critics also point out that there is substantial variation in the number of net new jobs small businesses create from one year to the next. Most jobs created by small firms originate in start-up firms, which typically begin small in employment size. According to a 2011 report by Ian Hathaway and Albert Palacios, firms in existence less than a year accounted for an average of about 3 million jobs per year from 1990 through 2009. By contrast, firms aged from 1 to 5 years lost an average of 622,000 jobs a year; firms aged from 6 to 10 years lost an average of 348,000 a year; and firms that had been in business 11 or more years lost an average of 574,000 a year.[45] This is to say that non-start-up firms lost an average of 1.5 million jobs a year in that period. Hathaway and Palacios also found that the average annual job creation from 1990 to 2009 among start-up firms was 2.906 million, whereas small firms aged 1 to 5 years lost an annual average of 703,000 jobs; those aged from 6 to 10 years lost an annual average of 401,000; and those aged 11 or more years lost an annual average of 849,000.[46] Relatively few start-up firms accounted for most of the job growth.

A 2010 study by economist John Haltiwanger and Ron Jarmin and Javier Miranda from the U.S. Census Bureau supported the findings of the Hathaway-Palacios study.[47] Haltiwanger, Jarmin, and Miranda used data from the Census Bureau Business Dynamics Statistics and Longitudinal Database to test the widely held belief that net job growth over time is negatively related to firm size. The results confirmed the belief when the researchers did not control for the age of firms. But when they did, the evidence for a systematic relationship between firm size and net job growth disappeared. What emerged instead was a systematic relationship between gross and net job creation and the age of firms. More specifically, the results showed that start-ups accounted for disproportionately large shares of job creation and job destruction from 1992 to 2005. They also

---

economy as a whole would realize a net job gain of 75, and the share of that gain attributable to firms with 100 or fewer employees would be 133%.

[45] Hathaway and Palacios, *Small Business and Job Creation: The Unconventional Wisdom*, p. 8.

[46] Ibid., p. 11.

[47] See John C. Haltiwanger, Ron S. Jarmin, and Javier Miranda, *Who Creates Jobs? Small vs. Large vs. Young*, NBER working paper 16300 (Cambridge, MA: August 2010).

indicated that firms over 10 years old and with more than 500 employees accounted for 40% of job creation and destruction. Haltiwanger, Jarmin, and Miranda concluded that young firms exhibit an "up or out dynamic," meaning that they either grow fast or quickly go out of business.

Birch and Medoff discerned a similar trend in their analysis of the small business jobs created during the late 1980s and early 1990s. They called the few firms responsible for this job growth "gazelles," as they grew swiftly from few employees to many employees.[48]

Critics also contend that even if small firms were to create more lasting, well-paying jobs than large firms do over time, there would be no reason to expect government support for small business to generate faster employment growth. Economic analysis shows that an economy generates jobs through a natural process of growth, decline, and structural change. The size distribution of firms seems to be nothing more than a byproduct of this process. This implies that the level of national employment at any point in time is the result of a mix of forces that is bound to overwhelm the employment effects of any government support for small business. Most economists would agree that the key forces are fiscal and monetary policy, consumer spending, business investment, and U.S. exports and imports.

Small Firms and Technological Innovation

Research and development (R&D) is the lifeblood of technological innovation, which, in turn, serves as a powerful engine of long-term economic growth and transformation. Economists generally agree that without government support, business investment in R&D would fall significantly short of socially optimal amounts. Left to their own devices, firms are likely to invest too little in R&D for two reasons. First, they cannot capture all the returns to R&D investment, as other firms find ways to capitalize on the results of research despite patents and other forms of intellectual property protection. Second, some firms (mainly start-up firms) lack access to the funds needed to undertake planned R&D projects because potential lenders and investors lack the information they require to

---

[48] Birch and Medoff, "Gazelles," pp. 162-164.

assess the projects' profit and the firms' survival potential.[49] Economists generally view the predisposition of businesses to invest suboptimal amounts in R&D as a market failure. This is because the external economic benefits (or positive externalities) from the investments seem to have little or no influence on the investment decisions of private companies. To remedy this shortcoming, many economists call for the adoption of government measures aimed at spurring greater levels of business R&D investment than companies would undertake on their own.

Critics of government support for small businesses maintain there is no good reason for targeting such support at small firms only if the main intent is to spark faster rates of technological innovation. They note that small and large firms develop the new technologies that propel economic growth and encourage lasting shifts in the structure of developed countries' economies.

Moreover, say critics, it is often impossible to disentangle the contributions of smaller firms from larger ones. According to data from the National Center for Science and Engineering Statistics, larger firms typically perform the vast share of business R&D: in 2008 and 2009 combined, for example, companies with fewer than 500 employees accounted for more than 20% of the business R&D (measured in current dollars) conducted in the United States, whereas companies with 1,000 or more employees undertook nearly 76% of those investments.[50]

Available evidence indicates that small firms and large firms tend to have distinct advantages as agents of technological innovation.[51] Historically, small firms have had more success than larger ones in using R&D to generate new industries and dominate the industries' early stages of growth. Smaller firms may also have been more flexible than larger firms in identifying and pursuing commercial applications for emerging innovations. In contrast, large firms more easily raise the funds needed to

[49] Scott J. Wallsten, "Rethinking the Small Business Innovation Research Program," in *Investing in Innovation: Creating a Research and Innovation Policy That Works*, Lewis M. Branscomb and James H. Keller, eds. (Cambridge, MA: MIT Press, 1998), p. 197.

[50] National Science Foundation, National Center for Science and Engineering Statistics, *Business R&D Performed in the United States Cost $291 Billion in 2008 and $282 Billion in* 2009, NSF 12-309 (Arlington, VA: March 2012), table 1, p. 1.

[51] See Wallsten, "Rethinking the Small Business Innovation Research Program," p. 197.

finance the sunken costs involved in many research projects. They are also likely to capture a larger share of the returns to R&D investments through marketing campaigns, the use of intellectual property protection, and the creation of regional, national, and international distribution, service, and repair networks.

According to critics, studies that have looked at the effects of firm size and market structure on innovation have found no consistent proof that a certain firm size is ideal for generating and disseminating new commercial technologies. Rather, their findings indicated that in some industries, small firms were more innovative than large firms, but that in other industries, large firms had a decisive edge in the generation of new technologies.

Critics also point out that the vast majority of U.S. small business owners have no intention of developing a new idea and bringing it to the marketplace. A 2011 study by economists Erik Hurst and Benjamin Pugsley from the University of Chicago noted that only 10% of new businesses that participated in a 2006 survey conducted as part of a Panel Study of Entrepreneurial Dynamics II reported that they planned to develop "proprietary technology, processes, or procedures in the future."[52] By contrast, nearly 80% of the businesses indicated that they had no plans for research and development "to be a majority priority."

Small Firms and the Productivity and Efficiency of Business Supply Chains

Critics of government support for small businesses also challenge the notion that small firms in general play critical roles in improving the efficiency of business supply chains. They cite certain findings of the study by Hurst and Pugsley to make their case. Among other things, Hurst and Pugsley found that about half of the new small businesses they surveyed intended to provide an existing product or service to an existing customer base. In addition, few of those firms showed much desire to grow into big

[52] Erik Hurst and Benjamin Wild Pugsley, *What Do Small Businesses Do?* August 2011, p. 25, available at http://www.brookings.edu/~/media/Files/Programs/ES/BPEA/2011_fall_bpea_papers/ 2011_fall_bpea_conference_hurst.pdf.

firms or to innovate "in any observable way."[53] When asked about their primary reasons for starting a new business, over half of the small business owners said that "nonpecuniary benefits" played a leading role. These benefits included being one's own boss and having a flexible work schedule.

According to Hurst and Pugsley, such behavior was consistent with the industries in which most small firms were concentrated. Using data from the Statistics of U.S. Businesses compiled by the U.S. Census Bureau, they found that two-thirds of small businesses in 2007 were either restaurants, skilled professionals (e.g., doctors, lawyers, accountants), skilled craftsmen (e.g., general contractors, electricians, plumbers), professional service providers (e.g., clergy, insurance agents, real estate agents), or small retailers (e.g., gas stations, pharmacies, grocery and clothing stores).

Critics maintain that these findings call into question the validity of the argument that small firms deserve government support because they serve as indispensable agents for productivity growth and greater efficiency within business supply chains. In their view, the typical small business owner has little or no interest in developing new products or processes that could be sold to large firms. Rather, say critics, he/she is mainly concerned with selling existing goods and services to established customers in the geographic areas they serve.

Small Firms and Economic Renewal and Change

Critics acknowledge that start-up companies that become what Medoff and Birch called "gazelles" can exert a transformative pull on the fabric of markets and industries. Cases in point include Google, Microsoft, Facebook, and Amazon. But they dispute the notion that small firms in general are critical to the processes of economic renewal and change. In their view the gales of creative destruction stirred by such innovative big companies as Amazon and Walmart have done as much as any gazelle to transform entire markets and industries, often to the benefit of consumers. Some say that firms such as these are likely to do more to advance

[53] Ibid., p. 2.

productivity growth and promote economic change over time than any cluster small firms could do.

Hidden Tax on Small Business Growth

Yet another concern raised by government support for small businesses, according to critics, is that the subsidies may offer a robust disincentive to grow to the point that the firms no longer qualify for the government support. This effect, which has been called the "notch problem," is likely to become an issue when the loss of a tax preference effectively penalizes the firms that had benefited from it.

A case in point is the Section 179 expensing allowance. The maximum allowance is set at $1 million in 2018, and the allowance begins to phase out when the total value of qualified assets acquired and placed in service that year exceeds $2.5 million. Firms that purchase and placed in service more than $3.5 million in qualified assets cannot claim the allowance, as the amount that can be expensed is reduced dollar for dollar when a firm's total spending on such assets exceeds the phaseout threshold. Critics maintain that such a design gives firms a tax incentive not to invest more than $2.5 million in qualified assets. Firms that invest more than that amount face implicit tax penalties in the form of higher marginal effective tax rates that increase as the amount of investment over $2.5 million approaches $3.5 million.

CONCLUSION

Available economic data indicate that small firms make significant contributions to the U.S. economy. The magnitude of the contributions depends, of course, on how a small firm is defined. If a small business is defined as a firm with fewer than 500 full-time employees, then it can be said that small businesses account for a majority of private-sector jobs and about half of private-sector output, generate many technological innovations, and serve as agents of renewal and structural change in a variety of industries. But if the threshold were set at fewer than 100 employees, the small business shares of output and employment would be smaller.

The economic contributions of small businesses, however defined, appear to explain part of the longstanding bipartisan support in Congress for government programs to assist small firms.[54] Some of this support is in the form of tax preferences (or expenditures) available to many small firms. The combined revenue loss from these expenditures may top $17 billion in FY2018 (see Table 1).

Current federal small business tax benefits serve one or more of the following four purposes: (1) improving access to equity capital, (2) simplifying tax compliance, (3) promoting capital investments, and (4) achieving other policy objectives. Supporters of these benefits and other federal programs to support small businesses argue that they are needed to eliminate or reduce barriers to the birth, survival, and growth of small businesses, which, in their view, make invaluable contributions to the growth and transformation of the U.S. economy. They point to the vital role played by small firms in job creation and in technological innovation as proof of the special economic importance of small businesses in general. The biggest barrier, they say, is the difficulties many small start-up companies experience in raising the financial capital they require to fund operations, including R&D.

Yet the findings of some studies and recent changes in federal policy toward start-up firm financing raise questions about the accuracy of this economic rationale. In particular, they suggest that current federal support for small businesses may be less effective, on the whole, than it could be in promoting faster job growth and increased investment in such firms.

A 2010 study by economists John Haltiwanger, Ron Jarmin, and Javier Miranda from the U.S. Census Bureau used data from the Census Bureau Business Dynamics Statistics and Longitudinal Database to test the widely held belief that net job growth over time is negatively related to firm size.[55] When the researchers did not consider the ages of the firms, the results

---

[54] Small business owners are also valued for their work as community leaders.

[55] John Haltiwanger, Ron S. Jarmin, and Javier Miranda, "Who Creates Jobs? Small Versus Large Versus Young," *The Review of Economics and Statistics*, vol. 95, no. 2, p. 348.

indicated that smaller firms had faster rates of net job growth than larger firms from 1976 to 2005. But when they considered the age of firms, that relationship fell apart. What emerged instead was a strong correlation between gross and net job creation and the age of firms. More specifically, the results showed that start-ups had disproportionately high rates of both job creation and job destruction over the first 10 years of their existence.

A 2011 study by economists Erik Hurst and Benjamin Pugsley, using a database composed of individuals in the process of starting a business, found that most small business owners are not the entrepreneurs that economic models and lawmakers tout as the prolific job creators and intrepid innovators who open up new pathways for economic growth by accelerating the demise of older technologies.[56] Instead, their research showed that relatively few small firms bring new ideas to the marketplace, and that most small business owners are content to sell existing products or services to buyers in local established markets.

Hurst and Pugsley also discovered that relatively few small business owners have a strong desire to grow large and innovate. This disposition was consistent with the main characteristics of the industries in which the majority of small businesses operated: skilled craftsmen, lawyers, real estate agents, doctors, small shop owners, and restaurateurs. It is also consistent with another key finding by Hurst and Pugsley: for about half the people who started a new business in 2004, the primary motivations were nonpecuniary, especially being one's own boss and having flexible work hours.

The findings from the two studies raise questions about the justification for current federal policy toward small businesses. Specifically, the findings suggest that most of the job growth and technological innovation by small firms is likely to come from the activities of a relatively small number of new companies. Therefore, Congress may consider whether new ways to target federal support at small start-up companies would help more of them raise financial capital. Identifying these companies is itself a significant challenge for public

---

[56] See Erik Hurst and Benjamin Wild Pugsley, *What Do Small Businesses Do?* NBER working paper 17041 (Cambridge, MA: May 2011).

policy. Hurst and Pugsley suggested as one option having the SBA work with venture capitalists to find new entrepreneurial small firms that might benefit from early-stage federal financial assistance. They also maintained that a better understanding of the costs and benefits of current federal support for small businesses may help lawmakers determine which current programs address the needs of those firms and which should be jettisoned as unnecessary and ineffective.

Most economists believe that departures from uniform or neutral taxation of the returns to capital are warranted only to correct identifiable market failures. This raises the question of whether existing federal government support for small firms is intended to remedy any market failure. For example, in light of the contributions of start-up firms to employment growth and technological innovation, one might argue that too few such firms are being formed, largely because of barriers in debt and equity markets to small business startup financing.

Is there evidence that too few small entrepreneurial firms are being formed? Imperfections in capital markets arguably prevent some individuals from getting the funds they need to start a new business and grow it. This can happen for a variety of reasons, including asymmetric information between aspiring entrepreneurs and lenders or investors, and excessive caution on the part of lenders and investors. A 2010 study by Alicia M. Robb and David T. Robinson of the financing choices of firms in their first year of business indicated that most of the firms in their sample relied much more on external debt than family and friends to obtain start-up capital.[57] They found that the start-up capital for over 80% of those firms was split evenly between bank debt and owner equity. The findings suggested that well-functioning credit markets are critical to the formation and success of new small firms.

The federal government is using several measures to improve access to capital for new businesses, including SBA loan guarantees, tax preferences for investment in small startup firms and business startup costs, and the

---

[57] Alicia M. Robb and David T. Robinson, *The Capital Structure Decision of New Firms*, NBER working paper 16272, National Bureau of Economic Research (Cambridge, MA: August 2010), p. 25.

recent dismantling of regulatory obstacles to using a method of raising equity capital known as "crowdfunding." Under this method, aspiring small business owners can raise small amounts of money from a large pool of investors, usually through the Internet, without running afoul of federal securities laws. Congress might consider whether additional measures could accelerate the rate of new entrepreneurial business formation and growth.

INDEX

A

B

C

D

E

F

G